the GUINNESS guide to mountain animals

René Pierre Bille

guinness superlatives ltd.

◁◁ **Two eaglets a few days before
leaving their eyrie in the Zinal area
(Valais).**

Translated from the original French by
Geoffrey Lovett and
Michael Hopf
Editorial adviser:
Gerald L. Wood FZS

Original copyright
© 1974 by Éditions Denoël, 14, rue Amélie 75007 Paris.
Les Animaux de Montagne,
René Pierre Bille, Denoël

Published in Great Britain by
Guinness Superlatives Limited, 2 Cecil Court,
London Road, Enfield, Middlesex, England.

ISBN 0 900424 57 5

Photoset in Great Britain by
REDWOOD BURN LIMITED
Trowbridge & Esher

Printed by Mussot, Paris, France

the GUINNESS guide to mountain animals

Contents

Mountain fauna.

Sub-alpine forests and glades

Mountainous terrain

Endangered species

Mountain fauna

The mountain fauna and in particular the fauna of the Alps is without any doubt one of the most attractive in the world. On one hand its extreme shyness, its wildness, its prudence and perhaps even more so the isolation in which it lives all make its observation difficult. On the other hand the solitary and grandiose regions, often difficult of access, where this fauna prefers to live give it an extra attraction in the eyes of the naturalist, the photographer or even the hunter, an attraction which only the more spectacular big game of Africa seems able to equal.

In fact, the surroundings in which mountain animals live is never commonplace, be it the dark conifer forests intersected by deep gorges where raging torrents foam against the rocks or even the chaotic mountain scree, twisting its stony slopes above the vast pastures where, every spring, incomparable flora appears. How could the infatuation, even passion, which seizes so many people at the discovery of their first chamois or their first grouse be explained if it were not for the wild scenery amongst which they live? How would they react without these immense empty or wooded spaces which are so conducive to peace of mind, to a return to one's self? How would they react without the beneficial solitude, and the marvellous silence which almost always accompanies such an experience, immediately enhancing it with a grandeur and an extraordinary dimension?

The longer the approach or the more hostile the terrain, the more symbolic the value acquired by the animal which is seen for just a few minutes or even seconds: it becomes a rare jewel, like the last flower before the glacier . . .

Those animals which now inhabit the Alps are of complex origin. Certain species are present everywhere and can be seen both on the plains and at higher altitudes: the fox or the chaffinch are such examples. Others may be described as mountain dwellers for preference, but they are also able to exist at medium or low altitudes. The beech marten, the coal-tit, the crested tit, the mistle thrush, the song thrush and the woodcock seem to be more frequently seen in the mountain forests than in the forests of the plain, at least in central Europe.

The effects of the glaciers

Finally, there are certain species which are strictly mountain dwellers and, at breeding time, can only be seen at high altitudes. These species are by far the most interesting; amongst them are to be found those of Arctic origin, seeking the cold and the snow of the mountains. They are justly described as the descendants of the Ice Age; their presence in the Alps and the Pyrenees can be explained in the following manner. In the Quaternary period the climate became considerably colder, so that the mountains were gradually covered with glaciers. Under the pressure of this change the tertiary fauna of the high altitudes was obliged to beat a retreat in order to survive. It took refuge at the base of the high mountain ranges, where it came into contact with the animals from the north which had also been forced to migrate southwards when the immense Arctic glaciers covered northern Europe. Both animals and plants from the Alps and the north became closely intermingled on the western plains, which by that time had become extremely cold. Subsequently, an increase in temperature caused the glaciers to melt and so to retreat, some to the north, others to the mountain peaks. In this way certain ancient tertiary species

Tracks of black grouse in the fresh snow at dawn.

such as the chamois, the ibex, the alpine accentor and the snow finch returned to the high areas and regained possession of their old territories, while the animals which had come from the tundras of the north, — like the reindeer and the musk ox — inhabited the wooded areas. Certain examples of this type of creature did not return only to the north but also followed the withdrawal of the ice to high altitudes and found on the mountains conditions of life which were similar to those of their ancient homelands. This is the explanation of the presence in the alpine and sub-alpine areas of species such as the ptarmigan, the mountain hare, the redpoll, the three-toed woodpecker, Tengmalm's owl, and certain others, including insects like the white butterfly, *Colias palaeno* and beetles like *Helphorus glacialis*, the little water-scavenger found in stagnant water. These animals have flourished up to the present time not only in their northern homeland, but also in the Alps, where they have remained, as it were, in an Arctic enclave, surrounded by more temperate regions. Parallel with this phenomenon, certain species which were originally of alpine origin, like the water pipit and the ring ouzel have not only regained possession of the mountains, but have also emigrated to some extent towards the north.

Seasonal moultings

Many of the species living in the Alps have been able to adapt themselves remarkably well to the severity of the climate. The mountain hare and the ptarmigan, which are closely related to certain of the fauna of the far north, have done even better. Neither had any fear of the cold, but summer in the mountains presented some problems initially, as originally both these species remained largely white in colour throughout the Arctic year. Seeking the coolness of the glaciers during the fine season, their fur and feathers gradually became more and more pigmented after the spring moult, so as to blend perfectly with the colours of the snow-free landscape, but became white again at the approach of winter. This protective capacity to camouflage became so developed in the alpine and Pyrenean ptarmigan that the bird now has four types of plumage annually, two of which are variegated (the spring and autumn moults), the third white (winter plumage) and the fourth brownish (summer plumage). It would even be possible to add a fifth type – the September plumage which the bird carries for a very short time and which is more grey than the summer feathers. At moulting time the ptarmigan lives on ground which is partially covered with snow and completely merges into the colours of its habitat. The physiological and anatomical complexity of this bird's plumage still astonishes naturalists as it can be said that the bird moults for the greater part of the year.

A very interesting fact is that when the mountain hare from north Norway was taken to the Faroe Islands, which are influenced by the warmth of the Gulf Stream, it changed, according to Couturier, its white winter coat for a light blueish grey one in less than forty years. The thermal factor is therefore evident in influencing the changes of colour of the mountain hare and the ptarmigan but other factors are also responsible for these changes. Russian physiologists have proved that the light factor also plays an important rôle.

Another species which exchanges its fawn summer coat for a fine white fur in winter is the stoat. It is a curious fact that the weasel, which is closely related to the stoat, remains brown during the alpine winter. However, it seldom lives above the tree line and its living habits are far more nocturnal.

Hibernation

Apart from these remarkable examples of protective pigmentation, certain types of mountain fauna are capable of a remarkable adaptation to low temperatures. The alpine salamander, for example, which is found up to an altitude of 10 000 ft (3000 m) does not go to water to lay its eggs like most members of its generic group, but gives birth to its young after two or even three months of gestation. The young are born in pairs, and are 1.5 in (4 cm) in length, completely developed and able to withstand the rigours of the climate. Many rodents spend the winter in a state of deep lethargy. A typical example is the alpine marmot which, at the approach of autumn, builds up large reserves of fat, buries itself several feet under the ground and curls itself up on a thick bed of dry grass, after having carefully blocked up part of the entrance to its lair. It would seem that the advent of sleep depends on the temperature of the surroundings. The lethargy becomes increasingly profound as the temperature falls; at 50°F (+10°C) sleep is total, according to Couturier. The temperature of the body follows naturally that of the surroundings. Breathing is reduced to two or even one

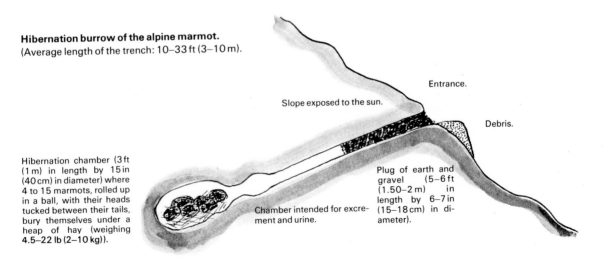

Hibernation burrow of the alpine marmot.
(Average length of the trench: 10–33 ft (3–10 m).

Hibernation chamber (3 ft (1 m) in length by 15 in (40 cm) in diameter) where 4 to 15 marmots, rolled up in a ball, with their heads tucked between their tails, bury themselves under a heap of hay (weighing 4.5–22 lb (2–10 kg)).

Slope exposed to the sun.

Entrance.

Debris.

Chamber intended for excrement and urine.

Plug of earth and gravel (5–6 ft (1.50–2 m) in length by 6–7 in (15–18 cm) in diameter).

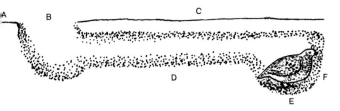

Cross-section of the gallery and winter domicile of a black grouse (Lyrurus tetrix).

A Surface of the layer of snow.
B Entrance to the gallery.
C Thickness of the layer of snow above the gallery 2–4 in (5–10 cm).
D The actual gallery. Greatest length: 10 in–49 ft (25–150 cm): Average length: 22 in (55 cm).
E Main chamber with a pile of droppings at the bottom.
F A blackhen in her domicile (average dimensions: 12–16 in (30–40 cm) in depth and diameter)

single inhalation per minute. Professor Mangalini has calculated that the alpine marmot, which normally makes 72 000 inhalations in two days during its active life only makes 72 000 inhalations during the entire months of its hibernation: this gives a clear idea of the deep sleep of the animal, a sleep which is very close to death.

During its sleep the marmot uses its reserves of fat very slowly, so that on its awakening in the spring it often has lost half of its weight. Apart from its thermal factor which has already been mentioned and which plays a fundamental rôle in the hibernatory mechanism of this rodent other factors also intervene in controlling the hibernation, in particular the endocrinal glands and the nervous system which plays a regulating part in the hibernation. In the course of its hibernation the marmot wakes up several times either to discharge some faeces or to urinate. This takes place in the lower part of the lair in a fairly large hole which has been dug especially for this purpose. The spring time awakening can take place from the end of March to the beginning of May, depending on the position of the lair and the degree of exposure of the terrain, the severity of the winter or the unexpected arrival of a warm south wind. The marmot is often obliged to clear away, apart from the block of earth which separates it from the fresh air, several feet of snow. In the latter case the exit from the lair is visible from a distance because of the mud which dirties the surrounding white area.

The marmot is not the only alpine mammal which sinks into a deep lethargy in winter. The garden dormouse, covered with a thick layer of sub-cutaneous fat, also buries itself together with several companions in the hollow of a tree or in a hole in the rocks and sleeps at a high altitude from October onwards to awake only in the following April. Its sleep however is not as deep as that of the common dormouse. A special mucus seals the eyelids of the former during the entire period of hibernation so that, when spring arrives, it takes the garden dormouse, although definitely awake, several days to open its eyes fully. Finally the bat, a rare animal in the mountains, takes refuge in caves or hangs in the vaults of grottos which penetrate reasonably far beneath the earth thus maintaining a constant temperature and a certain humidity. Its sleep during hibernation is very deep with water often forming in drops on its body. It scarcely shows any movement when it is touched. It is as well to note, in passing, that the mating season of the bat takes place in autumn and that its sperm remains stored in the genital passages of the female during the period of hibernation. It is only in the spring, when the bat awakes, that ovulation takes place and the ovary is then fertilised.

The approach of winter

The large alpine mammals, such as the chamois and the ibex, leave the highest areas which are already covered with snow and take refuge in the forests. There they are able to find a definite supply of food and an effective protection against avalanches. However many of the ibex, for reasons which are still not clear, dislike penetrating the fir or larch forests and prefer to remain at a high altitude. They are then at the mercy of avalanches and heavy falls of snow and so many of them die of hunger during the severe winters. Red deer and roe deer abandon the northern slopes and take up their winter quarters in the wooded slopes which receive the most sun. Their fur becomes much greyer and thickens considerably at the approach of the severe weather and this effectively protects them from the cold. But the roe deer has shorter legs than the red deer and a much weaker constitution than the chamois, this means that it becomes quickly exhausted in heavy snow and often sinks in it up to its chest. When this happens it soon succumbs to the attacks of mountain foxes or dogs. This graceful deer is without any doubt the least suited of all the mammals to survive the severe winters in the high mountains although it is often seen at the upper edge of the treeline in the alpine forests.

During snowstorms the red squirrel is able to remain for several days in its nest of mosses and twigs. When the weather is extremely cold it leaves its nest only very early in the morning, but never falls into a hibernatory sleep. The yellow-necked mouse and the snow vole remain active throughout the winter, living partly from the stores which they have built up during the autumn, and the vole in particular moves frequently between soil and snow. Finally, the brown bear and the badger are sometimes known as 'false hibernators'. Their activity in winter is only slowed down, as they never fall into true hibernation like the marmot. It has been proved several times that the brown bear, when it retires into its cave or its hole in the rocks in winter, falls into only a light sleep and quickly awakens at the sound of the approach of man.

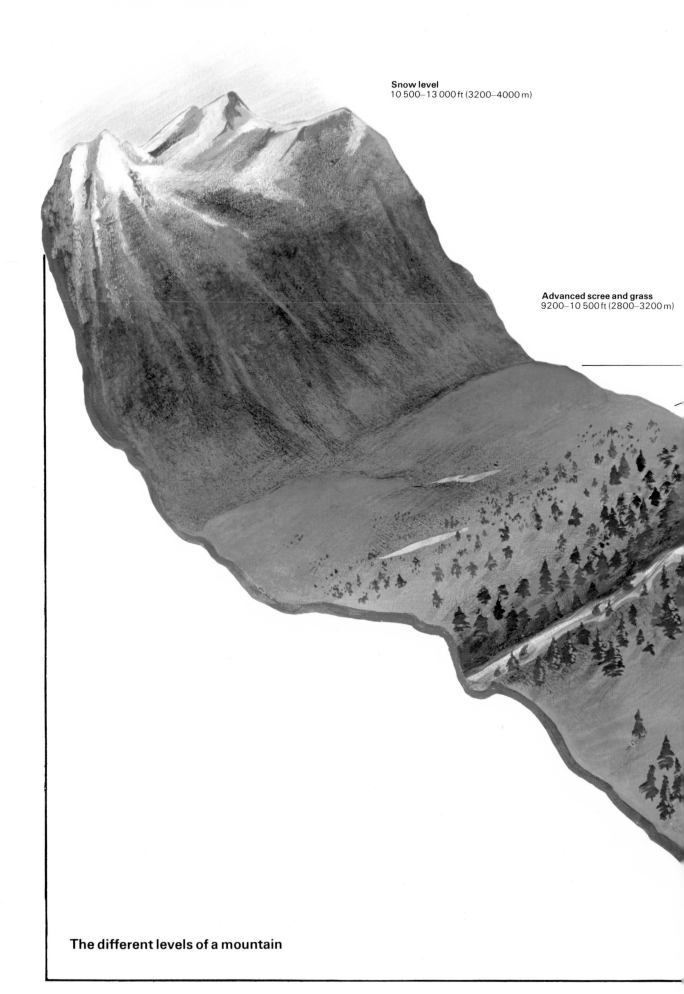

Snow level
10 500–13 000 ft (3200–4000 m)

Advanced scree and grass
9200–10 500 ft (2800–3200 m)

The different levels of a mountain

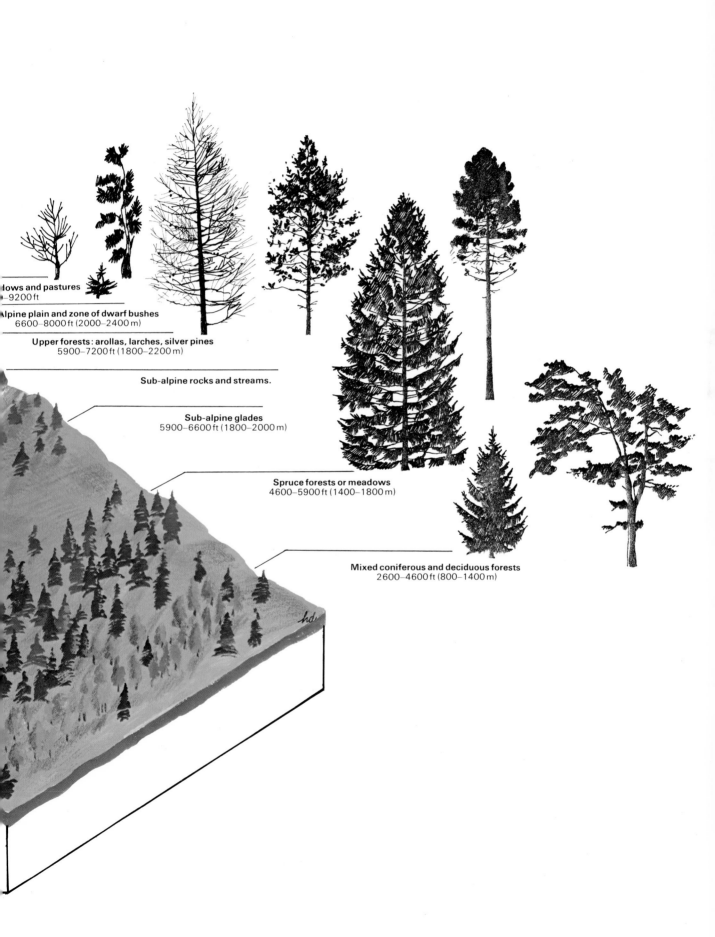

lows and pastures
–9200 ft

Alpine plain and zone of dwarf bushes
6600–8000 ft (2000–2400 m)

Upper forests: arollas, larches, silver pines
5900–7200 ft (1800–2200 m)

Sub-alpine rocks and streams.

Sub-alpine glades
5900–6600 ft (1800–2000 m)

Spruce forests or meadows
4600–5900 ft (1400–1800 m)

Mixed coniferous and deciduous forests
2600–4600 ft (800–1400 m)

Reptiles, batrachians, insects and birds

Reptiles and batrachians of the high altitudes spend winter hidden beneath stones which are more or less deeply embedded in the ground and so sheltered from the frost which would prove to be fatal to them. The case of certain brown frogs, which live at 8000 ft (2500 m) in small pools which freeze up completely in October, is rather perplexing, and where exactly they spend the winter is uncertain. Many of the insects living in alpine areas die at the onset of the first period of cold weather and only their eggs, their larvae or their pupae, hidden in a thick covering of snow, are able to perpetuate the species. Without this covering of snow many plants, or small animals would be unable to survive. The ground does not freeze under such a soft eiderdown which forms a truly protective covering, beneath which many seeds, bulbs, eggs and larvae are able to continue their existence, albeit at a slow rate. Many beetles spend the winter beneath tree bark or inside dead wood, either as larvae, pupae or even in the form of imagines. Such is the case with the majority of the long horned beetles, the bask-beetles and the wood-boring beetles. A curious fact is that the eggs and the chrysalises of certain insects cannot hatch without having undergone a relatively long period at a low temperature. A similar situation exists with the seeds of certain plants. The subject is therefore much more complex than it would seem to be.

It should also be noted, with reference to the life cycle of insects, that the number of generations decreases with increasing altitude. A butterfly capable of two or three generations at a low altitude would only have a single generation above the tree-line. In certain cases even the complete life cycle of the species will only be achieved at the end of two or three years: this is the case with the alpine grayling – Oeneis glacialis – of which the caterpillar completes its metamorphosis at high altitudes only in July of the third year.

What is the situation of the birds of the Alps? As has been seen certain species are superbly well adapted to the cold and to the snow. The ptarmigan hardly ever leaves the high altitude which it has taken as its habitat. At the very most it descends to the foothills in winter and it has to be an exceptional year for it to penetrate the forest zones. The black grouse and the hazel hen burrow beneath the snow in areas where they are able to camouflage themselves perfectly from the eyes of their enemies, and where they are protected from the danger of the lowest temperatures. Many sparrows, feeding on seeds of conifers, move in small groups from one forest to another, spending the greater part of the winter in the mountains. Certain of them, however, reach the plains in search of the seeds of the alder and the birch trees; such birds are the redpoles and the siskins. The bullfinch even reaches inhabited areas and ravages

orchards in its search for buds. Birds as hardy as the alpine accentor leave their lonely heights when bad weather approaches and fly into the mountain villages where they seek their food on the balconies of houses. The dunnock and the robin, which are less hardy, descend to the plains and to gardens near towns where they spend the winter in company with other sparrows. Amongst other less mobile species which spend the entire year in the mountains are the black woodpecker, the nutcracker which lives on its store of seeds built up during the autumn, certain types of tree creepers, the nuthatch and the tit. There are also certain nocturnal birds of prey which are particularly resistant to the cold, and which are incidentally descended from the Ice Age, together with certain other diurnal birds of prey like the sparrow hawk and the goshawk, and finally, the golden eagle who takes little heed of even the lowest temperatures.

Migration

Most of the insect-eating birds, however, leave the plains and mnuntains in September and spend the winter further south. The problem of their migration across the Alps is one of great complexity, and it is extremely difficult to convey a satisfactory concept of this migration in a few lines. Suffice it to say that it varies greatly according to weather and to the diurnal or nocturnal character of the migration. In the words of Paul Géroudet: 'There is a concentration of birds between September and October on a fairly wide route to the north of the alpine range where certain valleys act as funnels towards the south-west, giving rise at their narrower points to spectacular concentrations of these birds. This is particularly the case in the Cou-Bretolet, Forclaz, Balme, Hahnenmoos pass etc. Regardless of whether they are open to the north or north-east each valley is a transit point only; the importance of the migration depends on the size and the direction of the "funnel" which exists there. Bad weather, wind and, above all, low cloud levels modify conditions for the birds and give rise to local congestion and drifting etc.' (P. G. in letters Works. 18 May 1973.).

In recent years enormous numbers of migratory birds have collected in the valleys of Cou-Bretolet, in Valais, and in several other places in the Alps. Naturalists are just beginning to notice the importance of this phenomenon, observation of which is made ever more difficult due to the vast nocturnal movement of the birds often beyond the scope of any detailed investigation.

I

sub-alpine forests and glades

from 3000 ft to
the upper limit of the
coniferous tree-line

A forest of larches near
Chandolin (Anniviers valley).

1
Inhabitants of the mixed coniferous and deciduous forests

The capercaillie – the hazel hen – the roe deer – the badger – the jay – the woodcock – the great spotted woodpecker – the black woodpecker – wood boring insects.

The capercaillie

In mid-April the great spring festival begins . . . The voices which greet spring at dawn become more and more numerous: there are the clear and emphatic songs from the throats of thousands of thrushes seen in the tops of the pine trees, the lively, piercing notes of the tiny wren, its tail lifted, always hidden in the bushes, the melancholic and soft trill of the solitary robin, the lilting melody of the dunnock, and the song of many many others . . .

In the least frequented parts of the forest, amongst the slowly rotting tree trunks, an entire range of plant life is in the process of being reborn; there are the young shoots of strawberry and raspberry plants, the myrtle and the bramble, and the tall green lances of the bracken. There, in the heart of this kingdom of mosses and rotting bark, beneath the low branches of the pine trees and the rust-red buds of the beech tree lives, divorced from the rest of the world, the most amazing bird of the forest: the capercaillie, that giant of the European bird world.

Everything about this bird appears somewhat strange, not least of all its song, which is scarcely audible at a distance of fifty paces . . . Can one really give the word 'song' to this series of bizarre popping noises which precedes the famous 'noise of a cork being drawn', followed in its turn by a sort of grating noise comparable to a scythe being sharpened? It is still dark when the bird, with a noisy flutter of wings, leaves the top branch in order to crop the tough needles of the old pine tree on which it spends the greater part of winter. With a slow supple step it paces its domain, head in air, its eye missing nothing from beneath the thick red lid formed by its wattle. The woodcock, already in full retreat, has uttered through the foliage its guttural over-sharp cry, the screech owl has already retired to the depths of its hole which is nothing more than the old home of the black woodpecker . . . The capercaillie, a dark shape difficult to

distinguish in the undergrowth at any time if it w[ere] not for the white mark on its shoulder, leaves its dr[op]pings, opens its beak and utters a first clucking no[ise] which rings clearly through the silence; a little vap[our] leaves its throat at the same time as the base of [its] breast is shaken by a spasm. Its tail is lifted and op[ens] into a large black fan marbled with a little white. L[ike] a great lord the bird circles, lowers its wings, stiff[ens] its neck even further so that every feather stands stiffly beneath its powerful yellow beak. Its s[ong] quickens and the clucking noise ends with the fi[nal] typical popping sound. This is the only note whic[h is] audible at any great distance and it is followed by [the] final phrase of this bird's unique call, the gratin[g of] the scythe being sharpened, uttered in an unbeli[ev]able posture, with its neck stretched right out, he[ad] raised vertically and its beak opening and shutt[ing] with frantic movements as if the bird was swallow[ing] air! This is the moment of ecstasy, the moment wh[en] the grouse sees and hears nothing, the supre[me] moment when the trained hunter can appro[ach] within range. This is the game of life and of dea[th.] The great bird begins its song again and, in the li[ght] of the dawn it appears even more superb than ev[er] showing the typical blue green reflections of [its] breast in contrast with the brown of its wings and [the] steel grey of its neck. This is a rare spectacle [for] anyone who has the opportunity of seeing it and is [an] unforgettable experience as the last star disappe[ars] from the sky and the dawn breeze slips down [the] slope.

A little later the soft sound of beating wings in [the] branches and the sonorous 'cluck, cluck, cluck' [an]nounce the arrival of the hens. One lands on [the] ground, rust red in colour and round in shape, diffic[ult] to distinguish from the carpet of dead leaves and [so] different from the cock both in size and plumage t[hat] it is difficult to imagine they belong to the sa[me] species. Sometimes a rival comes to disturb the rit[es] of this ceremony and immediately the master of [the] domain faces up to the intruder, the feathers of [his] neck raised, his attitude threatening. Both birds d[efy] each other, uttering strange guttural sounds int[er]spersed with grinding noises, their powerful bea[ks] pointing towards each other trying to peck out [the] other's eyes or, even achieve a fatal attack on [the] skull. Brown wings beat furiously in the undergrow[th] as the two cocks roll down the slope until one of [the] adversaries retreats, leaving on the snow some g[rey] feathers or even a few drops of blood.

The capercaillie has become rare in the Alps a[nd] maintains its position more or less in the foothills [of] the Alps, the Jura Mountains, the Pyrenees and [the] Vosges. Its effective habitat, however, is consta[ntly] decreasing, in spite of the protective measures wh[ich] have recently been taken both in France and in Sw[it]zerland. It has disappeared from the Massif Cent[ral] and appears to be almost extinct in Belgium. Marte[ns] and foxes have ravaged the hens of this species, [the] goshawk and the golden eagle sometimes atta[ck] them – and even succeed in overwhelming [the] cocks. Finally, the disease coccidiosis has given r[ise] to epidemics which have attacked, above all, [the] young birds. Like all the ancient representatives [of] our bird life the capercaillie seems condemned [to] disappear from western Europe unless immedia[te] steps are taken to ensure its survival.

The hazel hen

This is the classical type of shy bird, inhabiting the depths of the woods, revealing unexpectedly in its flight through the branches russet coloured wingr, or the ash coloured spread of its tail shadowed in black.

It is also a bird given to long periods of silence, hiding its rich bark-coloured plumage in solitude. This plumage covers a surprising range of colours from white through beige, brown and grey to black.

The hazel hen is also a bird that is seen in the hunting season, but only then it is seen falling from the branches, its beak opening and shutting spasmodically, its wings beating the ground frantically, while a trickle of blood colours the moss around it and the black eyelid closes beneath the scarlet wattle.

Of all the grouse, the hazel hen together with the capercaillie, are the ones certainly the most at home in the forest. This bird can easily pass unnoticed because of its modest size (similar to that of a partridge), its very discreet habits and the secluded spots where it prefers to live. This cunning hen is adept at concealment and, at the first sign of alarm, it either becomes motionless amongst the brambles letting the cause of the disturbance pass by or else suddenly flies up from the ground, with a characteristic beating of its wings, without moving very far away. However, before taking flight, this prudent bird takes great care to leave a thick curtain of trees or foliage between itself and the human who disturbs it.

Crouched against a tree trunk with its head hidden under its wings, the hazel hen remains perfectly still and merges in with the bark of the trees so well that it is almost impossible to see it. This camouflaging plumage and the habitat which it normally frequents does not make its study easy. Shy by nature, this chicken of the hazel trees' wants nothing more than to be unnoticed; it seeks silence and tranquility and hardly ever shows itself in the daylight, seeming to be surrounded by a certain atmosphere of mystery. It quickly abandons forests frequented by man and takes refuge in the glades of deep forest where, in the dense undergrowth, it can find nuts, the young shoots of birch trees and all kinds of berries. The hazel hen can be found in the Alps up to an altitude of 6600 ft (2000 m); that is to say as far as the upper limit of the forests. At the height when the trees begin to thin out, however, the hazel hen concedes its place to the slower, more common grouse which is in its natural habitat at this altitude.

The hen of the hazel trees is an enthusiastic hatcher of eggs. Its nest, like that of most hens, consists of a simple depression scratched in the earth and decorated with a few feathers. It is always well sheltered by a tree trunk, a low branch, or perhaps a young fir tree. It is even more difficult to discover the nest when the eggs are in an advanced state of incubation. The bird stays permanently on its nest until only extreme danger forces it away. Recently some tree cutters told the author that a hen even allowed itself to be crushed on its eggs when a tree was being cut down rather than move. They had no idea of the existence of the nest before this drama because it was so well hidden under a small bush. The extraordinary fact was that neither the noise of the saw nor the coming and going of the workmen had been enough to force the unhappy mother to leave her eggs!

Catching sight of the hazel hen in the forest is always a pleasant surprise. It is usually at the least expected moment that this bird suddenly leaves a branch or the ground with a typical beating of its wings. This noise is certainly not comparable to the impressive noise of the capercaillie when it leaves a slope but it has its own unique charm and character. For a few seconds one can follow the russet coloured silhouette until it is hidden behind branches or concealed by tree trunks. However fleeting the glimpse of the bird is, it is still much appreciated by those who like to wander alone through the large forests and those few last areas remote from civilisation. During the mating season, in March, April, May and also in the autumn, it is possible to attract the hazel hen and observe it at a close distance by imitating its call, either with the help of a bird-call or even better with a tape recorder. Its call is a series of sharp notes which become more hurried just before the end of its stanza. The author, by imitating the call of the hazel hen, has seen a male bird rush straight to his hiding place in order to defend its territory, obviously convinced that it had to deal with a rival! In this way he was able to put on film the image of this fierce little grouse. Its rarity, its discreet habits, its capacity to blend in with the colours of its habitat and the areas in which it prefers to live makes the hazel hen the true jewel of the great forests of Europe.

A hazel hen among
the lichens
of an old spruce.

◁ A capercaillie singing
on the staddle of
a young beech.

A young female roe deer in flight.

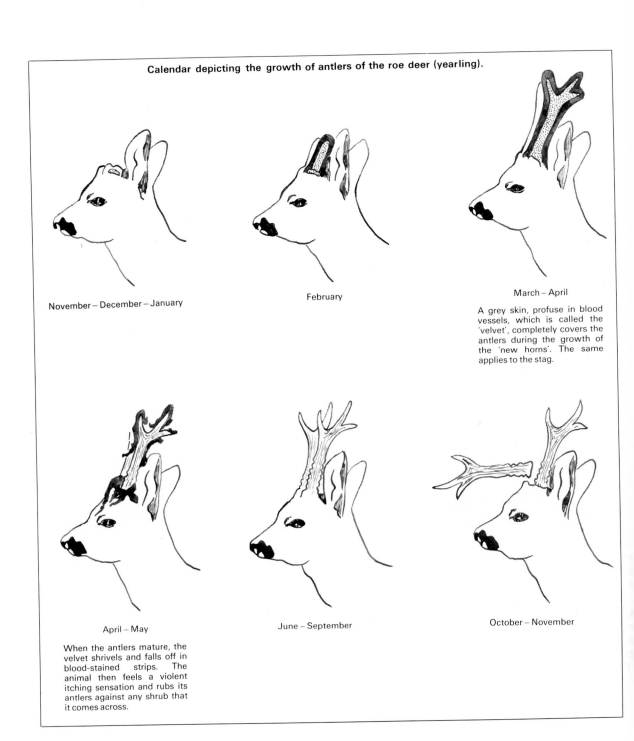

Calendar depicting the growth of antlers of the roe deer (yearling).

November – December – January

February

March – April

A grey skin, profuse in blood vessels, which is called the 'velvet', completely covers the antlers during the growth of the 'new horns'. The same applies to the stag.

April – May

When the antlers mature, the velvet shrivels and falls off in blood-stained strips. The animal then feels a violent itching sensation and rubs its antlers against any shrub that it comes across.

June – September

October – November

The roe deer

The spring is the best season to see the roe deer. Starved by the privation of winter and greedy by nature, it leaves the protection of the trees early in the morning and seeks out the clearings where it can graze on the young shoots of plants. At the first sign of danger, however, it will bound into the nearest thicket. This graceful small deer seems to be so suited to the forest habitat that a wood without roe deer would be sad and lifeless. Meeting it always gives pleasure to the naturalist and its graceful leaps enchant the eye even if, for the most part, it is only possible to catch a glimpse of a gracefully proportioned silhouette running through the trees on extremely delicate legs. Only the 'mirror', that is to say the famous light patch on the buttocks of the animal, allows the observer to follow it for a second longer before the forest swallows up this little animal.

Much has been written on the roe deer but it still seems that writers have not laid enough stress on the vocal sounds uttered by the animals. In fact amongst all wild European mammals it is possibly the roe deer which possesses the most astonishing voice in relation to its size. It is difficult to imagine that such a terrible clamour can be produced from the throat of such a graceful animal. These raucous, gutteral sounds, emitted with a sort of contained rage and amplified by the special natural acoustics of its habitat, make at night a very strong impression. When these sounds are heard from the shadows of the forest their wildness is certainly unexpected and sometimes even frightening. It is difficult to compare them with the cries of other known mammals. Only perhaps the yelping of the fox can be said to have something in common with the ill-tempered cries of the yearling when it is surprised by man.

The roe deer is careful about the time and place for uttering its cries. It is normally very silent in the middle of the day, and it is only towards the end of the afternoon and above all in the evening, at night or in the very early morning, that this deer reacts violently if it finds a human in its territory. Very often the male roe will give the alarm before leaving his cover. Even deep in the wood its excellent sense of smell can give

it a warning and, even though down wind of the animal, one can be certain of hearing its enraged cry sometimes at a great distance. If taken by surprise the yearling reacts with unbelievable violence; it first gives a gutteral cry of extraordinary force, comparable to a sort of barking or raucous bellow which it then repeats two or three seconds later at a lower pitch. It is possible for the animal to give several cries in this way while increasing the distance between itself and the disturber. Very often its mate replies with a higher pitched cry, which it repeats even more hurriedly.

This can be well illustrated by an incident which happened to the author at the beginning of April. Having spotted a tawny owl the previous day, he went into the forest which was at an altitude of 3000 ft (1000 m) so that he could tape the cries of this nocturnal bird, which is a descendant from the alpine Ice Age. On arriving at the spot he installed himself and his equipment at the base of an enormous fir tree and waited, without moving, for night to fall. A little fresh snow covered the ground here and there and there was the smell of moss and humus in the air, while a very light breeze was blowing. A song thrush was singing its last melody from the top of a nearby tree, when suddenly the author had the strange feeling that something was passing behind his back. He heard a slight noise and as he turned a terrible clamour broke the silence, making him jump. Although long used to the sounds of the forest this cry of the roe deer, uttered no more than 20 feet (6 m) away really froze his blood! The yearling took an enormous leap to one side and, as it escaped, repeated its cry even more loudly and with obvious bad temper. Without being aware of it the author had placed himself in the path of the animal, who was merely making its way towards its favourite pasture, a small glade a few hundred yards away from the fir tree. It is difficult to say which of the two had been more afraid but the strange echo of that infinitely wild voice, a true voice of the great mountain forests, will be remembered for a very long time.

The badger

The badger is mainly a nocturnal animal and to find it by day is something of a problem. If one wishes to observe it closely one must first of all discover its set. It can happen, however, that it goes about its business at unexpected times. The author once surprised a badger, one April afternoon when the sky was blue and a light breeze was blowing, as it was in the process of scratching an ant hill in the forest. One year previously, in the same area, while paying a visit with a friend to the badger's set, they were fortunate enough to see it at only a few paces from one of their observation points, stretched out in the sunlight and fast asleep. From time to time the animal gave some noisy snorts or heaved a deep sigh. His observers, placed a few feet down wind from the sleeper, had great difficulty in controlling their desire to break into laughter. Would the animal wake up of its own accord? In any case it seemed to have no inkling of their presence. Finally, in despair, the author indicated that his friend should touch it with a stick while he held his camera ready to take a photograph. The reaction of the badger was so sudden and so violent that the animal almost knocked both people over in his rush for his lair, which was right at their feet. It disappeared into its set so quickly that the observers were left quite amazed! Some years later, when the author was busy filming the mating dances of the grouse at the beginning of June, a badger crossed the pasturage at dawn and entered the forest quite close to him. It was at that moment that he understood, what great distances this animal must cover in the course of a single night despite its sluggish appearance. In fact its ambling gait seemed extremely supple and light, and although it is low built and bulky in size, it disappeared quickly behind the nearest available bush.

The author's first meeting with this rather engaging little creature was a long time ago, but it is tha meeting which left him with his clearest memory the animal. It was early in May, and up in the mou tains. For a week it had been noticed that each mor ing, on a small path partly covered with snow not fa from the author's house, the track and the dropping of a badger had appeared. This very clean carnivo has, in fact, its own 'private lavatories' which it visi regularly; they consist of small square or conic holes in which it leaves its droppings which sme strongly similar to musk. Wishing to know exact what was happening, the author decided to spend night outside in the hope of observing the coming and goings of this animal which fascinated him. H took up his position in a tree overlooking the pat made himself more or less comfortable a few fe above the ground and, warmly clad, waited patient for the arrival of the night-walker. The greater part the night passed without any incident and the silenc was only broken from time to time by the far o passionate cry of a tawny owl. As it was not too col it was difficult for him not to fall asleep despite h precarious position and, so as to overcome h sleepiness, he concentrated on even the smalle sound that was made. Now and then a fragment crystalised snow fell from a tree and the cracklin sound helped keep the author awake. Finall towards three o'clock in the morning, the sound of tengmalm's owl broke the monotony of his vigil wit its distant cry of 'pouh! pouh! pouh!', soft and mela choly but presenting a sad sort of beauty. Although was quite dark he could still make out the badger path by the faint reflection of the star-light on th snow. The author was convinced that no anim could move along that path without being see However, as night reached its end and the darknes gave way to the first hint of dawn there came a sligh sound from the path. Suddenly there appeared greyish shape with dark and light stripes: it was th badger. It advanced at a slow trot over the froze snow but, on arriving at the base of the tree, it sud denly sensed the author's presence, gave a sort disdainful grunt, jumped to one side and went noisi down the slope, leaving the author unable to mak any move for several minutes, and bemused by th brief appearance of the badger in the semi-darknes Even to this day, the author cannot recall this distar visit without thinking that the discomfort of the entir night spent under the skies was a low price to pay f such an unforgettable sight: like some ghostl shadow, the badger had suddenly appeared on th snow covered path that winter evening and ha transformed the experience into something magica allowing a glimpse for just a few seconds of all th wild mystery of the forest.

Cross-section of a badger's burrow

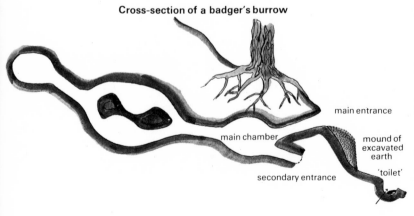

main entrance

main chamber

mound of excavated earth

secondary entrance

'toilet'

The jay

The author had scarcely entered the pine forest when a discordant cry burst like a trumpet fanfare from the depths of the nearest group of trees. Then, there flew out a handsome looking bird, red and black with a patch of white on its rump. With heavy flight, the jay flew off and disappeared into the thickest part of the woods. Despite this hasty exit, the author was able to glimpse for just a few seconds the blue flash of the marvellous little feathers which covered part of the wings.

Again the raucous cries echoed in the foliage, but this time the bird remained prudently invisible, although it continued to watch every movement that was made. This is usually all that one sees of the jay, one of the most richly coloured members of the crow family in Europe, but a bird which is very reluctant to show itself in open terrain. It is about the size of a pigeon but has a head and a beak much stronger than those of a pigeon. The jay has brilliant plumage, but is clumsy in flight and needs dense cover to enable it to hide quickly from its enemies, the sparrow-hawk and the goshawk. It is an obvious inhabitant of the forests and is very careful although at times fierce. Its habitat is found up to quite a high altitude in the mountains and it has been observed on several occasions amongst the last trees on the edge of the forests. However, in general it prefers to build its nest at a lower level and is particularly fond of the small woods of the sub-alpine zone where pines and larches mix with deciduous trees. It especially prefers those bushes which offer it safe refuge. Whenever it is even

slightly disturbed the jay raises its crest and scream its discordant cries through the trees, warning othe birds even a considerable distance away.

Like the nutcracker, which prefers to live in th upper reaches of the forests, the jay plays the rôle of guard throughout the sub-alpine levels. Its voice no only announces the arrival of man but also the fox the wild dog, the wild cat and, in the Pyrenees, th bear. Its vocabulary is much richer than one generall imagines. Apart from its famous alarm cry, which i both lengthy and unpleasant, the jay can also imitat the mewing of the buzzard, the cry of the owl an even on occasions the human voice. In early spring joins up with other jays and together they produce a extraordinary mixture of sounds, which are some times gutteral, sometimes whistling or mewing.

In spite of its wildness this bird, if taken from th nest, can be tamed very easily and exhibits qualitie which are psychic in character. The author had young jay as a pet for a very long time and this be came an inseparable companion, even though livin in total freedom in the garden adjoining the famil house. It shared all the family meals and knew exactl at what time they were served. If by chance a windov or a door were shut at meal times the bird announce its presence by a few taps with its beak against th window or the door. It adored taking a bath an would play for hours with small oval pebbles which allowed to run down its beak into its extending cro and from there back again, several times over; whe it tired of this game the bird finally, obeying th

Jays at feeding time.

The woodcock

This is the first bird to start flying before dawn. This is the bird of the twilight which each spring appears at the top of a tree against a leaden coloured sky revealing its strange bat-like silhouette. It has a guttural voice and the serious 'caw caw caw', followed by a 'psit' which it makes in sharp tones generally announces the arrival of this bird which skims over the branches with a slow beating of its wings . . . In the distance the harsh wild cry of a song thrush echoes. Then silence descends again. Darkness spreads through the forest and slowly hides the bark and the moss so that nothing more will be seen of the woodcock that day. So much has already been written about this strange bird. What hunter, ornithologist, or photographer at the fall of night has not hidden behind a tree in order to surprise this beautiful bronze creature and catch a mere few seconds' glimpse of its famous silhouette cutting across the grey sky? Everything about the woodcock attracts and retains the attention. Its twilight habits, its extremely discreet and lonely life, its marvellous plumage coloured like dead leaves, its tricks, its capacity to imitate and its tasty flesh have made it a special game bird, well-known to hunters and naturalists alike.

The author's personal experiences of the woodcock are very limited, apart from the fleeting glimpse of that bronze form which he has had in the mountains at an altitude of about 6600 ft (2000 m). He has twice discovered its nest, and on one occasion had the opportunity of seeing a bird hatching its young. Each of these encounters has created a deep impression on him. The most memorable occasion was probably when he discovered one of these birds sitting on its eggs; whilst looking for mushrooms in a wood crossed by a stream, his attention was caught by a brownish mass. As it was near a rotten tree stump it appeared to be nothing more than a piece of old bark hidden in the brambles; on examining it more closely however the regular stripes and the wonderful patterns on this piece of wood made a deep impression on him. Leaning forward the author saw through the grass and bramble leaves a large eye staring at him. The bird, which was resting on the ground, made no movement; not even its eye flickered, and it continued to stare at him unflinchingly. It held its long beak very near its breast so that he was rather puzzled as to what to do. This staring session lasted for a full minute; he was both surprised and stupefied. At last the author had come face to face with a woodcock! Its strange immobility made one wonder whether the bird was perhaps injured, so, with the aid of a stick, he raised the creature to its feet: then suddenly it leapt into action and took off almost vertically, with a nervous flight, disappearing into the trees and revealing four yellowish eggs spotted with reddish brown. When he had recovered from his surprise he took some photographs of the nest and came back the following day to take further pictures of the sitting bird. He found that the woodcock was, of course, in the same position as on the previous day and could admire at leisure the extraordinary way its colours blended with the background. The wonderful shades of colours in its feathers were exactly like tree bark or dead leaves.

powerful instinct of its species, would hide the pebbles under some leaves or — if it happened to be inside the house — it would conceal them in various nooks and crannies.

It would hide food almost anywhere and liked to perch on a shoulder. From this position it would delicately take certain pieces of food offered to the bird. When it had eaten enough it hid the leftovers in all kinds of curious places. Playful and gentle in manner this jay, who became known as Coco, knew how to arouse respect and threatened with its beak anybody who tried to tease it. It disliked dogs and strangers in the house and immediately fled from cats. It would only venture into unknown territory when accompanied by its 'master' although its great passion was chasing grasshoppers. When walking in the country the bird would follow its owner from tree to tree for hours. One was able to find for Coco those grasshoppers with blue or red wings which are so common in the south of France. The bird would immediately snap them up skilfully with its beak and then fly into a tree to finish off its meal in comfort. It would always begin the meal by tearing off its victims' legs followed by the wing sheaths, the head and finally the rest of the body. Endowed with a healthy appetite, Coco was capable of swallowing a dozen of these insects at one go and even when the jay had its fill it continued to hunt for reserve supplies which it hid in holes or cracks in the tree bark to be eaten the following day.

Great spotted
woodpecker
(male).

The remarkable mimicry of the woodcock on its nest.

The great spotted woodpecker

How pleasant it is at the end of winter to wander through the forests when all the snow has finally melted. Far from the daily routine, far from worry and noise, one has the impression of walking over virgin soil, one fills ones lungs with the scents of moss and humus, better than all the perfumes of the world. One walks through complete calm, far from the bustle of the towns, far from industry's sickening pollutants. Everything is fresh, silent. One can feel the sap rising in the trees whilst on the ground, which is covered with pine needles, red ants, already awoken from their winter's sleep, hurry out of the way as one passes.

Slowly, as it gets lighter, the forest comes alive. Great tits chase each other on a larch tree: a tree creeper sings its lively song from the tree top and two red squirrels climb in spirals up a tree trunk, scratching the old bark with their claws. But what is that strange sound which suddenly echoes through the forest? From where comes that sudden vibration? One raises one's head to look for the source of this drumming in vain. Happily, after a little time, the sound is repeated somewhere much closer: it almost sounds like the chattering of a machine gun. Then, clinging to the trunk of a larch which has previously been struck by lightning one sees a black and white bird the size of a blackbird, but with a patch of red under its tail, staring at you, motionless. Could this be the creator of such a piercing sound? Such a thing seems almost impossible. Suddenly, a new burst of 'gunfire' breaks the silence, but at the same time one can see the beak of this bird strike hard and bounce back with such a rapid motion that its head seems to be blurred in outline, like a spring when it vibrates! The great spotted woodpecker has been located. Clinging to the dry wood, resting on its tail, with the feathers of its stomach raised, it seems to be gathering itself together in order to play an encore. This drumming, which consists of ten or twelve strikes of its beak, lasts for about a second and is the only way the bird has of marking its territory. It takes the place of song and is not peculiar to the species but common to most other woodpeckers, although for each of them there is a different rhythm. The great spotted woodpecker is the most spectacular and also the most common woodpecker in the Alps. Its alarm cry is a 'tick', sharp and vigorous, audible from a long way off. Near its nest, which is always in the hollow of a tree trunk, this magnificent bird, when excited, some-

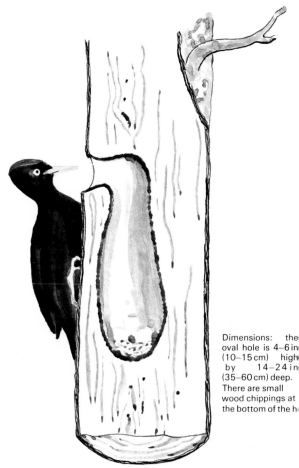

Dimensions: the oval hole is 4–6 in (10–15 cm) high by 14–24 in (35–60 cm) deep. There are small wood chippings at the bottom of the h[...]

Many birds make use of these deserted holes: owls, nuthatches, tits, etc.

Woodpeckers alone are able to hollow out and set up their home in a tree.

times emits a series of 'cicicirice' at a high pitch. The male differs from the female by having a small bright red spot on the back of the head, but the drumming is not exclusive to the male and its companion often replies from another fir tree.

These strange instrumental displays come to an end in March or April in the mountains, whereas at lower levels the great spotted woodpecker drums from January onwards if the temperature is at all mild. The noise should not be confused with the real hammering which is nothing more than a series of blows with the beak against the wood when the bird is seeking its food or digging a new home for its future family. Furthermore, the great spotted woodpecker feeds not only on insects and larvae of beetles but it also eats fir-cone seeds, especially in winter. It is able to push a pine-cone or spruce-cone skilfully between two pieces of bark which act as a vice, and then it methodically extracts the seeds. Often it licks with great satisfaction the sap running from cuts in a young birch tree after a nuthatch or a red squirrel has refreshed itself in the same way. Its definition as a mountain bird poses no problem, as the other variegated species only appear very exceptionally at high altitudes. Only the very rare three-toed woodpecker could lead to confusion at a distance, but it is much darker in colour and has no red on its plumage, while the male is the only woodpecker in Europe to have yellow on the upper part of its head.

he black woodpecker

Holes dug in a spruce fir by the black woodpecker so as to get at the larvae of wood-boring insects.

s the forest path continues to climb, the air ecomes fresher and the beeches gradually give way large silver fir trees and spruce. Suddenly, from the ees, there is a sonorous cry 'tru-tru-tru' and, at the ame instant, a shadowy form with a large pale beak ies noisily between the trees: this is the black wood-ecker! It disappears behind a tree trunk. The noise of s claws is heard as they grip the bark: then, suddenly black head, touched with scarlet, comes into view; iis fierce bird watches for a moment then vanishes reappear a little higher, this game of hide-and-seek howing how mistrustful it is ... Finally an extra-rdinary cry rings out, a sort of lengthy complaint vhich is almost human in sound 'cliu'.. ! The author nought that, if examining carefully the trees sur-ounding him, he might perhaps discover the hole rilled by this prince of the great mountain trees. The ntrance to its hole can be recognised by its oval or ointed arch form, and there are normally many vood chippings at the foot of the tree which the bird as chosen for its home. The noise of the bird's wings heard again, and this giant amongst woodpeckers resses its black body against the trunk of a fir tree, uddenly becoming silent. Then the bird could be een just by the entrance to its hole, its neck tretched out, its light coloured eyes seemingly ightened, making movements which can only be escribed as reflex, while carefully putting its veight on to its knife-blade shaped tail. The bird dips s red-crested head several times into the hole and nen, with one hop, it disappears inside. Generally peaking, the black woodpecker builds a new cavity or its young every spring, choosing for preference a ee trunk which is free from branches up to quite a eight. Both male and female share in drilling the ole, although the latter is the more active. The cavity quite large, normally reaching a depth of 20 inches 50 cm) or even more, and has an internal diameter of to 9 inches (18 to 23 cm).

The old holes of the woodpecker often act as a ome for tengmalm's owl, whose life in this way is onnected with the life of the woodpecker. The awny owl also occasionally lays its eggs in the voodpecker's hole although, in view of its large size it oes rather feel the lack of space. Even the little owl ests there sometimes as do the dove, the tits and ne nuthatch.

When March arrives in the mountains, the black voodpecker utters cries which are very similar to nose of the green woodpecker. In the wild and nountainous valleys there can be heard the 'ouk ouk uk ouk' of the black woodpecker; a sonorous and nelodious sound, emitted slowly, sometimes in a ong series. The female replies to the male with shor-er, more piercing cries, the couple giving rise to trange forest duets. Even more bizarre, perhaps ven more formidable, is the sound which the black voodpecker produces when it indulges in its drum-

ming. The author had the opportunity of hearing it on one occasion as close as 55 yards (50 m) and was amazed by the rumbling noise produced by this bird against the stump of a dead branch. This drumming noise can last for more than three seconds and although it is audible from nearly half a mile (1 km) away, it has nothing in common with the hammering of the bird's beak when it strikes the bark in search of its food or while drilling a new home. Like the tits' 'song' this drumming is part of the bird's mating ritual. The great spotted woodpecker similarly makes a hammering noise when mating though it is more frequent in the latter's case. Both black and green woodpeckers like to fly down to the ground in their search for ant-hills which they then dig up in order to eat the occupying ants. The woodpecker seems particularly fond of the giant black ants which they seek out of the old tunnel-ridden branches. Woodpeckers also feed on most wood-boring insects and are able to extract their larvae, even when they are concealed beneath the thickest bark. The female great spotted woodpecker differs from the male by a small red patch on her head. The black woodpecker, the giant among the European woodpeckers, is not frequently found in the mountains. It is not frequently seen and only its extraordinary cries reveal its pres-ence in the vast kingdom which it has chosen for itself – the wild and primitive forest.

A black woodpecker (male) at the entrance to its hollow.

Spotted icheumon (*Rhyssa persuasoria*)

Musk beetle (*Rhagium inquisitor*)

Larger capricorn beetle (*Ergates faber*)

Giant wood wasp.

Wood boring insects

In warm weather it is very rare to walk through a wood of pine trees in the mountains without seeing any insects. One only needs to examine carefully the bark of the trees which have been felled or uprooted by storms in order to make some interesting discoveries. Thousands of horned, wood-boring and bark beetles, sawflies, wasps and ants settle there and lay their eggs. One of the most widely found beetles at this time on the pine bark or on the old spruce stumps is the beetle *Rhagium inquisitor*. This medium sized beetle crawls quite quickly along the trunk when it is disturbed and the greyish brown down covering its black speckled wing sheaths blends perfectly with its background, making it difficult to locate. When it is not moving, *Rhagium* takes up a characteristic position, usually with its thorax raised. The female lays its eggs in a crack in the bark and the larvae dig long tunnels between the bark and the sapwood of the dead tree. Its pupa stage is completed in a casing, round in shape and surrounded by wood fibres. At the end of winter, by carefully lifting the old pine or spruce bark, it is often possible to find the adult beetle, still wrapped in this unusual type of nest. (See above, pages 8–12). Another horned beetle which is seen quite frequently in the mountain pine forests and which attracts attention from some distance away is the beautiful, violet coloured *Callidium violaceum* with its blackish antennae and legs, and a remarkable metallic blue round its body and on its wing sheaths. Its legs have a strange bulge at the top, and its larvae also burrow tunnels in the dry wood of the pine trees. This violet beetle is the same size as *Rhagium*, reaching just over $\frac{1}{2}$ in (15 mm) in length.

Walking through the pine woods on south-facing slopes it is also possible to find on the bark of the trees the longhorn beetle, *Ergates faber*, the giant of the family. Together with the great capricorn and the 'flying deer' common to the forests of the plain it is one of the largest beetles of Europe, reaching a length of $1\frac{1}{4}$ to $1\frac{3}{4}$ in (30 to 45 mm). The female, with her lengthened body, can be distinguished from the male by her winged sheaths which are blackish brown, and above all by her slightly flattened and corrugated thorax. This thorax is much rougher than that of her mate which, when viewed laterally, resembles two shining plates. In addition, the wing sheaths of the male, a fine reddish brown in colour, allow it to be distinguished immediately. The larvae attain a considerable size at the nymph stage, but growth is extremely slow, and very often several years pass before the adult leaves the dwelling where its metamorphosis has taken place. It digs deep tunnels in the stumps of pine trees. All the larvae of the longhorn beetles are actively sought out by the black woodpecker, the green woodpecker, the great spotted woodpecker and the three-toed woodpecker; they are also highly valued by trout fishermen for bait (they call them 'wood worms'). Although they are generally without feet, and are soft and whitish in colour, these larvae succeed in penetrating the hardest woods thanks to their large heads and pincer-like jaws. They should not be confused with the larvae of the wood-wasp *Urocerus gigas* which is somewhat similar in appearance and also bores long tunnels in the trunks of pine trees. The larvae of this enormous wood-wasp belong to an entirely different order, that of the *Hymenoptera*. The adult reaches a length of $1\frac{1}{4}$ in (30 mm). The abdomen of the female ends with a sort of needle rather like a very large sting, giving the insect a formidable appearance. This sting, the ovipositer, is completely harmless; the female only uses it in order to lay her eggs underneath the bark of pine trees, firs or larches. The larvae which are born there dig tunnels with their jaws which are enlarged as their size increases; their growth too is very slow and can last for several years. While the female is laying, she keeps her ovipositer buried deeply in the bark, which means she is unable to escape immedi-

Galleries of bark beetle larvae on silver pine wood.

ately and can be easily caught. The larvae of *Urocerus* would do serious damage to the timber of our forests if they were not, in their turn, victims of another *Hymenoptera*, the *Rhyssa persuasoria*. This handsome ichneumon, with its red legs and a black and yellow abdomen, is relatively common in the mountains and can grow to a length of $1\frac{1}{4}$ in (30 mm). It possesses, however, a thread-like ovipositer much longer than its own body $1\frac{1}{2}$ to $1\frac{3}{4}$ in (40 to 45 mm) and it is thanks to this extraordinary fine yet remarkably solid filament, that the female succeeds in reaching the tunnels of the *Urocerus* larvae where she lays her eggs. Beforehand the ichneumon spends a long time inspecting the trunks of fallen trees and testing the bark with her extremely mobile antennae. The female of *Rhyssa persuasoria* can locate the presence of the larvae with astonishing accuracy.

The author remembers his astonishment at seeing, for the first time, this large ichneumon rivetted to the bark of a dead tree trunk, its abdomen arched, forcing its long drill through the fibres of the wood up to a depth of several inches to reach the larvae of the *Urocerus gigas*. During this operation, which is always dangerous for the insect because it exposes itself to attack from enemies, only the probe is pushed through the woody tissue, while the protective casing, formed of two groove-shaped valves, remain outside; the egg, which can change shape to become longer and thinner, slips along the hollow probe to rest on the victim. The larva will then feed on the *Urocerus* larva devouring its live host in such a way that it attacks its vital organs only at the end of its stay – that is to say a little before achieving its own metamorphosis. This is the bizarre but true history of *Rhyssa persuasoria*!

Spotted icheumon (*Rhyssa persuasoria*)

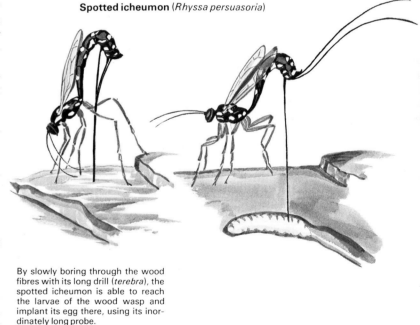

By slowly boring through the wood fibres with its long drill (*terebra*), the spotted icheumon is able to reach the larvae of the wood wasp and implant its egg there, using its inordinately long probe.

33

2
Inhabitants of the spruce forests or meadows

The tree creeper – the goldcrest – the pine marten – the robin – the siskin – the sparrow-hawk – the goshawk.

The tree creeper

In the mountains one can often walk through the pine forests without meeting any living creature. All around there is only silence, freshness, and a deep sense of mystery. The light itself only reaches one indirectly, flickering through the branches but not penetrating the shadowy corners. The smell of humus and moss rises from the ground, and one's view is limited by the base of the tree trunks where one can see only the bark and the innumerable lichens which grow there, or the confused tangle of twigs and the paths of pine needles.

In the heart of this strange kingdom something suddenly moves. More often than not it is nothing more than a small bird scarcely larger than a mouse, a small ball of greyish feathers climbing along a trunk with short hops, using its tail like a safety catch after each movement. The sight has something unusual about it; this greyish bird clinging to the old tree and constantly on the move resembles nothing more than a piece of living bark, the colours of its feathers blending so well with its background. The little bird, while actively searching in the smallest cracks with its beak, continues its spiral climb. When seen in profile it reveals the silky whiteness of its breast and the russet colours of its side and its sub-caudal areas. Then this tiny shape disappears behind the trunk, only to appear again a little higher, but on the other side, always moving, always using its tail and the long sharp claws it possesses. Suddenly the bird bursts into song; it is a pleasant sound, with several syllables, full of happiness, sharp and clear in tone. This song scarcely ever lasts more than two seconds and its volume is in keeping with the modesty of the performer. The tree creeper, instead of continuing its ascent, now changes direction and moves on to a large horizontal branch, which it explores feverishly, clinging on to the fine flakes of bark with great ease, like a fly crawling over the ceiling. We follow the progress of this little acrobat with increasing pleasure until, suddenly, it leaves the branch with a sharp cry and plunges like an arrow, its wings close to its side, and alights a few yards away from the ground on another tree trunk, where it starts its climb again . . . Very often the wood tree creeper, contrary to its close relation the garden tree creeper, likes to explore the upper part of the pine trees, showing a special preference for their bushy tops. It becomes difficult to observe the bird under such conditions, and it often disappears amongst the tangle of needles, lichen and twigs. When alarmed the tree creeper remains perfectly still, pressed against the bark, and great skill is required to detect the bird under these conditions. Here is a little anecdote which illustrates the marvellous blending of the plumage of this bird with its background and the advantage which it can draw from it . . . The incident happened in June at a height of 6500 ft (2000 m) not far from the upper tree line of the alpine forest; the author had been watching since dawn a black grouse which had settled in a thicket and emitted from time to time its harsh cry of alarm. The minutes and even hours passed by without there being any change in position. He was leaning against the trunk of an old spruce tree and half concealed by its lower branches, while still seeing clearly. 11 yards (10 m) away down the slope an enormous larch raised its knotty trunk, the rough bark full of folds and cracks. Upon examining this tree more closely, he spotted on its bark, for a split second, a sort of yellow flash in two places very close together. Intrigued by this, he paid even closer attention. A few minutes later these two yellow flashes appeared again . . . this time however he saw a tree creeper suddenly leave the larch and he realised that clinging to the bark were two young tree creepers waiting patiently for their food, perfectly still and invisible because of their brown striped backs. Each time the parent came to feed them they opened their beaks for an instant, revealing their presence by the yellow colour of their mouths. Without this movement the author would probably never have noticed them, as their feathers blended so well with the bark of the larch.

The goldcrest

The author's encounter with the smallest bird in Europe goes back many years, but he still has a very clear impression of the occurrence. He was returning one fine March day from a long cross-country ski trip travelling through woods in deep snow. The sun was sinking rapidly, and as his village was not far off he chose an old spruce in the centre of a small copse, broke off a few dry branches covered with lichen, spread them on the snow and settled down comfortably near the tree. The air was completely calm and the spot isolated; only a few tracks made by a mountain hare and a fox betrayed the fact that some sort of life had been there. Tired, but very happy, he was in the process of filling his pipe, when his attention was attracted by a small greenish bird which was moving from branch to branch, often poised, hovering in the air in one spot. The movement of the bird's wings was so rapid that sometimes nothing more than a little ball of feathers could be seen, surrounded by a sort of halo, looking as if it were suspended from the tufts at the end of the branches of the conifer. While vibrating its wings in this way, and without making any sound incidentally, the little fly-like bird was pecking at its invisible food with its tiny beak. The spectacle was fascinating and the author took in every detail. When it was tired of hovering in one place, the tiny creature alighted on the tree and crawled into its depths just like a mouse, to inspect every corner of the branches, every piece of lichen, every crack in the bark and the smallest twigs, constantly hopping or flying. It would disappear and reappear, never giving up its intense activity.

Highly intrigued by this little gymnast, the author attempted to follow it as best he could through its green kingdom; suddenly, with a series of scarcely audible high-pitched sounds of 'sih sih sih', a second bird announced its arrival. The newcomer began to fly-flutter like a butterfly under a branch quite close to him. Not more than two yards separated him from this charming acrobat which paid him no attention. Like a sphinx in the twilight the author watched it inspect, one by one, the dark needles of a fir tree. It alighted here and there, using its claws, which were so delicate they appeared almost transparent, revealing between two branches its little round olive stomach and the black patches of its wings which trembled incessantly . . . Suddenly the little bird, alarmed by a movement the author had made, raised its crest which glowed like a flame amongst the shadows of the conifer; it was a magnificent sight and doubtless responsible for the name of goldcrest, given to this bird. This small crest, in a setting of black feathers, normally appears only when the creature is frightened or when it is excited during the mating season . . . Usually the tiny bird keeps its crest flat on the top of its head; it is the only brightly coloured area in the whole of its plumage and the only sign which allows the observer to determine its sex; the female has a crest of bright yellow, while the male displays one of a delicate orange red colour. Later the author saw the goldcrest on a neighbouring tree, hopping from one branch to another, never tiring. It was no longer alone, as some coal-tits and crested-tits joined it in its frantic dance, uttering cries of encouragement. These sounds, blending together, gave the impression that the forest was full of mischievous imps. This was not to continue for long however because, when the sun slipped behind the horizon, the joyful group suddenly deserted the spot; silence fell again. The author started on his way again, thinking about this instinct of solidarity which unites these tiny beings and helps them to survive the rigours of the cruel winter. At night these birds assemble on a branch or in a hole in serried ranks and only the warmth of their combined plumage saves them from freezing to death. The nest of the goldcrest is difficult to locate, as the bird likes to build it under the end of the spruce tree branches, hidden amongst the protective foliage; normally the nest is built at a height of between 16 and 65 ft (5 and 20 m). It is solidly made from moss and lichens sewn together with threads from the spiders' webs and lined inside with small feathers or some pieces of plant material.

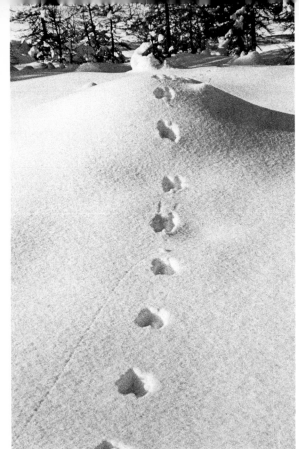

A pine marten . . . .   and its tracks in the fresh snow.

The pine marten

This is certainly the most mysterious carnivorous animal of the alpine fauna. Only the most exceptional good luck allows it to be seen. It is, however, not a rare animal as its tracks can be observed after every fall of snow. The pine marten, in contrast to the beech marten, is not fond of the presence of man. It retires into the spruce forests intersected with rocky banks, where there is more freedom of vision; it inhabits the wild, isolated valleys and seems to prefer the coniferous forests up to their tree line rather than the leafy woods of the plain. It is an animal which is both curious and savage, wandering through vast tracts of land; because of its preference for the twilight it is very difficult to observe even though it comes out during the day time more often than does the beech marten. It stands a little higher than the latter, with better developed ears and with far more fur on its feet so that the pads of its feet are largely covered with hair, allowing the expert to recognise which species he is following should there be soft snow on the ground. The beech marten marks the snow with the pads of its feet, under good conditions, in the same way as does the wild cat, while the pine marten leaves tracks which are far less distinct.

The author's encounters with this impressive musteline have unfortunately been very limited. He once saw it one morning when stalking some black grouse. It crossed a snow covered copse and made straight for the author's hiding place, only to stop suddenly underneath a larch less than 19 ft (6 m) away from him. At the click of the camera, the marten gave a curious growl and with a few leaps disappeared into the forest. On another occasion, a pine marten suddenly appeared on the edge of a forest track and, blinded by the lights of the author's car, remained motionless for more than a minute while he allowed the engine to continue running only a short distance away. He was able in this way to examine it at his leisure, without, however, daring to make any move. The animal stared at him with strange reflections in its eyes, obviously blinded by the strong lights, which accentuated the light patch on its throat and made it much yellower than it would have been otherwise. Then, suddenly driven by its instinct of self-preservation, it made a great leap to one side and literally plunged into the night. More recently, while author's eldest son was searching for a buzzard's nest in a lonely spot, he saw a pine marten approach him and, surprised by his presence, take refuge in a young larch quite nearby from where it stared at him for several minutes. It was an unexpected piece of good fortune for which the author is still waiting . . . Quite recently, while crossing a secluded forest one night, he heard a series of grating noises on the bark of a tree, noises which could only have been those of the claws of a pine marten climbing up to some old squirrel's nest.

The author regularly sees pine marten droppings on mountain paths and they always are in the same spots from one year to the next. Usually they are black in colour the size of the little finger or even smaller and, those seen at the approach of autumn, are of changed colour; he has seen some which were violet, others inky, while others contained raspberry seeds and were reddish in colour; in winter he often finds in the droppings of the pine marten the tough skins of the arbutus berry. Apart from wild berries, which the pine marten consumes in large quantities, it also catches the common vole, although its favourite prey appears to be the red squirrel. It pursues this animal relentlessly from tree to tree, climbing and from time to time making enormous leaps. The pine marten also successfully attacks young grouse and hazel hens, seizes their eggs and fledgelings — and even attacks hares; insects also form part of its diet, especially grasshoppers and cockroaches. It has been established that the pine marten leaves at various precise spots certain strong smelling secretions from its anal glands which act as boundary markers for its territory. This fact is well known to those poachers who succeed in outwitting the cunning of this animal and lay traps for it on its favourite paths. The pine marten leaves tracks in thick snow which are similar to those of the beech marten. In the snow it bounds along with short leaps and leaves its tracks in parallel pairs, although one of the tracks is always slightly behind the other. Much more of a forest and tree dweller than the beech marten, the pine marten normally hides its young in a hollow tree trunk, sometimes in the old nest of a bird of prey or a red squirrel, or even in the hole drilled by the black woodpecker, or holes in the rocks. The true mating season takes place from the end of June to September, followed by a gestation period of nine weeks, while the false mating season, taking place in January and February, is non-productive.

The robin

Whenever the author installs himself somewhere in the forest to await patiently the passing of a deer, a badger or a stag, a small round bird — always the same one — comes to examine him at close quarters, making little bows and nervous movements of its wings and its tail. He has become accustomed to this occurrence, and often asks himself what could be the attraction? With olive brown feathers on its back, its neck and its wings, it displays a superb orange patch on its breast and the upper part of its body. A few feathers, very soft blueish grey in colour, separate these two principal shades, its stomach alone being white. When it is seen in the shadowy undergrowth in the morning or the evening, the robin is not easily recognised immediately. Only its shape and its habit of paying one a furtive visit allow it to be recognised under such circumstances. In winter it is quite happy to approach houses and parks to such an extent that every garden seems to have its own robin.

Between March and April this little bird retires to its native forest where its song is heard, most often in the morning and the evening. Although it is discreet, the song of the robin is of great beauty, full of poignant melancholy. It is a series of crystalline notes, full of subtle modulations, cascading trills or quiet whistling. The varied melodies follow each other without any special order, as if the bird was confiding in itself. . . . Exquisitely sweet, the robin's song seems to be an integral part of the forest, of its smell of moss and humus and of the peace of its evenings . . . Its true meaning, however, is completely different. It is a solitary bird and extremely jealous of its territory. It is so aggressive that it will not accept the presence of any other male of its species in the domain which it has chosen for itself. It 'sees red' as soon as a neighbour with its red breast ventures to invade its territory. It takes up a threatening attitude, soon followed by a sharp attack. One day the author registered the song on his tape recorder and then played it back as loudly as possible. The robin immediately started to sing continuously with such energy that it hardly seemed

A tree creeper.

A robin singing.

A goldcrest in winter.

A pair of siskins at mating time (the male is on the right).

The siskin

Winter and spring are the seasons best suited for th
observation of this charming little member of th
sparrow family, although it breeds at times in th
Alps in a very irregular manner. Certain ornithologist
have noticed that the siskin builds its nest in th
mountains very early and lays eggs at the beginnin
of March. The abundance of these birds and the
desire to build nests seems to be connected with
heavy crop of cones on the conifers, but other, mor
obscure reasons also influence their erratic behaviou
from time to time. Very sociable by nature, they con
tinually emit metallic cries while they are in flight; an
when they are eating food they utter a more gentle
whispering cry, repeated more and more frequentl
so that it often becomes an extraordinary warblin
sound. Generally the siskin appears from the north i
great numbers at the beginning of autumn. They the
settle in the larch forests, but also visit the small birc
woods and develop a special affection for the alde
on the plains and in the mountains. The author ha
often seen them hanging from the outer branches c
the alder in acrobatic positions, carefully taking th
shell off each small cone, while continuing their joyfu
babble in spite of his close presence.

Their shape is typical enough to be recognised im
mediately; they are small greenish birds with a fla
tail and wings striped with yellow. The rump and th
base of the tail are also of the same colour in the cas
of the males but a little less bright with the females
whilst the greyish white breast has dark vertica
stripes. The author remembers particularly well on
spring when the siskins had invaded the forests c
Anniviers in such large numbers that their flocks ros
continuously into the sky, animating the sever
mountain scenery in an almost unexpected way. A
little before sunlight the siskins, having gathered to
gether in the first light, crowded the larch trees an
burst out with a crackle of metallic notes while break
ing open the cones in order to get at the seeds. Thi
pleasant babble, normally rather insignificant, suc
ceeded in drowning all the other sounds of the forest
it created a sort of constant chatter of joyful notes
while at the same time innumerable shapes move
from one large tree to another, dropping clouds o
russet husks on to the snow below. Looking at then
from below one immediately noticed the dark streak
on their breasts, the heads of the males capped with
black and the gold stripes of their wings. Against th
light, one of the trees on which the largest flock o
birds had settled seemed laden with thousands o
small fruit. There was an unbelievable clicking nois
which filtered through the high branches to b
echoed *ad infinitum*. All the time late arrivals joine
the throng and this tiny universe of birds swarme
through the trees and hung from the cones, each bird
trying to twitter louder than the next; there was a
ceaseless coming and going of greenish feathers an
of wings striped with gold. Then, suddenly as if at a
given signal, the entire flock took flight, looking like
light cloud of dust as they flew up the slope of th
mountain, which was by now in shadow, and leavin
behind them in the sky above the larch trees a charm
ing echo of silvery notes.

possible. When it realised that this achieved nothing,
the bird came up to within 6 ft (2 m) of him, very
excited and obviously furious, staring at him with its
large dark eyes and displaying continuously its
orange little breast. Then could be fully understood
the extremely combative nature of this small 'lord of
the forest', its ill-tempered attitude towards other
members of its own species and the great need for
solitude which it has. Also understood was the profound territorial meaning of its song, concealed beneath the strange sweetness it possesses.

The mating of couples in the spring is not without
its difficulties. The migratory males arrive first and are
hostile in their reception of the females. The latter,
instead of escaping, put up with their rebuff patiently
until two birds become accustomed to each other;
the couples then look after their affairs within the
strict limits of the territory conquered by each male.
The female alone builds the nest while her mate
keeps guard. The small bowl made of moss and roots
is often built on the ground, in a natural cavity on a
slope protected by ivy, roots or a heap of dead leaves.
The author has discovered such a nest in the mountains only by disturbing the sitting bird from beneath
his feet, and one frequently finds robins even at the
upper limit of the forests, although they are always in
the damp undergrowth. Their usual cry is a 'tic tic tic'
emitted in short groups of sounds.

The robins of the north are migratory birds; those
from the Alps descend to the plains where many of
them succeed in passing the winter more or less happily near towns or streams, but suffering heavy losses
when there are severe snow storms. In March and
April the males return to the high altitude and begin
again their crystalline song in the areas where they
intend to mate.

The sparrow-hawk and the goshawk

Apart from the golden eagle, two other birds-of-prey regularly inhabit the coniferous forests in the mountains as far as their upper limits. The author has sometimes even seen them at much higher altitudes, hunting their prey on the bare slopes above 10 000 ft (3000 m). They are, however, above all two species which live in the forests, but they also build their nests on the plains. In recent years, however, industrial pressures and the intensive reorganisation which has taken place has been sufficient to force the sparrow-hawk and the goshawk to be constantly pushed back towards quieter areas. They have therefore been more than happy to seek out the wooded slopes intersected with small valleys, the isolated copses or the gorges in which the waters of streams still chatter freely. From time to time one discovers a nest not far from a little-used forest path; both birds seem to have a particular affection for the old forests of spruce and larch trees where there may or may not be mountain pines. They are skilful hunters of birds and small mammals and are capable of following their prey with unbelievable speed amongst the thickest confusion of branches and tree trunks in the forest.

Unless one knows the whereabouts of their nests, they are difficult birds to observe. Even with such knowledge, one must take every precaution to be completely concealed and a lot of patience is needed. The sparrow-hawk and the goshawk are almost silent, except during the mating season; they are wild and fierce, very swift, and are armed with long powerful and sharp claws. Both these birds would for the most part remain undetected, were it not for the feathers which they often shed in the undergrowth. Thanks to these feathers it is possible to locate the areas inhabited by these remarkable birds. The author is far from claiming to know them well, but he is fascinated by their strange beauty, the speed of their flight, the proud way they look at one and their discreet habits.

It is September in the mountains and the author is looking over a vast rocky amphitheatre at the edge of which cling a few larch and spruce trees. Some nutcrackers ply from one mountain side to another; those who fly up from the lower reaches have dropped their pine seeds into cracks sheltered from the snow. Those birds, however, which come from the upper forests are heavily laden. Some of them alight regularly on the same tree — an ancient larch partly struck by lightning — before plunging into the abyss. With their throats full of seeds and their necks distended, they seem very grotesque, and the author can never help thinking, when seeing their shapes, that they would be perfect material for a caricaturist!

On a tree a short way off a small squirrel darts now and again between the tufts of needles; it is a red squirrel. The animal is searching here and there along the branches for the last pine-cone. It reaches the end of a branch near the top of the tree, which starts to shake in an unusual way. The squirrel seems to have found what it was seeking; it is absorbed in its work and is trying to bite off a pine-cone covered with resin. Suddenly a grey shape hurtles toward the tree at unbelievable speed. A nutcracker gives the alarm. The squirrel tries to scramble down from its tree, but it is too late! At the same instant the goshawk stretches out its talons, and using its wings and its tail to stop its flight almost completely, it plunges its terrible talons into the soft fur. The bird lands on a lower branch, silences its victim with a few blows of its beak, and then raises its head — less than 55 yds (50 m) away. Suddenly the bird sees the author, makes a strident 'kik kik kik', and flies off slowly but powerfully towards the nearby forest, its quivering prey clutched in the long, greyish claws. Only those who have seen the attack of a goshawk can imagine the speed at which it is carried out. It is true, however, that larger prey like the hare for example, sometimes puts up a strong fight. Nevertheless, the author has seen this bird on two other occasions catch mountain hares without any apparent difficulty. It is true to say, however, that in one instance the hare was a young animal. Apart from the red squirrel, which seems to be one of its favourite foods, the goshawk likes to catch the jay, the nutcatcher and the carrion crow. As to the raven, the author witnessed one day, not far from the village of Chandolin, a desperate struggle between one of these giants of the crow family and this energetic bird-of-prey. It must have been a question of a territorial struggle because the incident took place at the beginning of March. The raven, using its beak, tried to intimidate its adversary; the goshawk, however, replied with some daring counter-attacks, thrusting its feet forward, while trying to seize the raven with its powerful talons. Without the help of an ally who arrived on the scene the goshawk would probably have been victorious in the end. This fine bird of prey is also successful in hunting pigeons and thrushes; it attacks the mountain hens such as the hazel hen, the grouse, the rock partridge, and sometimes hunts the ptarmigan on the higher mountain ridges. The sparrow-hawk and the kestrel too are not safe from its talons and sometimes fall victim. As Paul Géroudet, the eminent ornithologist from Geneva, said quite rightly 'Amongst all the European birds of prey, this is the bird which, without doubt, possesses the widest range of hunting capabilities, and it uses them most efficiently'.

The same could be said for the sparrow-hawk, bearing in mind its far smaller size (approximately the size of a pigeon in the case of the female). This bird is a great hunter of sparrows. It is bold, swift, silent and rash to the point of madness.

The rest of the morning passed without any new developments. From time to time the young sparrow-hawks raised themselves on their legs, beat

A young goshawk.

their wings energetically and circled around the eyrie in all directions, sometimes seizing the branches with their talons as if they were playing. They still had tufts of fledgeling down in places, their heads were still more or less white, their eyes dark, their breasts very pale with wide stripes of brown, while their shoulders, backs and wings were brownish grey flecked with rust colour. Towards midday the smallest of the three, probably a male, suddenly left the eyrie and perched on a neighbouring branch, only to disappear from there into the forest. The two others dozed for the greater part of the afternoon, but towards three o'clock they began to utter plaintive cries. At half-past-three the female arrived at the nest, quite silently, bringing with her a large victim which by the telephoto lens was shown to be a headless blackbird. The young birds were beating their wings before the adult, who continued to hold the blackbird in its talons at the edge of the nest, and then began to pluck the feathers from its prey. Very soon the female began to tear the first pieces of flesh from the prey and distributed them, first to one of the young birds, then to the other. There followed a very entertaining scene: the more impatient of the two young birds tried on several occasions to seize the blackbird but the adult kept watch and constantly drew its prey back under its talons with powerful pecks. Suddenly, the young male who had disappeared into the sur-

roundings for part of the day returned to the nest a received its share of the food, the other two appea ing more or less satisfied. In a short while all th remained of the blackbird were the large bones a the wing feathers, the young having eaten the feet well as the flesh. Three days later the nest was emp and the young nowhere visible being perfec camouflaged in the high branches of the tree.

The nest of the goshawk is much larger than th of the sparrow-hawk or even the buzzard. It is usua built in the highest third of the tree. It would se that a pair return to the nest almost every year unli the sparrow-hawk. The goshawk, always has seve nests at its disposal which it inhabits in turn with the sector chosen for raising its young.

One of the most striking facts about these tv species, which are very similar to each other in a pearance and habits, the sparrow-hawk being smaller version of the goshawk, is the marked diffe ence in size between the sexes. In fact the males a always a good third smaller and lighter in weight th the females, this fact being the origin of the wo 'tercel' used to describe the birds in ornithologic terms. This is also the reason why it is difficult identify with certainty in its natural habitat the fema of the sparrow-hawk in relation to the male of t goshawk. In flight, the wing span of these two bir of prey is more or less the same, while the colours

The sparrow-hawk in pursuit of its prey.

An adult goshawk tearing its victim (a brown hare) into pieces.

ir lower parts are identical. There is, however, no iculty in distinguishing the male adult sparrow-vk thanks to its small size, its breast striped with owish brown, and the slate grey, almost blue of upper parts of the wing and the back. The female the other hand has the upper parts of its plumage oured brown, while its white breast is covered h numerous horizontal stripes, greyish brown in our. The colouring of the latter is similar to that nd in both sexes of the adult goshawk. Due to the rming decrease in their numbers during recent rs all birds of prey are now protected by law in nce, Switzerland, Belgium and many other coun-s. It has finally been understood that they have ir part to play in nature. The goshawk exercises a trolling influence over the numbers of the crow nily, while the sparrow-hawk, in hunting the more nmon sorts of sparrow, helps to control their ex-sive breeding. Let us close this section by observ-that, in general, the birds of prey have a beneficial ct on European fauna, eliminating the creatures ich are weak, sick, defective, or imprudent!

Do not let us treat them as 'harmful' any longer t, as the writer Paul Géroudet says, 'Let us salute m as the living expression of nature in all its ength and richness!'

3
Inhabitants of the mountain streams, rivers and their banks

The dipper – the river trout – the bullhead – the white wagtail – the grey wagtail – the wren.

The dipper

What would the mountains be without the sounds of the streams, without that white foam chattering happily amongst the mossy rocks and the saxifrages? What would the Alps be without their springs, their waterfalls and their clear waters flowing calmly through the wild valleys as they have done for thousands of years, giving even in the heat of summer a delicious freshness? From beneath the old wooden bridge joining the two banks, there appears a dark coloured bird similar to a blackbird but far more squat in form. With a short cry of 'zrett' it flies downstream with short beats of its wings and comes to rest on a large stone bathed in the foaming water ... If it were not for the brilliant white patch of its breast it would pass almost unnoticed, the rest of its plumage appears so black or slate coloured. The author seized his binoculars and distinguished the brown sectors of its head, its neck and its stomach. The bird, watching him, balanced its body in a curious way, bending forward constantly as if it wished by these little bows and the movements of its short tail to express its emotion. Then, suddenly, the 'water blackbird' left its stone and dived into the tumultuous water, only to reappear a few seconds later at some distance from the place where it disappeared, with a larva of the Tridopterus in its beak. Perhaps with a little patience one might be able to discover its nest. The author decided to hide himself on the bank a little distance from the bridge where he already suspected that the dipper had lodged its family. Concealed behind some alder trees, he was able to observe the bird with his binoculars as it went about its business and plunged into the water on several occasions. When it emerged from the water, small drops fell from its plumage, without it seeming wet, doubtless thanks to the particularly fine, close texture. The movements of this bird are all the more interesting as the dipper is the only thru[sh] like bird which can both dive and swim; its life see[ms] closely linked with the element of water and [one] wonders how this bird succeeds in holding its p[os]ition underneath the current while looking for its fo[od] with its beak? It must certainly use its wings and [its] claws to advance against the stream. The period[s it] spends under the water are short, from seven to [ten] seconds, but it never fails to emerge from the stre[am] with some food in its beak. Then the bird flew awa[y to] its original starting point. It dived beneath the [ ] bridge without any hesitation, stayed there for a c[er]tain time and then set out again upstream, its fli[ght] being almost along a straight line.

This time there could be no doubt, the nest m[ust] have been hidden somewhere underneath the h[uge] larch wood arches of the bridge and the author [set] out to look for it. But on both sides he saw noth[ing] more at first than piles of moss on the rocks be[ing] continuously sprayed with water. A little [dis]appointed and with his feet already soaked by the foam, he was on the point of leaving when he notic[ed] a bowl of moss shaped like a bell which was sligh[tly] larger than the other piles. On examining it closer [he] finally discovered an entrance at the side of the ba[ll] which was well concealed; this was the corridor [by] which the dipper enters its nest. Five of its alrea[dy] well-developed young were hidden there, complete[ly] dry.

Doubtless they left their droppings outside [the] nest after each feeding time and the water from [the] stream washed it away immediately. The author w[as] amazed by so much skill and ingenuity. This n[est] made from moss, positioned so naturally betwe[en] two rocks was yet another example of a masterpie[ce] created by nature.

Dipper.

Head of a bullhead.

A brook trout in a stream.

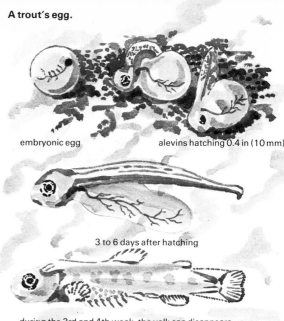

A trout's egg.

embryonic egg   alevins hatching 0.4 in (10 mm)

3 to 6 days after hatching

during the 3rd and 4th week, the yolk sac disappears and the troutlet measures 1.2 in (30 mm) in length.

The river trout and the bullhead

It is true that the river trout, that most noble of fishes, can create dreams and that the trout alone has an attraction which no other fish in the world can create. It is also true that this fish needs pure cold water, rich in oxygen, and that it is a born individualist, voracious, home-loving, faithful to its breeding ground, knowing how to conceal itself marvellously well beneath a stone or a root in the water. Everything about the river trout is astonishing; its unusual strength, the delicate flavour of its flesh, and its colouring, which varies from one to the other and blends perfectly with the surroundings in which it lives. There are some trout which are greenish in colour, others which are brown or golden, still others which are of a silvery greyish green, but they all have on their sides magnificent red or black spots, surrounded by white rings. Such is the harmony of their appearance and the beauty of their shape that trout have always attracted painters, given great pleasure to naturalists and excited innumerable fishermen.

The trout generally spawns between November and February. It swims quite far up the mountain streams and feeds on various insects, small crustaceans and above all on the larvae of the Trichoptera. These larvae are always found in rapid flowing, sandy streams and rivers, even at high altitudes. The larvae are in the form of small cylindrical cases about $\frac{3}{4}$–1 in (2–3 cm) in length. The cases are made from sand grains or small pieces of gravel stuck together with a secretion from the larva. In this form it crawls on the bed of the stream, only showing its head and black legs. When alarmed, the larva of the mayfly retires into its protective casing and remains immobile, but this does not prevent the trout from swallowing it, complete with its casing. The adults are similar to certain butterflies and moths, and hold their front wings together when resting, rather like the gables of a roof; they are almost always to be found near water. They have a short life, a few weeks at the most, sufficient to give them time for reproduction. The trout is extremely fond of them as food and fishermen use them as bait on lines with great success. The same is also true of the larva.

In most of the rivers inhabited by trout there lives another fish which remains carefully hidden under the stones; this is the bullhead. It can be recognised by its small size, its brownish colour, its squint eyes close together on a flattened head and by the ventral fins, which are fan shaped. The fish is almost always found on river beds, only moving over short distances and then strictly at night. This fish feeds on the larvae of the Trichoptera and also on eggs and tiny fish When it swims in the running waters inhabited by the trout, the latter give it a warm welcome as it is one of their favourite foods. The gills of the bullhead are, however, protected by sharp spines and it often happens that a small trout chokes and dies after having partly swallowed this strange fish which cannot be confused with any other. The skin of the bullhead has no scales; it is entirely covered by a coat of sticky secretion which protects it for a certain time from drying when the level of the water suddenly falls.

The white wagtail and the grey wagtail

How marvellous it is to quench one's thirst at a stream after a hard climb; what pleasure to plunge one's hands and arms into the icy water which cascades from stone to stone, splashing one as it passes and occasionally throwing its fine spray over the moss and the saxifrage on the banks. 'Tsitsip!' . . . a sharp, metallic cry disturbs the stillness and, pattering along at the bottom of the ravine cut by the tumultuous water, a little yellow and grey patch can be seen, followed by a long black and white line which is constantly moving. This bird's silhouette is striking for its slimness, its elegance and the light-footed way in which it hops from pebble to pebble, snipping up a gnat or pecking at some tiny aquatic larva. By its cry, which is harder than that of the grey wagtail, by the length of its tail, and its dark bib bordered with white and, above all, by the fine sulphur yellow shades of its stomach, this bird can be immediately recognised as the male white wagtail.

There are few birds whose movements are so graceful as those of the 'yellow washerwoman'. What would the mountain streams and rivers be without the presence of this elf? With a single beat of its wings it can rise in the air with a joyful cry, crossing the wild gorge apparently without reason only to return immediately and perch on some large mossy stone protruding from the torrent. From this pedestal, the bird watches you, constantly wagging its tail, while uttering unexpectedly a plaintive, drawn-out cry which it repeats at regular intervals.

The female is darker in plumage and without the black patch at its throat, but just as graceful as the male. The bird has arrived at the bottom of the ravine with pieces of food in its beak. After some hesitation it takes flight again, whilst the male continues to watch the author uttering its sharp cries of 'siiht'. He draws away a little from the bank and hides behind the trunk of a large larch, amongst the rhododendrons, in order to observe the bird through his binoculars. When it sees his movements, the wagtail gains confidence; the bird moves to the bank, snaps up a gnat and then swiftly flies into the depths of the ravine. It half disappears into a small natural cavity formed by the overhang of the rocks, re-appearing a few moments later carrying some droppings. The nest must be there, firmly lodged in this natural recess and very difficult to discover from the outside. Meanwhile, the wagtail has dropped its load into the stream and dips its beak several times into the water, doubtless in order to clean it. Five minutes later the female who has also brought food to the nest repeats the same operation. On this diet the young grow rapidly. They leave the nest at the age of only twelve days, with their tails still very short, and hide more or less successfully in their surroundings although they are frequently the prey of the sparrow-hawk. The white wagtail can often be seen well above the tree line, near alpine springs, at an altitude of almost 9000 ft (2700 m). In general, however, these species nest at a lower altitude in the forests of the sub-alpine area and also in the plains although it is almost always to be found near water. It seems, however, particularly fond of deep slopes, mountain streams and rocky banks as opposed to the grey wagtail, which is quite happy on the river edge preferring more open areas and even seeking out spots near man. It also appears very eclectic in the choice of a place for its nest. The nest is, in fact, found in the most varied and sometimes unexpected spots. Although the grey wagtail is quite similar to the white wagtail, it can be easily distinguished by its shorter tail and the complete absence of yellow in its plumage. Both male and female are almost identical: they both have black on the top of the head, while the front and the sides of the head and the sides of the neck and stomach are white, the throat and the breast being black. The wagtail normally spends the winter in the south of Europe and the north of Africa, although it sometimes reaches the eastern parts of Africa, being found in countries like Uganda and Kenya. Certain individuals of the two species appear, however, to be more or less sedentary and do not migrate, remaining practically in the same place, in particular the low lying areas of Switzerland, France and Belgium.

The wren

Practically everyone must have spotted this tiny brownish bird with its raised tail emerging from branches or thickets towards the end of winter. After a moment's hesitation, this ball of russet feathers with small round wings finally flies off just above the ground, and when it is at a certain distance away utters its penetrating trill. This song continues vigorously for a good five seconds with a very rapid cadence. The sound is so loud, sharp and strident that it is difficult to connect it with the insignificant shape which escaped from the undergrowth. However, there is no doubt it belongs to the wren, which together with the goldcrest and the firecrest, the inhabitants of the coniferous forests, are the three smallest birds in Europe. It would seem to justify its German name 'Winterkönig', that is to say 'the king of the winter', as this little bird seems to brave the rigours of the winter so well, maintaining its good humour amidst a very hostile nature! The wren is remarkable in more ways than one and it would be difficult to confuse it with any other bird. Very eclectic by nature, it frequents the most varied surroundings, showing a preference in the mountains for slopes covered with bushes, mossy scree, banks of streams and rhododendron groves, although it can also be found well above the tree line. Everything about this bird is surprising: first and foremost its squat form, and its method of creeping through low vegetation like a rodent without flying much, its sonorous song, its furious alarm cry, 'trett! tritt! trterrettettet!' The male is polygamous and as soon as the fine weather begins, that is towards April or May at high altitudes, it is he who builds several nests made from moss. Generally speaking these are spherical balls, pierced with one opening and usually placed at the base of an embankment, between old roots in a hole in a cliff, a rock, in the middle of a thicket or a tangle of branches. These nests usually blend so well with their surroundings that they are scarcely visible. As soon as a female enters the territory of the male, the latter becomes very excited and enters one of its nests, emerging and re-entering several times, while it sings vigorously with its wings lowered and its tail spread out as if to invite the female to visit the wonderful dwelling. If the female finds the nest suitable, it inspects it, makes its final decision and completes the work by lining it with pieces of wool, hair and feathers. This work is carried out by the female alone and while it comes and goes, the male pursues the female very assiduously. At the same time, however, the male attempts to attract other females to its territory and invites them to visit the other dwellings which it has constructed. The author amused himself one day by reproducing on his tape recorder the song of a wren which he had just recorded. This incident took place in the mountains during May, on a forest track which had been widened the previous autumn and which offered in consequence excellent, half excavated slopes beneath which the bird found very suitable places for its nests. As soon as he started to play back the song, the male flew towards him just above the ground, perched on a small larch a few metres away and began to sing frantically. With its throat distended, its wings vibrating and its spread tail opening and shutting, this tiny Don Juan paid no attention to the author whatsoever and devoted itself to its trills with so much enthusiasm and strength that he will never forget the strange spectacle of that tiny ball of russet feathers almost lost in its surroundings, but nevertheless able to drown the noise of the nearby stream with its song on its own.

A young white wagtail.

A grey wagtail (female) near its nest.

A wren on a willow branch in February.

4
Inhabitants of the sub-alpine glade

**The common vole – the field vole – the buzzard –
the honey buzzard – the rock bunting – the insects
of the sub-alpine meadows – the whinchat.**

The common vole and the field vole

As soon as the snow retreats from the fields, and the clearings in the woods reveal their covering of grass and moss, strange furrows, bordered by plant debris or earth leading to small holes, can be seen on the sides of many banks. These are the winter tunnels of the voles. These small rodents, who do not hibernate like the marmots or the dormice, are accustomed to moving between ground and snow in the winter season. Protected from the cold by the deep covering of snow, they tunnel through the thickness of the vegetation, throwing aside any debris. These easily identifiable tunnels terminate either in a large pile of chopped up grass or in small holes scarcely larger than the thickness of a thumb. Only the common vole and the field vole are responsible for these, as the much larger snow vole – described later – and the water vole build burrows distinctly wider in diameter. During the entire winter both the common vole and the field vole are able to exist without any danger from their many predators. They live on reserves built up during the autumn in their 'store houses'. These underground store houses are usually surrounded by a complicated system of twisting tunnels. They open into the characteristic furrows made between the ground and the snow. Once, in February, at an altitude of 6000 ft (1800 m) the author opened up one of these 'provision chambers' and found it to be com-

pletely dry and quite spacious. He found there roots of various umbelliferous plants and the seeds from several wild grasses. The vole can best be observed when the snow melts in the sub-alpine meadows near the lowest tree level. To do this one should sit at the foot of a tree near the tunnels remaining downwind and perfectly still. When evening falls, the tiny rodents emerge from their holes and come and go feverishly along the paths or furrows created in the dead undergrowth; one can see them running close to the ground, often stopping to lift their heads and sniff the air before biting off the first green shoots or the stems of the crocus flower, of which they seem very fond at this time of the year. Aggressive by nature, they fight amongst themselves sometimes very fiercely, doubtless excited by the mating season. The author witnessed one of these fights one evening. Two voles stood on their hind legs and hurled themselves at each other, uttering sharp squeaks, their fur and whiskers bristling, their eyes sticking out, and they tried to bite each other. It is also in this season that the nocturnal beasts of prey seize them without difficulty; the fox emerges from the wood silently and stalks them patiently at the edge of the trees waiting to pounce on any rash creature who wanders too far from its hole and thus becomes an easy victim. The author once saw a fox starving after the winter, in a clearing in the afternoon seize through the melting snow a vole who doubtless considered himself perfectly safe and was using this last protective covering of snow to improve its tunnel system. The fox leapt on the small animal with his two front paws and then seized it in its jaws; or seeing a human it rushed back into the nearby forest

The weasel, the stoat and marten actively hunt the vole while to the viper it is a favourite prey; the buzzard and the kestrel also kill them in large numbers. Yet even with so many enemies, there is little danger of these rodents becoming extinct as their rate of breeding under favourable conditions is so rapid that the young can reproduce when only one

Field vole.

The buzzard and the honey buzzard

'Hyayhuay! Hyayhuay!' These mewing cries ring out above the spruce wood. In the March skies, two large birds, their wings and tails fully extended slowly climb into the sky describing enormous circles. On their almost silvery bodies can be seen two dark patches at the base of the wing while the tips also appear black; their tails, which have several reddish stripes, end with a much wider, darker band. These birds could easily be mistaken for small eagles were it not for their much smaller wing-span, their more rounded heads which are less visible in flight, the greater width of their wings, proportionally speaking, and their mewing, piercing cries which have something savagely beautiful about them. In fact, unlike the golden eagle which is silent for most of its mating period, the buzzard 'mews' frequently while in flight, thus announcing his presence from afar. Widely found on the plains, this imposing bird of prey is progressively more difficult to find at higher altitudes, although its appearance in the mountain skies is common enough. Very often a pair will fly to a great height, skilfully taking advantage of rising currents of air. Buzzards are excellent gliders. Without a movement of their wings, these birds can stay aloft for hours at a time, moving in wide spirals and usually in opposite directions to each other, until one of the pair suddenly closes its wings and glides down in the direction of its nest, to be quickly followed by its companion. It is not uncommon to see the male join the female and have the latter clenching its talons while performing a strange turn on to its back for a few seconds . . . then the pair settle on the nest or in the immediate vicinity and mating takes place, almost always accompanied by grating or plaintive cries. During their mating flights, buzzards, which are normally rather mistrustful of man, lose this sense to a

month old. These tiny mammals may proliferate to the point of becoming a real scourge for the crops. Both types of vole are greyish brown and resemble each other so closely that it is almost impossible to distinguish them under ordinary conditions. Seen close up, the fur of the field vole seems a little longer, coarser and thicker than that of the common vole. Its head is more furry and a small tuft of hair extends into the animal's ear, but it is clear that such characteristics, which can vary from one individual to another, are insufficient to determine the species. Only the second upper molar which, in the case of the field vole has three projecting points on its internal face as opposed to only two in the case of the common vole, makes identification certain. Finally, it would appear that the field vole prefers damp ground, close to water and brushwood while the common vole is more at home in the open fields where the vegetation is short and sparse. Both species are commonly found both on the plains and in the sub-alpine glades; they are also found in the high alpine meadows, where their tunnels and holes can be seen up to an altitude of 6600 ft (2000 m). It is probable that the common vole lives at even greater heights. The author once captured one of these voles at 8000 ft (2400 m) without being sure to which of the two species it belonged.

Buzzard.

Rock bunting.

Young honey buzzards in their nest.

certain degree. This is particularly true lower down, but in the mountains they always remain remarkably prudent. As the buzzard is most frequently seen in flight, it appears heavy, solid and somewhat apathetic when it is seen resting on a mound or in a field hunting the vole. Although its colour is generally brownish there exists a great variety of shades; certain birds are very dark, others have the lower part of their body touched with brown and white, while there are even some which are very pale in colour with a completely white breast. When a vole emerges from its hole this bird of prey stretches its neck, opens its wings and glides noiselessly towards it with its claws outstretched; the vole is taken by surprise, killed on the spot and often swallowed whole.

In the Alps, pairs usually settle in the sub-alpine zone with a marked preference for the spruce and pine forests.

These forests are interspersed with vast meadows rich in small animal life. This forms the basis of the buzzards' diet and dictates to a large degree their living conditions. The author has, however, noticed on two occasions that snakes were brought to the nest as food for the young. Due to a lack of light, however, it was unfortunately not possible to determine whether the snakes were adders or grass snakes.

In the mountains the buzzard usually has several nests, changing from one to another according to the year. These nests sometimes reach an unexpected size. Sometimes they occupy an old eagle's eyrie, which they fill with a voluminous mass of twigs in the centre of which the young are found. While the young are being raised, the adults continue to decorate the edge of these nests with green pine branches until the fledgelings fly away.

At high altitudes, the trees which are normally chosen for these nests are spruce, mountain pines, or larches, normally situated near an open space or a meadow. The nest is built half-way up the tree or in its upper third, for preference in one of the forks of the tree, or at the spot where a large lateral branch begins. If one attempts to visit the young birds, the adults circle the spot ceaselessly, uttering plaintive cries; only if one puts up a hide not far from the nest is it possible to observe under good conditions what

prey is brought to the young and the way in which the parents behave at the nest. Very often the adults arrive there one after the other, each carrying a vole; the young buzzards, already well covered with feathers, greet them by uttering sharp cries and adopting rather subservient attitudes; they then settle down in the nest, beating their wings frantically, and the young snap up the voles very quickly, often swallowing them whole or tearing them up on the spot. This is not the case with larger prey which is swallowed piece by piece. One day the author saw one of the young buzzards seize a large snake which the adult had just brought to the nest. Having partially torn it into pieces, the bird of prey tried to cram the remains of the reptile into its crop. In spite of its energetic efforts, however, it failed in this and the young buzzard, being unable to breathe, rapidly disgorged the snake and then began to tear it up again into smaller pieces. In the first weeks after hatching it is always the female who keeps the chicks warm, while the male attends to their feeding. When they reach the age of forty-five days, the young normally leave the nest and spread into the immediate vicinity, where their frenzied cries, repeatedly uttered, enables them to be located without any trouble! Moreover, their tawny breasts, with vertical stripes of brown, make them easily recognisable, especially as the adults are constantly mewing above the intruder, as they dive rather rashly over his head. That is even more true of the species from the north, the buzzard with feathered legs, whose white tail has a large white band at its end. Once when the author was travelling in Finnish Lapland, two buzzards of this type attacked him with unexpected violence, diving vertically towards his head and only stopping at the last moment!

Numerous buzzards are to be found in central Europe. But those birds which nest in the north generally migrate in mid-September towards the southeast, only stopping at the Pyrenees. This hardy bird of prey, which used to be much more common, can be confused with the honey buzzard which is slightly smaller, with a longer tail. This bird has a wide, dark coloured band at the end of its tail and two other dark stripes near the base of the tail, as opposed to the eight to twelve stripes which are characteristic of the ordinary buzzard. Its shape in flight is a little slimmer, the wings appearing longer, but its head is carried further forward on a longer neck. However, from a certain distance it is possible to confuse these two species. Seen close up the iris of the eye which is light yellow in colour will eliminate any remaining doubts as the ordinary buzzard has brown eyes. The honey buzzard chiefly inhabits the deciduous forests of the plain and the foothills although it is sometimes seen flying above the sub-pine meadows where it occasionally builds its eyrie up to a height of 5000 ft (1500 m). The species however is much more localised than the normal buzzard as its staple diet is insects, with a particular preference for the nests of wasps and bees, supplemented by lizards, frogs grass snakes, and sometimes young birds. The honey buzzard spends the greater part of its life in tropical Africa and its return to European countries is therefore much later than that of the ordinary buzzard rarely taking place before May and sometimes as late as June in the mountains.

The rock bunting

It was early spring. The author, having left the surfaced road running through the centre of the deep valley was making his way along a track which clung to the sides of the hills, climbing towards the mountain. On this steep slope, exposed to the south, the air which was already warm moved gently in different directions ... Small stunted oaks, wild rose bushes, berberry bushes, juniper trees and other types of small trees clung here and there to the thin covering of soil from which emerged large greenish boulders, covered with houseleek. The snow had only recently disappeared; even though the old grass which had survived the winter already seemed dried up. A stone lizard ran across the track, while a large yellow and black bee flew laboriously along, inspecting each crack in the ground; higher up, amongst the grey grass of the scree, the first anemones had opened, offering to the light a little of their golden powder and the dark violet of their petals. Somewhere, from the depths of a bush rose a soft twittering song which the author took at first to be that of a dunnock. After a moment's silence, the high pitched sound started again. He realised that it was not a dunnock and wanted to find out what bird it was. With great care he approached the bush from which these harsh little notes seemed to come ... Before he had taken two steps however, a russet bird the size of a sparrow emerged; the little songster was frightened and fled directly into a nearby bush. It watched the author for a moment with nervous movements of its tail and wings, then disappeared, slipping skilfully into the vegetation. However, he had the time to notice the soft grey hue of its head, which was also decorated with fine black stripes, the magnificent orange red colour of its breast and its stomach and finally the white patches which become visible as its tail opens and shuts with a jerky movement. A drawn out, throbbing cry emerged from the bushes at intervals. Would this be its cry of alarm? With the aid of his binoculars he searched through the bush as best he could and finally he saw a part of the russet plumage of this fierce bird which had been looking at him the whole time. Even when hidden behind the screen of branches and spiky leaves, it did not seem at all reassured and finally disappeared completely in the heart of the undergrowth. This bird which takes such care to conceal itself from the author is a rock bunting – the least well known of all the buntings and one of the most difficult to observe in its natural habitat. The female is very similar to the male, but its plumage is less brightly coloured and seems darker. Its nest is almost always placed between two tufts of grass or hidden at the foot of a bush, choosing from preference the berberry; sometimes the nest is even built in the hollow of a rock. The discovery of its nest depends all the more on luck as the rock bunting will scarcely ever approach to feed its young if it knows it is being watched and finally the observer loses patience ... This species prefers for its habitat dry sunny slopes in the mountains between 3300 and 3600 ft (1000 and 2000 m) and in general does not appear to be migratory. However, great numbers of them descend to the plains in the winter while some of them migrate to the south of France.

The insects of the sub-alpine meadows

It would be impossible within the limits of this book to comment on all the insects living in the mountains, in particular the Alps. They are without number and therefore only the most common of them will be described.

As soon as the snow melts, in March or April, you will see on those grassy slopes exposed to the sun a strange little butterfly. It has smokey wings, a black, hairy thorax, feathery antennae and can be easily mistaken for a fly! This is the male of the *Oreopsyche plumifera* which, together with the small tortoiseshell butterfly, are the first butterflies to appear in the mountains in spring. The female is wingless and the caterpillar is somewhat similar to the larvae of the Trichoptera, as it lives in a case of twiglets, in which it spends the winter as a chrysalis. A moth of the geometrides family also makes its appearance very early, revealing itself as soon as the snow disappears; this is the *Brephos parthenias*. Thanks to its upper wings, which are brownish grey and hide the lower wings marked with orange yellow, it blends perfectly with the soil on the tracks. If it is disturbed it flies quickly off and frequently reaches a considerable height. Some weeks later, the splendid *Malacosoma alpicola*, another moth, flies through the glades in the middle of the day. The males, brilliantly coloured, actively seek out the females as soon as they emerge on the banks. The latter are far bigger than the male, without any trace of yellow or red on the back wings and their antennae are much less hairy than those of the male. The small tortoiseshell butterfly already referred to, is a beautiful insect with tawny colours and the back wings are edged with a line of light blue patches surrounded with black. These insects are found everywhere in the mountains and they spend the winter under the eaves of chalets, in attics and in stables, there being able to withstand low temperatures. As soon as the atmosphere warms up a little they emerge from hibernation. One sees them flying everywhere as early as March at an altitude of 6600 ft (2000 m) and above, while the earth is still completely covered with snow. The small tortoiseshell is not a typically alpine butterfly as it can be found from sea level up to more than 10 000 ft (3000 m) and its habitat is vast since it covers the whole of western Europe as far as the North Cape. The same is true of the painted lady – *Vanessa*

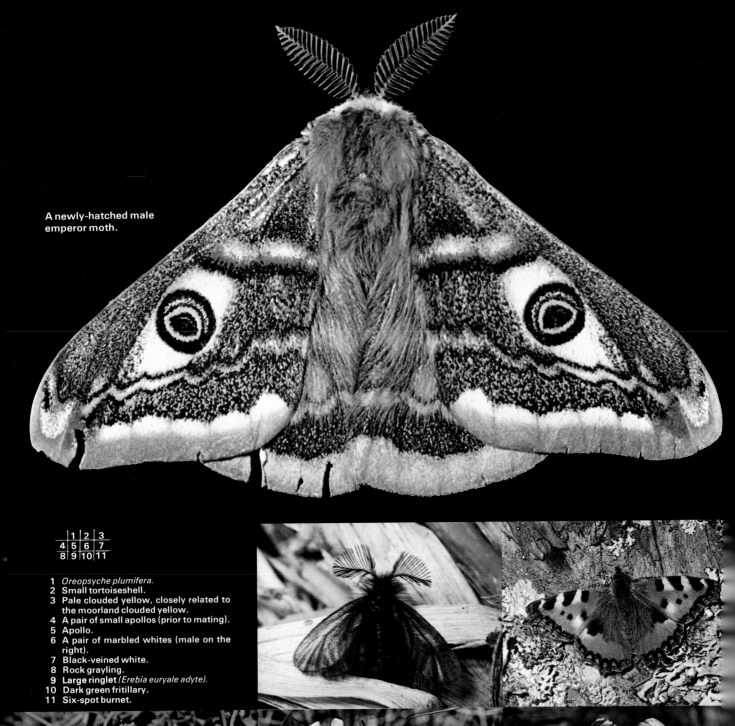

A newly-hatched male emperor moth.

1	2	3
4	5	6	7
8	9	10	11

1 *Oreopsyche plumifera.*
2 Small tortoiseshell.
3 Pale clouded yellow, closely related to the moorland clouded yellow.
4 A pair of small apollos (prior to mating).
5 Apollo.
6 A pair of marbled whites (male on the right).
7 Black-veined white.
8 Rock grayling.
9 **Large ringlet** *(Erebia euryale adyte).*
10 Dark green fritillary.
11 Six-spot burnet.

Grayling.

Apollo.

cardui – a migratory cosmopolitan species which one even finds above an altitude of 8000 ft (2500 m).

It is impossible to write about the butterflies of high altitudes without referring to the apollo butterfly. Unlike the painted lady this is the most typical of the mountain butterflies, although it lives at different levels, depending on the species, the exposure of the ground and the climate. The apollo can be easily recognised by its white wings, a little transparent at the edges and often glistening, decorated with magnificent red patches and black spots. The apollo flies only in bright sunlight between June and September, and seeks out in particular the thistle flower, the centaury flower and scabious, on which one can often find it resting during bad weather. Three species live in the mountains. The first, the small apollo – *Parnassius phoebus* – is certainly the most alpine of the three. It is not a rare butterfly but is strictly localised in the marshy areas and the edge of the streams in the sub-alpine meadows, between 5600 and 8500 ft (1700 and 2600 m). Its appearance is rather similar to the normal apollo – *Parnassius apollo* – which is much more commonly found and larger in size (wing span of 2¾–3 in (7–8 cm)). The centre of its wings, however, have a slightly yellow tinge which allows it to be distinguished from its larger cousin. The caterpillar of the alpine apollo (*Parnassius phoebus*) is black with orange patches on its sides and feeds mainly on the aizoid saxifrage and certain types of stonecrop. Both sexes have a hairy abdomen, which, however, is not the case with the female of the apollo (*Parnassius apollo*) which is smooth and has, at the end of its body when it has been fertilised, a strange brown horned pouch. Its caterpillar is also blackish in colour but has wart-like blue points on its back and a line of orange patches on its sides; it feeds mainly on the white stonecrop and different types of houseleek. The apollo which is found throughout vast regions and which inhabits the greater part of the mountainous areas of continental Europe from 2000 to 8200 ft (600 to 2500 m) represents a wide variety of ecological races and sometimes breeds with the alpine apollo. There are at least twenty-five types in France alone and it is impossible to name them all in this book. The apollo butterflies of the Pyrenees represent a pronounced dimorphism and are larger than those apollo butterflies found in the Alps. The third species is the black apollo (*Parnassius mnemosyne*) – which is found frequently throughout the sub-alpine meadows of the mountainous areas of central Europe, from a height of 1650 ft (500 m) to more than 6500 ft (200 m). This butterfly, which is smaller than the alpine apollo, can be easily recognised by the black patches on its more or less transparent wings and the complete absence of red eye marks. The abdomen of the female is black and smooth, with a large sphragis.

During the fine weather, species of butterflies which are normally found on the plains can be seen in the mountain glades; some of them because they are able to adapt to the altitude, others because they are migratory. This is the case with the swallowtail – *Papilio machaon* – a splendid, large species which can be found up to an altitude of 8200 ft (2500 m) on occasions; its fine green caterpillar has oblique black bands spattered with red dots on its sides; it feeds on various umbelliferous plants, particularly the wild carrot. The same is true of several whites, such as the black veined-white, (*Aporia crataegi*) which is completely white apart from the dark veins of its wings; it lives from sea level up to a height of more than 6600 ft (2000 m). Another example is the clouded yellow, (*Colias croceus*) an inhabitant of the alpine woods, the peat bogs and marshes of northern Europe, the Vosges and the Black Forest but which lives in the Alps only between 5200 and 8200 ft (1600 and 2500 m). More information about this species will be given when describing the butterflies of the alpine meadows.

Numerous browns of the less complex types fly from flower to flower in the sub-alpine meadows and are found up to a height of 6600 ft (2000 m) and even higher. The marbled white – *Melanargia galathar* – is widely found and is easily recognised by the black (sometimes brown) patches on its wings often arranged like a chess board. In dry and rocky areas, along deep ravines or paths in the pine woods, it is also possible to see the small wood nymph (*Hipparchia alcyone*). It likes to rest on tree trunks, against which it becomes almost invisible. The same is true of the grayling – *Hipparchia semele* – which blends admirably with tree bark or rocks, once its wings are closed. These have been photographed in the region of Chandolin, in Valais at altitudes of more than 6600 ft (2000 m).

Numerous types of browns, butterflies with dark brown wings decorated with fawn bands, fly through the sub-alpine glades. These are difficult to distinguish accurately owing to the similarity of the various species. Some of them are found at great heights, often up to the snow line, and these will be described, with details of the most characteristic species in Chapter 2 dealing with the high alpine meadows. In the fields which are surrounded by spruce and pine trees, one can certainly find *Erebia euryale*, usually between 3300 and 6600 ft (1000 and 2000 m). The sub-species *Erebia euryale adyte* replaces *Erebia euryale* from the Alpes Maritimes to the Savoy and from the south of Switzerland to Ortles. In Italy this species can be found in the areas of the Abruzzi and Gran Sasso. The *Erebia ligea*, also known as the great Hungarian brown, is a very similar species and is found throughout a vast area, in the majority of the mountainous regions of Europe as far as Kamtchatka and in Japan, and mainly in the wooded prairies and the forests where there are conifers.

Still in the same areas during the fine months
numerous butterflies of the important Nymphalidae
family can be seen. The dark green fritillary (*Mesoaci-
lia charlotta*) for example seeks out the scabious
flowers; the underneath of its back wings are decorated with beautiful silvery patches. This species,
whose span can reach almost 2 in (60 mm) is found
from sea level up to an altitude of 8000 ft (2500 m). It
is widely scattered throughout western Europe, from
the Mediterranean to the North Cape. The caterpillar
of this butterfly feeds principally on violets and wild
pansies. The fritillaries are also well represented in
the glades of the mountainous regions. But the
species which is most broadly scattered through
Europe, from the plains to the mountains up to an
altitude of 8200 ft (2500 m), is certainly the spotted
fritillary (*Melitaea didyma*) which is of medium size,
the upper part of the fawn coloured wings being uniform reddish in the case of the male; the female is
larger with the upper part of the front wings paler,
sometimes even yellowish. This fritillary shows
marked changes in form depending on geography
and these changes take place even between one generation and another depending on the time of the
season. The caterpillar is covered with spines which
are surrounded with hairs and when it is fully grown it
fixes the end of its abdomen to any support it can
find, most frequently a stem of a plant or a piece of
bark; it hangs there with its head downwards before
changing into a chrysalis. The latter is whitish in
colour but covered with stripes and spots which are
black or rust colour and it also has a series of small
spines on its back. There can be nothing more interesting than watching the emergence of the butterfly.
A little before this takes place the chrysalis changes
colour; one can trace through the shell, which has
become slightly transparent, the wings of the adult.
Suddenly the chrysalis moves; splits along two lines
separating the sheaths of the antennae from those of
the wings and the butterfly lifts this sort of panel
through using pressure, causing it to open on the
ventral side of the shell. It then frees itself rapidly
from the chrysalis, pulling out its antennae, its six
legs and the two threads of its proboscis from the
casing which has imprisoned them. Almost as soon
as the antennae are freed the proboscis curls up beneath the head and the butterfly, releasing through
its anus a reddish liquid, emerges, clinging immediately to the empty shell. Its wings are still weak, small
and crumpled, but they stretch and smooth out very
rapidly. During these crucial minutes, the spotted fritillary rolls and unrolls its proboscis, swallows a large
amount of air, and stretches its muscles, thereby giving greater pressure to its blood so that it can fill the
veins of its wings; the latter stretch more and more
and, after a few minutes, their development is almost

complete. The butterfly spreads them on the rock to
dry and harden in the sun; at the end of an hour or
two it will be able to take flight.

In the glades of the sub-alpine region the walker
will certainly catch sight of the Zygaenidae. These
tiny night-flying moths with wings marked in red,
bluish black or greenish black, fly rather clumsily on
to the flowers of the thistles and scabious where they
like to mate. When they are caught, they emit —
through the joints of their legs and their antennae —
a yellowish toxic fluid with a disagreeable odour
which serves as a defensive weapon. The most abundant species is the six-spot burnet (*Zygaena filipen-
dula*) which is extremely common in the wild glades
of the mountain regions up to a height of 7500 ft
(2300 m); also common is the transparent burnet
(*Zygaena purpuralis*) which flies at a slightly lower
altitude than the former; its caterpillar feeds on wild
thyme. Other types of *Zygaenidae* inhabit the alpine
meadows up to the snow line; these will be further
discussed in the section on the insects of the high
meadows.

Finally, on the southern slopes of the Alps wherever the 'small cypress' grows can be found the
splendid caterpillar of the spurge hawk (*Celerio euphorbiae*). It can attain a wing span of $3\frac{1}{2}$ in (9 cm)
and on its body has a dark velvety background
scattered with whitish spots and numerous red or
yellow patches; it also has a dorsal line of the same
colour which ends with a sort of small horn with a
black point. The adult, which can be found up to a
height of 6600 ft (2000 m) and whose colours are remarkable when it first emerges from the chrysalis,
flies in the twilight during June or September. This
hawk moth has the habit of sucking up the nectar of
certain flowers by unrolling its proboscis, which is of
considerable length, from some distance away. It
then vibrates its wings some 60–80 times a
second, to maintain its position.

Spiders are also very numerous in the mountains.
There, on the dry rocky slopes of the southern valleys, it is possible to surprise a very handsome
species which is still rather rare – *Eresus niger*; the
abdomen of the male is orangey-red marked with
four black spots. When it is alarmed it raises its stomach as high as possible and agitates it with a
strange trembling motion while it holds its head
lowered towards the enemy. This intimidating position, together with the strident colours of its abdomen, are enough to repulse would-be predators. The
female is much larger, reaching a length of just over
1 in (28 mm) and is completely black; she digs a
shallow hole and surrounds the entrance with a
number of threads. Field spiders, closely related to
the common spider, have globular bodies and extremely long fragile legs. They are normally found in
fields and woods, but some species are found up to
the snow line.

During the fine weather, even until the autumn,
large numbers of crickets and grasshoppers enliven
the glades and plains of the sub-alpine zone. One
needs only take a few paces through the grass to dis-

		2	3	4	
	5	6	7	8	
		9		10	
		11		

1 Caterpillar of the spotted fritillary.

2 Caterpillar of the spotted fritillary about to pupate.

3 Chrysalis of the spotted fritillary.

4 The chrysalis is ready to hatch.

5/6 The butterfly emerges from the broken chrysalis.

7 The butterfly has emerged from the chrysalis and has turned around so as to let its wings hang out.

8 The butterfly stretches its wings, which are quickly spread out.

9 A spotted fritillary settling on the chrysalis which bore it.

10 The butterfly spreads out its wings on a rock to dry and harden in the sun.

11 The spotted fritillary will soon fly away.

The caterpillar of a spurge hawk and its newly-hatched butterfly.

1	2	3	▷
		4	

1 Caterpillar of the swallowtail.

2 Chrysalis of the swallowtail about to hatch.

3 A newly-hatched swallowtail.

4 A swallowtail resting on a tuft of creeping juniper.

turb numerous tiny crickets with well-developed wings. One of them is *Stauroderus scalaris*, the male of which produces a characteristic chirping while in flight. The same is true of the *Psophus stridulus* which is larger and black, but which, when it takes flight, reveals wings which are a beautiful brick red. The yellowish brown, red legged cricket – *Arcyptera fusca* – is another beautiful species. The female of this species, when swollen with eggs, can reach a length of $1\frac{1}{2}$ in (40 mm), but the male is much smaller. By rubbing its thighs vigorously against its wing sheaths the latter produces a strange chirping noise, the typical sound of the mountains, which is repeated close at hand by hundreds of other insects in the hot August sun! The red legged cricket is fairly common in several regions of the Alps and Pyrenees up to an altitude of 7200 ft (2200 m). Also, in the rather more humid mountain glades can be found the *Metrioptera roeseli*, with its brown, shell-like body and a head decorated with brown and black bands; this insect can reach a length of 0.7 in (19 mm). The female, like all the Tettigoniidae or long-horned grasshoppers, has a sort of curved sabre at the end of its abdomen. This is the egg laying tube which it pushes deeply into the ground in order to lay its eggs. The *Metrioptera* always have wing sheaths which are shorter than the abdomen in both sexes; the species is found up to an altitude of 7200 ft (2200 m) and seems particularly fond of the sub-alpine prairies which are covered with marsh bilberries. The same is true of the wart-biter *Decticus verrucivorus*, a carnivorous species, usually large in size; it feeds both on grasses and other insects and is found on the plains and in the mountains, frequently beyond the tree limit. The wart-biter, of which the female can reach a length of 1.7 in (45 mm) excluding the egg laying tube, is variable in colour, depending upon the surroundings in which it lives. Although normally green, marbled with brown, it can in fact become entirely rust covered or even pink in areas where the bilberry is common. Thanks to its strong thighs and the great length of its rear legs, the female of this species is heavier than the male and takes enormous leaps when it is disturbed; the male, on the other hand, normally takes to flight when disturbed, thanks to its well developed wings. This large grasshopper likes both a certain humidity and full sunlight in the mountains. Its 'song' is a series of clicks, at first spaced out, then closer together, in rapid succession. The insect makes this noise by rubbing its wing sheaths which have special veins at their base. These thickened, rough veins on the left wing sheath are transformed into a bow, while on the partly transparent right wing sheath they are thinner and rounded in shape. The rubbing of the bow on the edge of the membrane of the right sheath produces vibrations which creates the 'song' of this insect. The same method is used by all the species belonging to the Tettigoniidae family which can be distinguished immediately from the Acrididae or short-horned grasshoppers by their threadlike antennae which are longer than the body.

There are also numerous beetles which can be found by the visitor crossing the glades of the mountainous regions. Many of them are particula fond of the large umbelliferous plants or the this flowers.

The majority belong to the family of longhor such examples are the small strangalie with its bla tail – *Strangalia melanura* – *Strangalia macula* the mottled variety, which is larger and has str coloured wing sheaths marked with several cr bands in black, the red leptura – *Leptura rubra* which is the same size as the previous species has brick red wing sheaths in the case of the fem and pale brown in the case of the male, and also ha black head and body. Finally, one can find the co mon clytus – *Clytus rhamni* – which reaches length of up to $\frac{1}{3}$ in (10 mm) and has dark wi sheaths decorated with golden yellowish bands.

On the flowers of the centaury plant a handso beetle catches the eye. It is the banded Trichius *Trichius fasciatus* – $\frac{1}{3}$ in to $\frac{1}{2}$ in (from 10 to 13 mm) length, which has fawn coloured wing shea crossed with three black bands. Also to be seen the large leaves of the umbelliferous plants growi at the side of the paths is the *Chrysochloa gloric* from $\frac{1}{3}$ in (8 to 10 mm) which glistens with meta blue, gold, purple or green, like a living emerald.

The author remembers his astonishment when discovered for the first time on the moss at the ed of a wood the splendid ground beetle which h golden tints – *Carabus auronitens* – as it w devouring the remains of an earthworm. Another d while looking for larvae of longhorned beetles insi a rotten tree trunk he was surprised to see shini there the superb green-gold wing sheaths and the coppery body of the same beetle, one of the most markable representatives of the famous family Ca bidae. This insect, which measures from $\frac{3}{4}$ to 1 in (to 28 mm) apparently spends the winter insi decomposing wood, where its larva then takes refu to achieve its transformation into a chrysalis; it c be found in fine weather up to the tree line and ev well above it and is found both in the Alps and in t Massif Central, the Dauphine, the Jura and t Vosges, where every forest has its local variety.

Many other beetles, butterflies and moths inha the high glade of the sub-alpine area; the reader mu have the pleasure of making his own discoveries, these pages only aim at the description of certa species amongst the most typical and common these insects.

The whinchat

Near mountain villages the meadows which have been mowed are always a little richer in grass than elsewhere. Towards the end of June the earth, which has been well fertilised and irrigated by man, is covered with large umbelliferous plants. These plants attract multitudes of insects, and bend their strongly smelling flowers in the least breath of wind. Perched on one of these plants a bird starts to sing excitedly at the author's approach, emitting a curious 'tac-tac' noise which echoes clearly along the slope. This bird has rather a short tail and reminds one of a sparrow because of the underside of its body and its wings; it is, however, much darker and more elegant. A large white eyebrow above the eye is underset with a wide blackish band on the cheek, and this, in its turn, is underlined by a light patch, allowing the bird to be easily identified. Added to this a breast which is orangey-fawn in the case of the male and pale fawn in the case of the female, whose eyebrows are also yellowish and less distinct than those of the male, and one has a reasonably accurate portrait of the whinchat in its nuptial dress. The bird is not at all timid and allows the author to sit within a few yards of it. It stands almost vertically on its black feet, which it shakes nervously while at the same time flapping its wings and its tail more and more; it repeatedly cries 'tac-tac-tac' while, a little further away on an old gate, the female, which is browner on the upper part of its body, flaps her wings and displays clear signs of alarm. Without any doubt the nest must be very close, hidden beneath the dense grass. The two whinchats then fly away, revealing as they do so the white patches on their wings and tails. Using this opportunity to retire to a distance of some 50 yards, the author leans against a slope, half concealed by a bush, brings out his binoculars and surveys the entire meadow. One of the whinchats — the male — comes back to perch on the gate with its beak full of food. After some hesitation it settles quite close by on the tallest of the umbelliferous plants, wags its tail and suddenly disappears into the depths of the meadow. Now the difficulties begin of finding a hiding place in the middle of all this greenery and at the same time trying to hold the binoculars trained on the exact spot where the bird disappeared into the grass. A few moments later the author can see it emerge at the same spot, with white droppings in its beak. The nest is certainly there. Fortunately some high branch of a cow-parsley displays its pink parasols only a few yards away to the right on which the female whinchat settles with a butterfly in its beak. It seems to hesitate for a moment, then fly directly into the vegetation and appear a few moments later,

A female winchat on the lookout from the top of a larch tree.

again carrying droppings. Soon the author finds the nest. He would have to move quickly in order not to disturb the pair and must at all costs avoid squashing the grass near the nest. He parts some stems carefully and via a small entrance passage, finds the nest firmly embedded in the slope and well concealed beneath the dense foliage of the meadow. The young birds, already covered with some feathers, are huddled at the bottom of their cradle. They could easily be mistaken for some lumps of earth and the author refrains from getting any closer in order to avoid forcing them to leave their nest prematurely. The two adults, highly alarmed, fly from plant to plant uttering loud cries and he moves away quickly in order to cut short their anguish.

1
Longhorn beetle *(Leptura dubia).*
2
Longhorn beetle *(Leptura maculata).*
3
Rose chafer *(Trichius fasciata).*
4
A pair of *Chrysochloa gloriosa* **beetles**
5
Chrysocarabus auronitens **devouring an earth-worm.**
6
Carmine jumping spider *(Eresus niger)* **in a position of repose.**

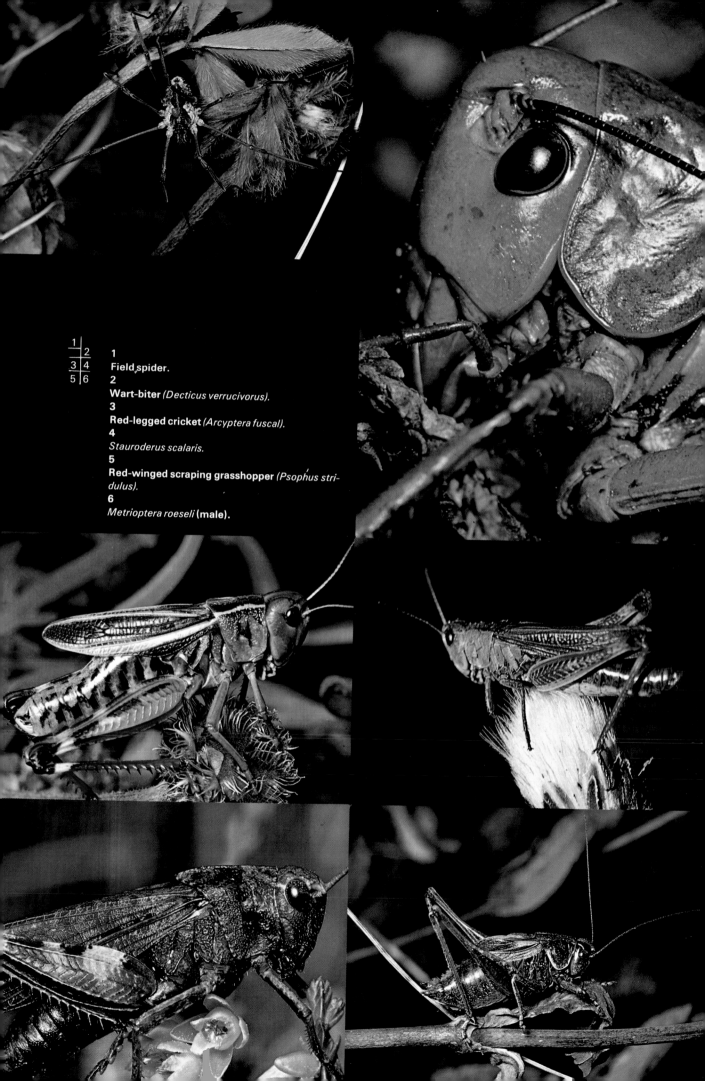

1
Field spider.
2
Wart-biter *(Decticus verrucivorus)*.
3
Red-legged cricket *(Arcyptera fuscal)*.
4
Stauroderus scalaris.
5
Red-winged scraping grasshopper *(Psophus stridulus)*.
6
Metrioptera roeseli (male).

5
Birds of the sub-alpine rocks

The raven – the crag martin – the alpine swift – the kestrel – the golden eagle.

The raven

Through the cold, clear air of the mountains a raucous and echoing cry is heard, 'croak-croak-croak' from somewhere in the sky. On looking up can be seen a large black bird beating its powerful wings making a harsh sound like 'voup, voup, voup!'. One can also distinguish now the enormous beak outlined against the blue firmament and the strong wings, which, as they beat, display a metallic sheen in the sunlight. But this swift silhouette quickly flies away to plunge towards the valley; after one or two cries the bird disappears into the shadows and is swallowed up by the mist. One is alone again, lost in the silence amongst vast snow fields which slowly merge with the hard blue sky above the mountain tops, and the pearls of water on one's skis. What could this bird have been? What could bring it to these heights and this deserted spot? What could be the meaning of its echoing cries? Its shape certainly had something in common with the common crow of the plains, the carrion crow. But it is some other type of bird, a crow, certainly, but a special sort of crow, much larger, with a powerful beak and a completely different way of flying from that of the carrion crow. As for its cries, they were more raucous, as if they came from the depths of the bird's throat; they were completely different from the banal 'kroa! kroa! kroa!' made by the carrion crow. Other details attract one's attention, in particular the angled tail of the bird, the wide span of its wings and the impression of strength and vigour of its shape which is something out of the ordinary. This was in fact a raven.

It is true that the raven deserves its reputation. Amongst all the members of the crow family it is the largest. It has such a strong beak that it is difficult to believe it is closely related to small birds like the tits, the goldcrest, and the lesser whitethroat. However, this Goliath amongst the crows, weighing the equivalent of 215 goldcrests according to Paul Géroudet, is nevertheless very similar in its constitution to these tiny birds, and also comes under the same laws that control its development and even certain of its cries. Its vocabulary is remarkable from more than one point of view. Apart from the resonant 'croak croak' which it utters constantly when flying, the raven also utters other cries with various intonations. Hidden under canvas near the refuse of a mountain resort, I was able to listen to its nasal growling, its yelpings, its ventriloquist's sounds, raucous or metallic, and finally certain cries which were strangely similar in their resonance to those of a xylophone. This bird can also glide with great skill, and at the end of winter it indulges in daring acrobatics: vertical dives, spins, loops and glides during which the bird suddenly changes direction and flies frequently upside down . . .

Normally the raven builds its nest on rocky cliff faces in the sub-alpine zone between 3000 and 5000 ft (900 and 1500 m). Pairs, which mate for life, appear very sedentary, but they cover quite a wide territory. They can, in a few minutes, reach the snow areas where they can be seen patrolling, on the lookout for the remains of picnics left by tourists or skiers. Nothing escapes their keen eyesight and, as soon as the snow melts, these birds fall on the bodies of those animals which have succumbed to the rigours of winter. They then indulge in feasting and clean right down to the bones numerous decaying carcasses, providing in this way a real scavenger service.

This strange bird became a rare species in the Alps twenty-five years ago. For the last twenty years or so, however, thanks to the development of winter sports and tourism in general it has multiplied greatly. What is the connection here? Quite simply the raven is principally a great scavenger. No bird knows better than the raven how to exploit systematically the refuse dumps which exist near most resorts. It thus plays a very practical rôle and, in spite of its proverbial mistrust and its wildness, this bird has been able to adapt itself completely to the new activity of mountain visitors. As the raven can find its food almost anywhere and is able to build its nest in innumerable spots, it has been able to breed rapidly – particularly now that it is effectively protected. Although it does not have such a wide wing span as that of the eagle, it is nevertheless, a true master of the alpine sky and does not fear to attack even the golden eagle. The author watched these aerial battles many times and, on almost every occasion, the eagle finally fled from this black fury. It is not, however, always the same in the case of the goshawk, when the struggle can become desperate – especially during the nesting season. Let us bring this section to a close by noting that this bird, like all the crow family, is endowed with a highly developed psychic sense. The author had proof of this on several occasions, in particular in Morocco, where he has seen Arabs searching through refuse dumps almost side by side with ravens. When he appeared on the scene with his telephoto lens, the black bird immediately flew away, to return a little later and settle near the locals when he had retreated some distance away. In the Alps, these birds are always extremely prudent and, unless one is perfectly camouflaged and prepared to wait for long periods, it is impossible to take good photographs of this giant, as it is one of the most mistrustful birds of the fauna of the mountains.

The crag martin

On the south side of the valley the old road, which has been cut into the rock with pickaxe and dynamite, follows the precipice and disappears into narrow tunnels. From a window in one of these tunnels the gaze plunges through space to the depths of the gorge and gives one a foretaste of giddiness. . . . The wildness of this spot is such that one is fascinated by the enormous labyrinth of stone which stretches at one's feet, and one is only half aware of a small golden butterfly, the *Endrosa aurita*, as it flies past, constantly borne upwards by the currents of air from the gorge.

Suddenly a brownish bird looking rather like a bat flies along the rock face and, with a quick swerve snaps up the butterfly and continues its flight. Now it is grazing the rock face, twisting and turning with great ease, carried on the upward currents of air with its tail wide spread, revealing on the underside some white patches. This bird is so skilful in flight that it passes over one's head several times and one is not able to follow it. Its size and outline recall a swallow, but its tail, far from being forked, is almost rectangular.

What can this bird be? It rests on an outcrop of rock where its plumage, blending well with the colours of the earth and the rocks, make it almost invisible. Only its lighter coloured breast attracts the attention. After uttering a few short cries of 'chrri! chrri! chrri!' the small glider flies above the abyss, like a dead leaf in the wind, but constantly indulges in aerial acrobatics. . . . The bird swoops past again, and this time it enters the tunnel and perches on a greyish ball which must be its nest. The semi-circular shape, made of fragments of earth stuck to the rock and of the same colour, blends so well that it went unnoticed. At the same moment four yellow throats emerge from the nest and the crag martin pushes into one of them a supply of insects and then leaves immediately. As soon as it has left, however, a second bird arrives and unloads the provisions it carries in its beak. As it passes it utters a rasping cry. All these details help in identifying it as the species, crag martin. In September this bird leaves the shores to take up its winter quarters in the north-west of Africa, the north of the Sahara and the Sudan. The crag martin is the first to return in the spring and can be seen sometimes as early as the end of February. Its habitat is the Var, the Alpes Maritimes and Corsica.

Alpine swift.

The alpine swift

It is a fine June day and, for more than an hour, the author has been following a path which twists interminably through a larch wood on the side of the mountain. Immense outcrops of rock occur from time to time and, from one of these, the white foam of a waterfall emerges to fall in a snowy spray into the valley. Near this waterfall a wall creeper suddenly flies from the high rocks like a strange butterfly, with pink and black wings. . . . The bird flies away and settles on a wet rock, a small greyish ball which is quickly merged with the background. The pungent smell of the juniper bushes scattered along the slope fills the air which is already shimmering in the strong sunlight. From a hawthorn tree another bird, similar to a sparrow but with a bluish head striped with three black bands, suddenly flies off uttering a brief cry of 'tzit'; it is the rock bunting. The author just had time to glimpse the white flash of its outside feathers as it crosses the path.

Gradually the larches become less frequent and a breeze starts to make itself felt. Finally the author reaches the open meadows where tiny crickets fly away at each step, using their wing sheaths to make their characteristic sound. All of a sudden a strange whistling sound could be heard coming from the sky, and two long wings shaped like a sickle hurtling over the last of the larch trees could be seen. A moment later the same shape brushes the top of another nearby tree at a crazy speed and, again, the wings of the bird vibrating can be seen as they cut through the air . . . It is very similar to the house martin which is so common in towns, but it appears much larger and with a wider wing span; in addition, its throat and its stomach are white, separated with a pectoral band of brown, and these characteristics allow us to identify the bird without any difficulty — it is the alpine swift. However, it is not alone: flying over the valley close to the rock faces are other bow-shaped birds; some of them graze the pasturage and seem to be snapping at invisible insects with their beaks. They are so graceful in their movements and so powerful and rapid in flight that one can only envy these alpine swifts, which are more skilful in flight than any other bird in the world; they are even more skilful than their smaller cousins the house martins. There is no equal for these marvellous fliers, ideally suited to their calling. Their narrow wings are so long and their bodies so well tapered that they can slip through the air for hours, indeed for entire days, without any sign of fatigue, carrying out their endless acrobatics. When the rising currents of air carry certain insects to high altitudes, the alpine swifts follow them and are often lost in the clouds. A few minutes are sufficient, however, for them to make their way back to the rocks where their colonies are to be found. Distance has no meaning for these birds, who can reach a speed of nearly 100 miles (150 km) an hour when they are in pursuit of food or indulging in aerial games. On the other hand their legs are so short that they never use them for walking; they are, nevertheless, provided with powerful claws, with four toes pointed forwards, and this allows them to hang on to any vertical face, wall or rock in the cracks on which they 'attach' their nests.

Even though they often hunt above the snow line, these birds build their nests at much lower altitudes and normally use fissures in rocks of the sub-alpine zone, sometimes even inaccessible cliffs of the plains or at the edge of the sea. In the Alps their colonies are rarely found at greater heights than 6600 ft (2000 m). One curious fact is that the alpine swifts like to build their nests in old buildings of certain towns of Switzerland. They are to be found in Fribourg, Bern, Bienne, Solothurn, Zürich, Luzern and Schaffhausen, but no similar colonies have been found in France. At dusk the adult birds and those of the previous year who have not yet nested gather together in large groups near the colonies. They then go in for extraordinary chases while uttering loud trilling sounds which can be heard from a great distance . . . This noise, which decreases and increases in waves of volume, these wild and passionate cries coming from the sky, are one of the many attractions of these superb fliers whose little known migrations conceal many future surprises for the ornithologist.

The kestrel

Above the slope, bathed in the light, a rust coloured bird the size of a turtle dove but with much narrower wings and a longer tail, his head less in evidence, is poised, hovering in one spot. Sometimes this small falcon, facing the wind, remains almost immobile with its wings trembling, its body horizontal and its tail closed; at other times it climbs or falls, depending on the air current, but takes up its position again at a precise spot in the sky, beating its wings for a moment, then spreading out its tail and moving it to the right and to the left, its head bent forward studying attentively what is happening on the ground. One might suspect the bird was suspended on a cord, it is so successful in maintaining its position in one place. Only its wings, which it beats energetically at times, appear blurred and this gives this small bird of prey its popular name of 'Sifter'. Suddenly the 'cord' breaks, and the bird plummets to the earth like a stone. Its wings stay close to its sides until, with its claws extended and its wings spread to stop short its fall, it seizes the prey of its choice: a common vole. The animal is despatched with a few pecks from the kestrel's beak, and then the bird takes flight again slightly weighed down by its plunder, which it will tear into pieces at its leisure on reaching the first pine tree. With a pair of binoculars the author watches it greedily tearing out the liver, the heart and the entrails of the rodent which it holds firmly in its yellowish claws.

In the fine months, the kestrel will collect in the same way the large crickets which it normally devours while in flight, using its claws to bring its prey within reach of its beak. In calmer weather it likes to lie in wait for its prey by hiding in the tops of trees, in a rock or a thicket. But the author has seen it carry out its famous 'flying on the spot' for several minutes at a time, even when no breath of wind moved the grass of the meadows; on such occasion

A crag martin at feeding time and in flight.

A raven standing over the spoils of a hare.

the bird succeeds in maintaining its position in the air only by beating its wings vigorously, holding its tail extended; it is obvious that such action is tiring and it much prefers to save its strength by skilfully using the air currents which are so frequently to be found in the mountains. When a strong wind is blowing it is not unusual to see the bird poised for a long time at one particular point in the sky without the least effort being apparent; the bird, however, constantly maintains its balance by slight movements of its wings or tail. This method of hunting, which is peculiar to the kestrel, allows it to cover a vast area; its sight is so keen that it can distinguish a vole at more than 160 ft (50 m) distance. Finally it is the only bird of prey in the mountains which uses this method of hovering in one spot, as the buzzard, which is much larger and heavier, only uses this method of hunting under rare circumstances when there are strong winds blowing. It is therefore difficult to confuse this bird with the sparrow-hawk or even the peregrine falcon. Seen from above the kestrel appears really russet in colour, with the ends of its wings blackish, the tail grey, terminated by a wide dark band in the case of the male, while the female and young birds have tails of a chestnut colour, striped in black before the final dark band. When it carries out its hovering it appears very light in colour, even silvery, depending on the angle of the light. In contrast to the sparrow-hawk and the goshawk it is active during the daytime; it can therefore be seen easily and is still the most common of European birds of prey, although its numbers have decreased severely in several areas during recent years both on the plains and in the mountains. It can be observed hunting for prey well above the tree line, on the high alpine pastures, even up to the desert crests of the Alps at more than 10 000 ft (3000 m). The kestrel not only hunts voles, lizards and insects, it also feeds on young birds which have not yet learned to fly properly. One day the author even saw a kestrel fall upon a young blackbird which had quite well developed wings. Without the quick intervention of his son, this little falcon would probably have achieved its purpose without any difficulty. On another occasion he saw a kestrel pursuing a stoat which only just succeeded in escaping by taking refuge in a hole. However, these are out of the normal run of prey and rodents form the basic essential food, together with lizards and large insects.

Like all the falcons, the kestrel does not build a nest. In the mountains the female lays eggs almost always on ledges on the sub-alpine rock faces. The female seems to prefer a small ledge protected from a sheer drop and edged with grass or a small thorn bush, rather than those rock faces which are above the tree line. The kestrel has also been seen using an old eyrie belonging to a golden eagle; on the plains it is happy to use the abandoned nests of carrion crows or buzzards and even takes advantage of old buildings not far from human habitations.

Bold to the point of foolishness, the kestrel never misses the opportunity of attacking the eagle when the latter enters its domain. They descend at full speed on the large bird of prey uttering cries of 'ki ki ki ki' which are harsh and pierced. It is a strange sight to see the enormous bird slowly sweep round on its broad wings with two tiny russet falcons on its track, harrassing it constantly and diving in on it as if they were fighter planes. If a sparrow-hawk ventures near their eyrie the kestrels immediately attack it violently with constant aggressive cries. Thanks to the speed of their flight and their surprising ability to turn quickly, they avoid being seized and finally succeed in driving off the intruder.

The young falcons are first covered with a white down, then with a second down of a russet grey colour. They are warmed and fed by the female alone. It is her who tears up the prey which is brought at regular intervals by the male, and who distributes the pieces to her progeny. The young grow rapidly and, three weeks later, they tear up themselves the voles or lizards which are offered to them in turn by the adult. When the adult arrives, there is a deafening barrage of harsh rhythmic cries which are magnified by the echoes of the surrounding rocks ... When the young are about one month old, the strongest of them leave the eyrie and perch on nearby crags from which they watch the arrival of their parents throughout the day. As soon as the latter appear in the sky, the young kestrels fly to meet them, beating their wings and demanding their food with plaintive cries so that the rock face is a scene of lively animation for some time. Gradually the family ties are relaxed, the young grow independant and scatter in all directions; the majority of the kestrels which are born in the Alps emigrate to the south of Italy and France or the east of Spain. Certain of these falcons even cross the sea and reach Morocco and Equatorial Africa. However, many adults remain more or less in the same area if the winters are not too severe.

The golden eagle

A golden eagle on the lookout for prey from a rock spur.

Above the shadowy valleys and the mists which arise from them a large brownish bird rises with a slow, calm flight ... Through one's binoculars one soon picks out two enormous wings, a little concave in shape, suspended in space on invisible currents of air: it is an eagle. It can be recognised by its imposing shape, by the ease and grace of its flight, by the spaced out feathers on its wings which look almost like the fingers of a hand. The royal bird flies slowly, describing large spirals against the background of the mountains. Endowed with superb strength and courage, with silence and solemnity, this enormous bird of prey is a symbol of the sky, shining above the dark forests. Now it gains height, and leaves the mists of the deep gorges. The proud bird makes for the areas beyond the forests, heading towards the white snows, even now without apparently beating its wings, still circling ... It rises even higher ... Following it as it flies, one will see how its neck turns silver, how the proud spirals of its flight carry it well above the ice, well above the snow, to the furthest limits of human sight ... There it is finally near the clouds, above the summits of the world, absolute master of space.

The golden eagle is without any doubt the finest of all the birds of prey; it is also one of the strongest and if it is not the biggest in size and weight it is, nevertheless, the boldest, the proudest and the bird which has more attraction and leaves one more impressed than any other.

The author has been extremely fortunate in his life, in that he has been able to observe this bird from afar and close up during its hunting and its mating displays. He has been able to follow the development and the first flights of a dozen eagles and on several occasions he has been able to observe the adult from less than 50 ft (15 m) away – on one occasion it was less than 10 ft (3 m). This occurred at the eyrie of Zinal in Anniers. The female arrived at the eyrie

of golden eagles, which usually use several eyries one after the other, do not breed every year. One or sometimes two young are hatched. The eaglet is able to breed only after four or five years and this fact limits the increase of this bird of prey to a very slow rate. Births only exceed natural or accidental losses by a small margin. However, since it has become protected in Switzerland and France, where no bird of prey may be shot, the golden eagle has recently been on the increase in the Alps, which will delight all friends of nature. Without such measures, no doubt the eagle would be almost extinct, like the bearded vulture was at the beginning of this century. If one realises what such a disappearance would mean for Europe, how much beauty would be lost and how much wild grandeur and atmosphere of the Alps would vanish, it is impossible not to be proud of possessing amongst our fauna today the most marvellous of all the eagles – *Aquila chrysaetos*. This great predator destroys numerous marmots, which provide its basic food in the fine months, and the author has seen it carry to its eyrie the young of the red deer and the chamois, the mountain hare, the black grouse, the red partridge and the ptarmigan, but he has also seen it kill young foxes! Wild cats, which are so destructive for game, are also often a prey of the eagle and, finally – a fact which should be stressed – this royal bird, through its constant inspection of an enor-

6
Inhabitants of the upper forests to the tree line

The nutcracker – the bank vole – the red deer – the crossbill – the weasel – the yellow necked mouse – the alpine tits – the bullfinch – the beech marten – owls of the mountains – the garden dormouse – the mistle thrush – the song thrush – the ring ouzel – the black grouse – the nuthatch – the chaffinch – the tiger beetles – the tree pipit – the green woodpecker – the red and black ant – the red squirrel – the fox – the citril finch – the brown hare – the redpoll.

The nutcracker

The autumn is certainly one of the most beautiful seasons in the mountains, and the enchantment which it creates is incomparably more intense and profound than that of the summer. The paths appear deserted, the colours are more subtle or more dazzling, and the russet gold of the larch trees contrasts with the dark conifers, covered on their upper branches with bluish pine cones. It is well worth gathering the small triangular seeds contained beneath the scales of the cones and extract from them their delicious contents. Mountain animals know best of all how to extract this marvellous food. During the long winter period they need to have something available for their table. Proceeding quietly through these forests of the alpine areas one will hardly ever go more than a hundred yards without hearing some harsh raucous cries. One can then observe on the top of a larch or amongst the branches of a conifer a bird the size of a jay but much more grey in colour: this is the nutcracker. Its large head, its strong beak and the black top of its head are easily noticeable; its breast and back are completely speckled with white on a brown background, giving a grey appearance from some distance away.

This bird makes itself known in such a noisy and characteristic way that it will be remembered for a very long time. 'Kre kre kre' it cries from the top of its larch tree, its head lifted and its beak wide open; this cry means 'What are you doing here, intruder? Return from where you came or I shall continue to announce your presence to the entire forest ...' In fact as long as it is observed, this mountain jay although not wild or curious by nature will remain in its tree continuing its noisy cry at intervals. This bird plays the rôle of guard in the Alps ... Its loud cries which are uttered frequently, warn game of the approach of man. The roe deer, the red deer, the chamois, the black grouse and many others pay heed to its cries as has been proved on numerous occasions. The nutcracker has been responsible for the author's missing several photographs because of its untimely alarm cry, and yet these strange birds are very sympathetic in many other respects. Huntsmen are quite right in calling them 'Informers'. The presence of th

A young nutcracker leaving its nest.

mountain jay in the Alps is closely linked to the presence of conifer trees. In September, if the conifers have a good crop of cones, these birds can be seen frequently, busy filling the extending pouch which they possess beneath the tongue with pine seeds. Very often the nutcracker tries to detach the cone from the tops of the trees, by pecking vigorously at the branch attaching it to the tree. During this difficult operation one can often see the bird beating its wings in order to keep its balance. Suddenly the cone drops from the tree and the bird carries it away in its beak, flying rather clumsily because of the heavy burden it bears ... The bird then hides in the depths of a tree and starts 'its meal'. Holding its loot tightly between its claws, it attacks it violently with its beak, and lifts one by one the seeds from between the scales. With its pouch full — which can hold more than a hundred seeds — this load makes the neck of the bird look like an attack of goitre. In the autumn the nutcracker is accustomed to build up stores which allow it to survive throughout the winter and even to supply its nest. It hides the pine seeds in numerous places, for example in cracks in the rocks which are well sheltered from the snow or even in the ground, or at the foot of tree trunks, beneath the large roots. Its memory is so good that the author has seen it locate stocks without any hesitation under more than 20 in (50 cm) of snow. It nevertheless happens sometimes that the bird forgets some of these 'larders' and, because of this fact, the nutcracker involuntarily contributes towards the reseeding of the conifer forests. It therefore plays an important rôle in the conservation and propagation of this essential element in the Alps, and the 'jay of the mountain' has been protected for a very long time.

When the nutcracker rests on the top of a tree with its pouch full of seeds, its shape is so deformed that the bird seems nothing more than a caricature. Its flight is more powerful than that of the ordinary jay, and it beats its wings regularly, flying quite quickly from one forest to another or even, on occasion, carrying out vertical dives into the valleys. It appears dark, almost black, with a white triangle beneath its tail and a border of the same colour at the end of the tail. The nutcracker, although normally a chatterbox, becomes very discreet and silent during the breeding season in March. The nest is large, well concealed in the depths of a conifer and normally built very close to the trunk in its upper half. It is very difficult to locate, as its exterior texture is made from lichens taken from nearby trees, and it thus blends perfectly with its surroundings. Young nutcrackers have been seen to emerge from the nest as early as the 25th April, at 6600 ft (2000 m) while 3 ft (1 m) of snow is still covering the earth. In the autumn the young birds often beg for their food with plaintive grating cries which are completely different from the alarm cries of the adults. The majority of nutcrackers in the Alps seem to be non-migratory, although the species is given to wandering and often moves from one valley to another. When there are heavy falls of snow, certain of them descend to the plains, but return to the higher altitudes as soon as the weather improves.

The nutcracker is a typical inhabitant of the large mountain forests, and is extremely fond of seeds. One might say that its rôle is the official guardian of the wild woods as the snow partridge is of the snowy ridges.

The bankvole

Unlike the alpine vole, the bank vole is hardly ever found beyond the tree limit in the mountains. At least the author has never found it beyond the zone where the small bushes grow beyond the upper tree line of conifers, gradually blending into the alpine meadows. It is much darker in colour than the alpine vole and has a fine brownish red back which is characteristic, while its sides are russet grey. The animal varies considerably in size depending on the region, but never attains that of the alpine vole. Like the latter, however, it often moves around during the day, although its main activity takes place at dawn or dusk. The author needed several years and some good luck to surprise this animal in its natural habitat, and this, in his own words, is how it happened: 'I was sitting at the base of an old conifer with my photographic equipment not far from a path used by deer, in the hope of surprising the latter on their return from feeding. It was scarcely day and a light breeze stirred around the slope so that I shivered a little, while paying close attention to the slightest sound in the forest. In the dawn the larches were just taking on a little colour, although the sky still had its last star, and a black grouse was hooting somewhere up the slope. There was a marvellous smell of dead leaves in the air. Suddenly, almost at my feet, I noticed a small animal run quickly past a juniper tree and come to a stop at the foot of a mossy bank. From its dark fur I was able to recognise immediately that the animal was a bank vole. The tiny rodent, completely unaware of my presence, started to chew a pine cone which had been forgotten by some nutcracker. Crouched forward, its back bent, holding the pine cone between its front paws which were a little raised, the vole, entirely occupied with its meal, gave me the chance to study it at my leisure. Its jet black eyes shone in the half-light like pearls and its movements seemed to be extremely lively. What surprised me the most was the loud noise made by its teeth against the pine cone, but as soon as the animal extracted the seed, silence fell again. When the pine cone was empty, the vole, after a quick wash, returned from where it had come, and disappeared as if by magic. I later discovered the entrance to its tunnel, which was hidden beneath a dwarf juniper bush.' This rodent seems to be faithful to the coniferous forests in the mountains, particularly those where the ground is covered with vegetation, although it can also be found in the brushwood and deciduous woods of the plains. Its food consists of roots, seeds, chestnuts, insects and the eggs of small sparrows. It is more agile than the alpine vole and runs quicker, jumps skilfully and even succeeds in climbing over the old bark of trees. As with all voles its numbers seem to vary in a strange way; in some years it is so common that one can find it in the glades of the alpine forests at every moment, crawling beneath the rhododendrons or running from one bush to another. In the twilight, however, it is hunted by many enemies: the bank vole seems to be the favourite prey of the little owl which even hunts it in the daytime. The author has seen the latter take many voles as prey for its young whilst in the forest of Anniviers. It is also eaten by the tawny owl, the tengmalm's owl, the long eared owl, the fox, the marten and the weasel and only succeeds in surviving thanks to its fast rate of breeding.

The red deer (elaphe)

Out of all hunts with the camera, the pursuit of the red deer seems to be the most difficult, apart from following the bear, of course. In fact this animal which is above all an inhabitant of the forest and which avoids the light, spending the greater part of the day concealed beneath vegetation, is extremely difficult to locate. There are of course exceptions and deer can, in fact, be surprised in the autumn as they rest in the meadows. The timidity and prudence of the mountain deer can bear no comparison with those attributes of the deer which live in the plain forests. This is even more so when the animals, as they normally do, live in regions which are little frequented by tourists and are difficult of access. Amongst all the large mammals of Europe, the deer is probably the animal which has the best developed senses of hearing, sight and smell. During the rutting season, when the male utters loud bellows, one can observe the deer with the least amount of difficulty. The rutting season ends in the mountains towards the end of the first week in October, but this can in certain years be a little earlier or on occasions somewhat later, so that the mating show can vary a little in its timing.

... 'One 4th October I took the car into a mountainous region where I knew there to be many deer. The forest road which I took came to an end and was not a suitable place to camp as there were small streams of water flowing everywhere. I therefore decided to spend the night in the car, put down the seats and made myself as comfortable as possible. But towards 2 o'clock in the morning, as I was unable to sleep, I made myself a drink, and took a path which was illuminated by the moon, carrying a bag laden with cameras and provisions for two days. Everywhere was perfectly calm and silent. The spruce and larch trees stretched before me black as ink, and even the large lichens growing on their trunks seemed black ... From time to time my feet hit against a root or a pebble, but I tried to make the least noise possible. The path climbed continually and I followed it without hurrying. The moon had just disappeared behind a mountain ridge and it became very dark. The first meadows could not be very far away, and as I could see nothing whatsoever, I decided to stop and wait where I was for dawn: so I put down my bag and sat with my back against a tree trunk. A chilly breeze blew down the slope, and I shuddered a little in spite of the thick pullover and the windcheater which I was wearing.

'Suddenly a slight crack towards my left side startled me and I held my breath, straining to listen for any further sound: there was nothing! A few minutes passed in complete silence. Did I really hear something a few minutes earlier? Was there really some animal near me? I began to doubt my senses when there was suddenly a formidable sound bursting through the night. It was raucous, lengthy, brutal and all-powerful. Another more distant cry echoed it.

Bank vole.

The growth of the antlers of the stag.

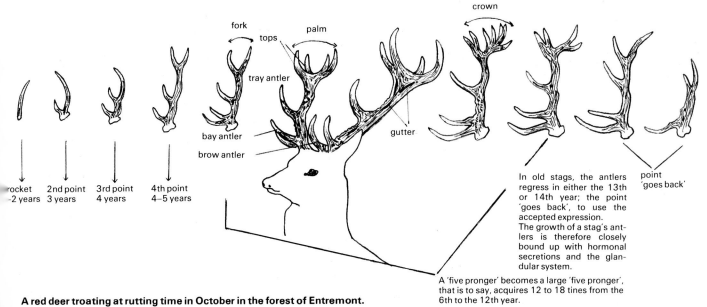

crown

fork

tops

palm

tray antler

bay antler

brow antler

gutter

rocket
—2 years

2nd point
3 years

3rd point
4 years

4th point
4–5 years

In old stags, the antlers regress in either the 13th or 14th year; the point 'goes back', to use the accepted expression.
The growth of a stag's antlers is therefore closely bound up with hormonal secretions and the glandular system.

point
'goes back'

A 'five pronger' becomes a large 'five pronger', that is to say, acquires 12 to 18 tines from the 6th to the 12th year.

A red deer troating at rutting time in October in the forest of Entremont.

dared not move and strained my eyes, staring at the spot from where this guttural cry had come; there was nothing except blackness, and I could barely discern the vague shapes of the tree trunks. The cry was repeated even closer and seemed deeper than ever. I pressed against the tree trunk, feeling very insignificant and didn't dare to move. The cry continued as if it were trying to crush me, as if nothing else existed in the black night apart from that sound. Then there was a further silence. Suddenly the cry was taken up again, wild, terrible and all-powerful . . . It seemed to me both like the bellowing of a bull and the roaring of a lion. Then the tone changed and the sounds became drawn out as if under the effect of a terrible pain which was continuous. It was a sound which could only come from the bowels of the earth and went back through the ages of history, covering thousands of years of combat, back to the first appearance of cell life. I seemed caught in the middle of this tempest, a small piece of flesh listening hard, placed there by miracle at the whim of some deity.

'Dawn started to break, and finally I was able to distinguish the animal: it seemed enormous, with antlers which had endless branches. I saw the beast paw the pine needles with its front foot then raise its head, open its mouth slowly and utter its cry at the same time as its breath appeared like steam. It apparently wished to remain on a small stretch of ground near a large spruce tree on the slope. The deer was not alone: two hinds, then three more appeared to surround it a short distance off, remaining silent and almost immobile, only twitching their large ears at each guttural cry made by their master. A little higher up the bank I noticed another young deer with three-branched antlers, its muscles tensed, its head pointing towards the hinds, and immediately I understood what was happening; the young male was trying to take the females from the older stag and the latter was trying to impose its will on the younger animal. The young beast did not dare to approach too closely but kept close watch on the situation, controlled by blind instinct. Day broke and the animals were less than 100 ft (30 m) from the tree behind which I concealed myself as best I could and they evidently did not sense my presence. It was still quite dark in the forest. The enormous stag bellowed from time to time but with less conviction, it seemed to me, as the light grew stronger; I waited impatiently for more light, hoping to take some photographs of this extraordinary spectacle. The light exposure on my camera was climbing extremely slowly towards the exposure for 1/15th of a second . . . I nevertheless took two photographs of the large male at the moment when it uttered its cry and kept my telephoto lens pressed against the tree trunk. Unfortunately one of the hinds noticed my movement, or rather heard the noise of the shutter and its two companions also turned towards me. The stag became silent and all the animals looked at me with surprise. I was very disturbed and tried my best to hide behind the tree; in fact I would have liked to disappear beneath the ground. But all my efforts were to no avail as all the animals, one by one, slowly disappeared into the forest. I saw their backs, their thighs and finally their legs disappear as the branches slowly hid them from view, and a little later the wood was deserted. I rubbed my eyes, thinking that I had dreamt everything, and finally fell asleep on the same spot where a few instants previously had been the most noble and most beautiful creatures of the forest.'

The crossbill

. . . 'Once again I am wandering along at the edge of a mountain meadow in late autumn. The light fall of snow from the previous night still covers the ground partially, but a harsh wind has arisen at dawn and is blowing away the clouds, leaving large spaces of blue sky visible. A marvellous light now bathes everything around me, while at my feet the last crickets of the season slowly start their daily lives . . . Several nutcrackers are constantly flying over the glade in the forest with their crops full of pine seeds. Suddenly a flock of birds settles on a nearby larch tree uttering continual cries of 'gup! gup! gup!'. Some of these birds are brightly coloured with brick red or ochre orange, while others are greenish or olive in colour although they all have dark wings and tails. They are a little larger in size than a finch but appear more thick-set, with a shorter, more indented tail, a massive head, and a large beak, the upper and lower parts of which cross in a strange way at the end. While certain of the birds keep watch on top of the larch, most of the flock busy themselves at this moment with the cones from the tree in order to extract the seeds, their basic food.

'It is an astonishing sight; in a few moments a shower of cones and needles turn in the air, caught in the wind. The tree itself shakes under the attack of the myriad beaks at work as the crossbills start their meal. Each bird holds on to a branch with one claw while with the other it seizes the cone it has chosen and pushes its powerful beak between the scales so that it can extract the seeds with the help of its tongue. If the bird's position becomes too acrobatic it nips off the cone from the stem . . . As soon as the cone is cut off the bird seizes it at the end before it can fall and moves to a lower branch where it can

Weasel tracks.

The weasel's coat stays brown in winter.

The weasel

finish its meal more at ease. Sometimes, however, the operation is a failure and the cone falls to the ground. In this instance the crossbill starts the operation from the beginning again. The same thing happens with the spruce tree. I have seen the crossbill go from one branch to another, holding on with its beak and using it like a lever, in exactly the same way as do certain parrots which the crossbill resembles somewhat in its shape.'

In the pure mountain air, it is most enjoyable admiring these red or greenish birds as they hang like ripe fruit from the branches of the larch. Soon the ground is covered with pine needles and the cries of 'gup! gup!' increase in strength until suddenly the entire flock takes flight and disappears into the forest.

The number of crossbills to be found in the mountains varies greatly from one year to the next and seems closely linked with the numbers of cones found on the conifers, larch, fir and in particular spruce. These strange birds do in fact feed almost exclusively from the seeds of the latter. They appear at times in very great numbers in areas where there has been a heavy crop of pine cones, although they will abandon the same area the following year if these cones are absent. The birds are justly considered similar to gypsies, constantly wandering in search of food. They are extremely hardy and can breed in the mountains during the depths of winter, although the most popular breeding season is March. In fact, one can see young in their nests at every season of the year! Everything about the crossbill seems therefore a little strange and their unexpected invasions of certain areas still raise numerous ecological problems which are far from being solved by ornithologists.

It is not quite certain why this small carnivorous mammal should be so rare in the mountains while the stoat is quite common. Can it be more nocturnal in its habits, or does it lead a more subterranean life? It is, of course, very possible! Whatever the reason, in the course of about thirty years spent in the Alps the author has found this gracious little animal only six or seven times. The majority of these instances have taken place in the forest and, more particularly, in the upper glades, where the land is principally covered with climbing juniper, rhododendrons and myrtle bushes. The weasel, like the stoat, makes excellent use of those piles of stones which are collected by the shepherds in the lower pasturages. When alarmed it takes shelter there and the author has had the opportunity of observing the weasel and photographing it in one of these artificial mounds of stones. The incident took place in late October... 'I had been tracking the mountain hare for the entire day in the snow and had not had great success in rather difficult terrain so that, tired out, I decided to take a rest and sat down to eat an apple not far from a pile of stones. The sun would soon sink below the horizon. The snow had largely melted during the day and there were only a few patches here and there in some sheltered folds of the earth. Lost in my thoughts, I had almost finished my apple when something attracted my attention as it began to move near the base of the pile of stones. I jumped to my feet, but the shape had disappeared. I decided to investigate and went over to discover near the large stones small fresh tracks. The tracks were visible on the soft snow, in pairs, at quite short intervals. On examining them more closely I could see that it was not a stoat which had been there, as this animal has tracks which are more

widely spaced. More and more intrigued I fetched my telephoto lens and concealed myself. I did not have to wait very long — a brown head with a white throat suddenly appeared between the stones and two beady eyes stared at me with disturbing intensity. I did not dare to make any movement for fear of frightening this small carnivorous animal, and my patience was rewarded as the animal came out from its hiding place moving quickly and lightly. I had immediately recognised that this was a weasel, and this encounter at 8200 ft (2500 m) was of special interest to me as I had never before taken a photograph of the species. I therefore decided to take a chance and set out to keep the tiny animal inside its castle as long as possible. When the weasel tried to escape towards the pasturage, I stood in front of it and made some noise so that it immediately retired within the pile of stones. As soon as it appeared again I took a photograph and then realised after a few moments, that the animal, gaining confidence, didn't even react to the click of the camera! Unfortunately darkness was rapidly approaching and this put an end to our game of hide and seek! However, I was delighted to have been able to study at my leisure this small creature which, until then, I had only glimpsed for a few seconds while wandering in the Alps.' On this occasion its spiteful expression had been registered on the author's film, and other details had also struck him: it was for example far smaller than the stoat, although in this case it may have been a young animal. Its legs were also much shorter and more fragile, and its tail was without the black patch at the end which is the characteristic and distinguishes it from the stoat at all times. It also had a triangular brown patch on the lower part of its cheeks and its throat and stomach were of pure white. Finally the surface of its back appeared darker than that of its larger cousin. An important fact to remember is that towards the end of October the alpine stoat takes on its white winter coat, although the end of the tail remains black. The weasel, on the other hand, (in the north) turns white in winter, but all the examples which the author has seen in the Alps during the winter months had kept their brown fur. This is probably one of the reasons why the weasel is less willing to leave the forest cover than the stoat. There are, of course, exceptions to this rule and the incident above is such an example. The weasel is a keen hunter of

moves in long leaps, thanks to its claws, which much longer than those of the vole. In its natural s roundings it is therefore relatively easy to know if c is looking at a mouse or a vole by studying the way which the animal moves. The vole presses its against the earth when it runs, whereas the yell necked mouse is more agile and jumps clear of earth. The tail of the latter is much longer, ev longer than the length of the body. It is larger than house mouse and its appearance, in spite of cert similarities, is quite different. It is necessary to h the two species to see that the head of the yell necked mouse is larger, and its nose longer and m hooked. The ears, also, are larger than those of house mouse and are very mobile, often trembli slightly. The eyes are black, protruding and mu larger; the fur is on the whole more fawn or r covered; the stomach and the lower parts of body, including the paws, are often very white in case of the yellow necked mouse and the cl change of colour is much more defined on the sid than with the house mouse. Finally, a pronounc yellow band round the neck distinguishes the yell necked mouse from the wood mouse, the latter ge erally having only a small yellowish patch under t neck slightly lengthened along the body, and its tai also a little shorter.

The habitat of these two similar species is r completely the same: the yellow necked mou seems to prefer the forest, and is found more often the mountains than its close relation. It sometim digs burrows, but generally uses holes dug by oth mice, cracks in the rock, the set of the badger, hollow tree trunks, and often leaves its store of fo beneath the large roots of certain conifers. T author once found its nest beneath an old tree stum it was a sort of ball of moss and dry grass which cc tained seven young, still naked and blind. This was May at an altitude of 6600 ft (2000 m). The yell necked mouse is an excellent climber and feeds pri cipally on pine seeds and wild laurel. In the mou tains the seeds of the pine cones would appear play an important part in its feeding during the wint as the author was able to confirm on one occasion finding such seeds in a hole in a spruce tree. It is ce tain that this mouse remains active throughout t winter, as its tracks are found more or less ever where on the fresh snow. It has a tendency howev to restrict its activity to the areas around villages this time of the year, and the author has caught se eral in traps left in his kitchen in Chandolin when t weather began to get cold. When it is held by its ne

The alpine tits

Coal tit.

Everything is motionless in the large mountain forests, covered with snow, where the small hares of the north have their being. There is no breath of wind, no movement, no cry apart from possibly the strange sound of a chamois disturbed in its quiet daily life, or the harsh voice of the fox, the wild hooting of the owl or high up in the sky, the proud call of the eagle.

These are forests of shadow and light, of dawn and night, intersected with gorges, close to the sky, and free of any human trace. These are the woods where the flight of the grouse can be heard, where trees die forgotten, their trunks scarred by the beautiful marten with its orange neck, or by the wild black woodpecker. This is the last stronghold of a world which is gradually disappearing.

Then, from the topmost branches, bathed in the perfume of resin and juniper, some sharp notes ring out suddenly. A small light shadow moves on the snow amongst the larger shadows of the undergrowth. The forest begins to come alive, other sounds are heard; the rapping of beats against bark, a quiet 'tock tock' noise, and the scarcely audible humming of wings amongst the branches . . . Suddenly a ball of feathers appears quite close on the branch of a pine, searching amongst every nook and cranny in the bark of the tree. Sometimes the bird reveals its back, the colour of slate, sometimes a wing with a double white stripe. On occasion the dark pearl of its eye, set in the steel blue of its head, is visible, setting off the white cheeks and the back of its head. This is the coal tit. Often called the 'little coalman' to differentiate it from the great tit, it is one of the most frequently encountered and typical inhabitants of the enormous conifer forests in the mountains. In a state of constant agitation, the frail bird methodically explores every branch, revealing from time to time for a few seconds its little round greyish stomach, or its black and white face; it then disappears again between two tufts of pine needles. With a few rapid beats of its wings the tit flies a little higher and there hangs at the end of a branch like an acrobat, or a large insect, with its legs and body twitching, and its wings beating with a constant trembling movement. Its slight, frequently uttered cries, very pure in tone, allow this bird to be recognised from far away, although it can on occasion be confused with the goldcrest.

The coal tit is very rarely the only bird to explore the vast mountain woods in the winter. Between two tufts of pine needles can be seen another bird of more or less the same size, a bird with a bold appearance, sparkling eyes, lead coloured beak, and an olive brown back. This bird has on its head a charming little crest which seems to be an elongation of bunches of needles. It has a pale breast with a superb black cravat which reaches to the back of its head in a double circle; it is the crested tit. One has scarcely had time to glimpse the bird before it has already moved somewhere else, onto another branch or the top of a tree, only to disappear a few minutes later, continuing its explorations on the ground, its wings vibrating, its body constantly moving, its claws gripping firmly the outer branches, its head below its body in positions which make the observer giddy. From time to time the bird utters a series of rolling cries which are so rapid that it is impossible to describe them. This curious sound is typical of the bird's liveliness, the intense excitement of the marvellous little winged acrobat and distinguishes it from the other species.

The crested tit and the coal tit are not the only birds to enliven with their cries and their constant acrobats the solitude of the high snowy forests . . . Other workers join their active daily round: the smallest of all, the goldcrest, is a tiny ball of greenish feathers, capped with red and so light that it is the past master of hovering in flight; then there appears the tree creeper, its back the colour of bark, climbing in hops along the tree trunks while uttering its sharp cry full of happiness. From time to time a softer cry, more silky in texture, dragging out the last syllables with a sort of teasing accent, announces the arrival of a third type of tit — the willow tit. Its head is black, its back the colour of the shadows, its eyes are surrounded with a paler area and its stomach is whitish. Slower and less agitated than its companions, this bird is also more prudent and doubtless less gregarious; its size is a little larger than that of the crested tit. Normally rather silent at the end of winter, it is most frequently heard from the tops of the larches or conifers, when it utters a nasal, piping sound. In the depths of winter, as long as there is light, the daily round of the tits takes place in this way, and they are almost always accompanied by goldcrests or tree creepers. In spite of the smallness of their size, these birds, together with the nutcracker and the nuthatch, are often the only ones to break the silence of the mountains and enliven with their cries and acrobatics the severe surroundings of the lonely high forests.

Beech marten.

Young long-eared owls in their nests.

The bullfinch

As early as March, when thick snow still covers the ground and the pine trees and larches are powdered, there arises from the forest at irregular intervals, in the heart of the black and white mountains, a very soft sound which could be mistaken for a flute . . . the notes are slow and musical, at times heard in brief snatches, and sometimes in long melodies — rising by half a tone or finishing unexpectedly with a harsh sound. Such a song makes a deep impression in this season because of its rhythm and the extraordinary clarity of its tone. One listens carefully to discover from where it comes, and then other similar songs reverberate: these sounds are more distant and even sweeter, a little indistinct and unbelievably sad . . .

The forest, wrapped in the silence of winter seems to abandon itself to a sort of melancholy. It is difficult to believe that such sweet sounds can be made by a bird! One would suspect that it was the intimate voice of the forest — the song of the bark and the snow — of solitude and silence . . . Everything becomes transformed: the rough alpine scenery loses some of its bleakness under the influence of the marvellous melody floating from the branches. There is possibly no other bird song which touches the heart and expresses secret suffering as well as the song of this bird. It is a prelude to the marvellous strength of spring in the mountains. On the top of a larch one might spot the blood-red breast of the bullfinch, which is a beautiful colour, and unexpected against the blue background of the sky. Three branches above the bullfinch sits the female, darker in plumage, but still delightful, with its head coloured like black steel, its slate grey back and its breast white as snow. The female does not seem to be unaware of the soft chords of the master . . . After a few further whistlings the pair, urged on by that vital drive, approach each other before disappearing rapidly into the forest looking for pine seeds.

In this way — above the wild forest — every morning can be heard the sweet, discreet, sad and tender song of the bullfinch.

The beech marten

This is one of the least known wild mammals in the mountains. However, the beech marten is not a rare animal and is even more frequently found than one might believe. A single snowfall will reveal, the next morning, its traces and presence near alpine villages, in forest glades, even at high altitudes. The author has often seen in the depths of winter how its track followed very steep rocky slopes or mountain ridges at an altitude of more than 10 000 ft (3000 m). What could this animal be doing in such deserted spots? Perhaps it was trying to surprise some mountain hare, a vole or perhaps a ptarmigan? The main reason is, however, following: in winter certain foothills are regularly exposed to the wind, and the snow hardly ever settles there; stretches of ground remain uncovered amongst the rocks, and grass from the previous season can be found there, together with berries on the arbutus bushes. These red berries, which are very tough and with a powdery but nutritional interior, explain the presence of the beech marten at such altitudes. Remains of the alpine arbutus berries are almost always found in its droppings in winter, and doubtless these small wild berries complement the carnivorous diet of the species during the winter months. A wanderer by nature, the beech marten can cover considerable distances in one night, crossing from one valley to the next, using the highest ridges of the mountains. The animal moves by short leaps over thick fresh snow and leaves very regular tracks, spaced at between 12 and 20 in (30 and 50 cm), depending on the condition of the powdery snow. These tracks go in pairs, one being parallel to the other, almost touching it, but always a little behind. Such tracks, when they are found in deep snow in the winter, cannot be confused with those of either the fox or the hare. The main difficulty is to know if the tracks belong to a beech marten or a pine marten, as the two animals move similarly. On melting snow or on mud the paws of the beech marten, which are not covered with fur, leave a much clearer imprint than those of the pine marten, which are more furry around the pads. Such a distinction is, however, impossible on normal snow and, in this case, only the place where they are found can give a clue to solving the problem: the pine marten prefers the large coniferous forests, rather than bare slopes or rocky places. Wild by nature, it leads a very retiring

Owls of the mountains

Several different nocturnal voices announce the arrival of spring in the mountains. Most of them are discreet, repeated untiringly for hours on end during the most silent part of the night in areas where man rarely ventures, and they owe their sad monotony to that strange sort of enchantment which inevitably takes control over the listener. March is the month of love for night birds, those beautiful creatures with golden eyes, and warm, downy feathers the colour of bark and dead wood. Their flight is completely silent, their claws are covered with feathers right down to the nails, their life is secret and retiring, lost amongst the rocks, the tree trunks, the moss and the roots of trees, so that without their song they would easily be completely unnoticed. The most noticeable cry is the echoing sound of the giant of the family, the eagle owl, considered later when species which are in danger of extinction are described; the next most noticeable cry is that of the long-eared owl, its little cousin. This cry seems even more muffled and is uttered with less force on the edges of the last trees before the high alpine meadows. Finally, in the depths of the wildest gorges can be heard the sonorous, passionate cry of the pygmy owl, a sort of long mewing sound, followed by a short silence and then taken up again with a loud clear trembling sound. In March or even February two other nocturnal birds are heard, these being creatures which remain very carefully concealed; the first is the tengmalm's owl which is so warmly clad that it can resist the most severe cold, and the other is the scops owl, which is almost the same size as a lark. These two species are descendants from the ice age in the Alps, similar to the ptarmigan and the mountain hare; and their favoured habitat is the large coniferous forest facing the north.

At dusk, but also during the day, especially when the weather is milder or when mists cover the mountains, the male of the pygmy owl utters repeated plaintive cries at regular intervals. They are very difficult to confuse with the whistling of the bullfinch; the sound is more grating, short and more desolate; the owl's cries are uttered with unbelievable monotony. This cry does not carry very far and even when a little wind is blowing it is almost inaudible at more than 100 metres. Sometimes the female of the scops owl replies to the cry of the male on a higher, more protracted pitch, resulting in strange duets through the forest. The couples, which are usually scattered, choose the old holes of the great spotted woodpecker and the three-toed woodpecker for building their nests; on occasion even choosing those of the black woodpecker and the green woodpecker. The owls seem non-migratory and remain faithful to the old spruce and larch forests in the Alps. The male and sometimes the female utter different cries in the autumn from those they make in the spring: it is a sort of ever-increasing song with sharp notes which become more and more hurried; the final sounds create the effect of a 'high-pitched falsetto' which can be blood chilling when hearing it at dawn or dusk on the edge of the deserted meadows.

The tengmalm's owl normally chooses as its domicile the most solitary spots, showing a preference for sparse forests which are mingled with large rocks

life, avoiding man if possible; this is in direct contrast to the beech marten, which seems to enjoy the presence of man, and hunts mice even in stables or outhouses. The beech marten is also a little lower on its legs than is the pine marten and is tamed more easily. Perhaps it served the purpose of the modern domestic cat in certain houses, before the latter was introduced to Europe.

The author admits that it is difficult to observe beech martens in the mountains as their mobility and their nocturnal habits conceal them from our observation for the greater part of the time. The same is also true of the pine marten which, although fonder of the daylight than the beech marten is even wilder by nature. The author has had little experience with these two animals: he has seen one trotting along at daybreak on the roof of an alpine building when he was on the look-out for black grouse. On another occasion, in bright moonlight, he also surprised a beech marten near a mountain village at 6600 ft (2000 m). With a few rapid leaps the animal took refuge beneath a pile of planks in a timber yard and it was impossible to get it out. Finally, more recently, one fine March afternoon, when he had been waiting for the arrival of an eagle for about two hours a little distance from its eyrie, a sound of gravel being dislodged amongst the rocks attracted his attention. He raised his head and saw a long supple body descending by short leaps straight towards his hiding place. The animal made use of every rough surface in climbing down and jumped gracefully over dead tree trunks or the roots of pine trees fixed into the scree. When it arrived near the author, the beech marten suddenly stopped at the foot of a tree, stared at him with its dark eyes, gave a sort of harsh cry, then, with a single leap, jumped up the slope and disappeared. He learnt subsequently that the animal had been disturbed from an old alpine hut while it was being demolished, and he found its tracks on the snow . . . These few encounters apart, the beech marten remains a rather mysterious animal for the author. Each winter mountain dwellers set traps for it and catch it from time to time for the sake of its fur. But the very keen instinct of the beech marten and the pine marten usually protects these rodents from the ambushes set for them and gives them some guarantee of survival.

A tengmalm's owl peering out from the former home of a black woodpecker.

A pygmy owl arrives clutching a bank vole.
Clearly visible on the left is the entrance to the hole dug by a great spotted woodpecker, at the bottom of which young pygmy owls grow impatient for their food.

and intersected with glades. Its presence seems connected with that of the black and green woodpeckers, as it regularly takes up its residence in the old holes of these birds and raises its young there. Its habits are the holes, a large round head with its round face.

... 'On the 13th May I was trying to track down the black grouse in an alpine pasturage, and was concealed beneath a refuge built of spruce branches. It had snowed the previous day, but during the night the temperature had dropped sharply and complete darkness had not yet fallen; there were a few stars shining like diamonds in the velvet of the sky, and these became more and more numerous. I looked at my watch – it was 3 o'clock! The cocks would shortly be crowing. Suddenly through the freezing air, breaking that pre-dawn silence, some clear, very soft sounds rose through the forest, in repeated series, broken off at regular intervals with a few seconds' silence. What could this night bird be, uttering in the border of the forest this 'pouh pouh pouh', filled with poignant melancholy? What is this shadowy voice, so pure and strange, seeming to come from another

world? It is the cry of the tengmalm owl, a small creature with golden eyes, downy plumage, indistinct colouring and mysterious ways of life. I listened for a long time in the chill of the air and the perfume of resin absorbed this nocturnal cry, seemingly from another age, praising the harsh mountain decor under the stars. It was a voluptuous voice from the shadows, a symbol of the all-powerful wild force ruling the mountains!'

The voice of the tawny owl is much more powerful than that of the tengmalm owl and is no less beautiful. The tawny owl is not as fond of the mountains as tengmalm's, being larger in size and found more frequently in the plains. Nevertheless the tawny owl can still be heard uttering its passionate cry up to the tree line. In the Alps it seems to prefer rocky outcrops which dominate valleys, doubtless because it can find holes suitable for its size there. It also frequently makes use of the abandoned homes of the black woodpecker although it feels the lack of space. On occasion it even uses the corner of some ruined barn. Although it is not commonly found at high altitudes its grating cry of 'kivick, kivick!' reveals its presence at a distance of more than half a mile ... The tawny owl is scarcely ever seen during the day; it prefers to sleep hidden in the depths of a conifer or against its trunk; it also seeks out the holes in old trees or in rocks, provided that these lairs can guarantee darkness and calmness. Its plumage is rust and greyish in colour with fine blackish brown bands; its shape is massive, and it is as big as a young chicken. Its large round head with dark eyes allow it to be distinguished from the other nocturnal birds, as the latter have an iris which is either pale yellow or orange in colour.

The long-eared owl is slightly smaller and slimmer than the tawny owl. The author has often seen it on the upper edges of the forests which border the high alpine pasturage. He has surprised it on more than one occasion in full moonlight as it hunted voles in the deserted land well above the tree line. It needs conifers for its breeding period and to guarantee a sense of security. Only the varied prey which it hunts take it into the high alpine areas, and it likes to fly over these open spaces once night falls so that it can return to the forest at daybreak.

Like the tawny owl, the long-eared owl is not a typical inhabitant of the vast mountain forests. It is far more frequently found in the small woods of the plains and becomes much rarer at high altitudes, its presence at a height of more than 6600 ft (2000 m) being scattered. It nests late, usually adopting the old nests of squirrels or the abandoned eyrie of some diurnal bird of prey. It is in April and May, when the mist covers a large area of the mountains, that its voice can be heard most often, uttering its low pitched muttered cries of 'whoo whoo whoo' from the tops of the last larch trees. This cry, heard at dusk and dawn, seems to be made by a ventriloquist and can in no way be compared with the powerful cry of the tawny owl. It carries at the most for a few hundred feet; as the snow still almost entirely covers the ground at this altitude the long-eared owl spends the larger part of its time unnoticed by man in the mountains. It is, however, another matter when the breeding season arrives. Then the young announce their presence from afar with grating cries uttered with great energy as soon as night falls. Their constant monotonous cries allow them to be the means of tracing those areas inhabited by the long-eared owl. At the approach of man, the adults also portray

A young song thrush at the exit to its nest (above).

A mistle thrush in a state of alert.

A male ring ouzel with its young.

A garden dormouse, shortly before going into hibernation.

their anxiety by strange yelping noises and clicking of their beaks. They do not hesitate to fly straight at the intruder as the author has noticed on several occasions, but they never attack deliberately as does the tawny owl when it believes its young to be in danger.

Apart from its low pitched cry and the long feathers which decorate the top of its head, the long-eared owl can also be distinguished from the tawny owl by its superb orange eyes. It has been noticed that the tawny owl has eyes of a brown, almost black colour, while the tengmalm's owl and the pygmy owl both have yellowish gold coloured irises. Because of their small size, they are difficult to confuse with the long-eared owl.

The presence of these nocturnal birds of prey in the mountains can also be ascertained, apart from their vocal manifestations, by their regurgitated pellets. These birds are accustomed to swallowing their prey whole as long as the size of the latter makes this feat possible. Then the feathers, hair, bones etc. of the prey which are not digested are rejected from the gizzard once or twice a day in the form of pellets. The discovery of several regurgitated pellets at the foot of a pine tree for example is a sure sign that a nocturnal bird has spent some time in the tree and it is probable that the bird is still using it or may even have its nest there. These pellets therefore can help in the discovery of owls. They also supply excellent information on the diet preferred by the species. Care must be taken however, not to confuse these pellets with the droppings of foxes and other carnivorous animals which are very often covered with hairs and are rather similar in appearance, but they are less round and more irregular in shape. In addition it is difficult to find many of them together, which is contrary to the way in which the regurgitated pellets are found.

Observation of these nocturnal birds of prey, although difficult because of darkness, can nevertheless give exciting results, and those moments spent in the presence of the birds can be an unforgettable experience.

The garden dormouse

This tiny woodland rodent always arouses many memories in the mind of the author. He once discovered in his youth a wood pigeon's nest in an enormous pine forest. Wishing to observe the hatching of the eggs of this bird, he was very surprised when looking into the nest to find on his second visit instead of the pigeon's eggs a charming garden dormouse comfortably rolled up at the bottom of the nest to which it had added a thick covering of moss. For the first time in his life the author had the possibility of examining this tiny creature at his leisure since, filled with its meal, it allowed itself to be picked up without difficulty. Its tail was quite long, forming a sort of black and grey brush at its end, while its ears which were fairly large and very mobile and its russet and white head, crossed with a dark stripe continuing along the sides of the neck and subtly coloured, together with its black, rather prominent eyes gave it a particular appearance rather unusual for a rodent. Very proud of his find, he slipped the little greyish ba into one of his pockets. During the walk, however, the dormouse recovered from its sleepiness and succeeded in slipping out of his pocket without being noticed. Since this little adventure the author has seen other dormice, often under very favourable circumstances. For example, on one day he was busy, together with a friend, in sawing down a tall larch at the edge of a meadow. As the saw had a tendency to stick, it was given a blow from time to time with a hammer. At one particular moment, when the author's companion was hitting the saw, the author's attention was attracted by a tiny greyish animal which was quickly climbing along the bark and trying to escape towards the top of the tree. The author immediately recognised it as a garden dormouse, and tried to catch it with the help of a long branch, but the very skilful rodent succeeded in escaping from his company. Where had it come from? On examining the old larch more carefully the author discovered at a certain height a small hole which could have been nothing else than the former home of a woodpecker. The two men started work again, highly amused by the experience, when to their big surprise after a few more blows of the hammer, they saw two other dormice suddenly leave the hole and run up the trunk of the tree. This time they both burst out laughing, greatly surprised by this 'miracle tree'. After a few more blows with the hammer even more little creatures emerged one by one from their retreat and took the same path as their predecessors. More and more entertained by this unusual sight, the two men asked each other how many more of these dormice could possibly emerge from the tree: however, at that moment the larch made some cracking noises, slowly leaned over towards the slope and came crashing down with a terrible noise. The two men immediately went in search of the rodents but failed to find a single one. They had probably succeeded in escaping into a neighbouring tree by climbing from one branch to another as squirrels do. What conclusion could be drawn from this experience? It was April and the dormice had probably spent the winter together in the depths of the hole in question and had just emerged from their hibernation. While cutting up the larch the two men found in fact a large nest made of moss mixed with hairs and a few feathers which gave off a very strong smell. Alarmed by the noise of the saw and by the violent blows of the hammer, the small creatures, aware of the danger which approached them, had hastened to leave their comfortable home in order to save their lives.

Apart from these accidental encounters, the dormouse usually leads a twilight or nocturnal life and is equally happy on the ground or in the trees, so that it is difficult to observe. It is, however, often attacked by nocturnal birds of prey, such as the tawny owl, the Tengmalm owl, the long-eared owl and the eagle owl. These birds find the creature very appetising, as do the fox and the marten. The author has been able on occasion at night to blind the dormouse with a pocket torch and then, as the creature remains fixed to the spot, he has taken photographs with a flash bulb. The dormouse is very fond of seeds, nuts, eggs, insects and fruits causing certain damage in gardens, but it prefers to live in the mountains up to a height of 6600 ft (2000 m), choosing from preference the large coniferous forests or deciduous woods. It can also be found in walls and in holes in rocks where it often builds its nest.

The mistle thrush and the song thrush

As early as the beginning of March when the snow begins to melt, a clear, extremely melodious song mounts from the southern wooded slopes. The ear is pleasantly surprised by this unexpected melody breaking through the silence like an explosion of joy. After the harsh winter such songs catch the attention through their beautiful clarity. This bird, singing from the top of the larch trees, uttering these warbling notes which are so similar to those of the blackbird in the plains but livelier, shorter and perhaps less varied, courageously braves the worst weather and is not afraid to announce spring a little before it arrives. If the March sky becomes overcast, the little singer becomes silent and it only needs a little sunshine, a break in the overcast sky with a breath of warm air, for the song to start again somewhere as intense and triumphant as ever ... The snow is still present, covering with its frozen crystals both forest and meadow. Nevertheless, near the high villages, little by little the first pieces of grass become visible, a first fly stretches its wings on a window pane and the alpine accentor on the gable of a mountain hut begins to weave its tiny melody while the anemone slowly opens its tiny downy buds close to the ground. Then this resonant song is heard more often and the melody carries further, rising from the depths of the valleys to float up the slopes as far as the last trees.

At the edge of the forest a greyish bird, a little larger than the blackbird, is perched on the top of a larch and seems immobile, facing the rising sun: this is the mistle thrush. With binoculars it is possible to see from a long way off the details of its plumage: it has a yellowish white breast, speckled with numerous black patches, its wings and back are both fawn coloured, while its claws are of a rather pale brown, so that the general effect is dowdy and attracts little attention. Suddenly, however, the bird opens its beak, its body trembles and the song begins again, louder than ever ...

The mistle thrush is the first to announce the arrival of spring in the mountains as certain of them do not emigrate, although in winter they become subject to very erratic behaviour. Wild and prudent, always on the look-out, the mistle thrush is difficult to observe closely. It is sometimes seen near villages moving with flexible hops along the slopes which are already free of snow. With its head high, its eye on the look-out for trouble, the bird seeks out for hours at a time the juicy earthworms or the larvae of the diptera (two-winged flies) which live on them. This is the essential basis of the thrush's diet in March, to which it sometimes adds wild berries. Often two mistle thrushes work over the countryside together at a little distance from each other. Seen from above their neutral coloured plumage blends well with the earth which is gradually becoming visible. Very often the birds are unnoticed and they certainly know how to keep their distance. If one approaches a little too close they leave the slope one after the other, uttering cries of 'trrr... tre tre tre... tra tra tra...' before hiding in the nearby forest. At the end of March the ring ouzel, recently returned from Spain and North Africa, invades the glades which have been freed from snow and joins the thrushes. In a few days there are certain fields that are teeming with these birds and their voices in the morning drown the sound of the streams, whereas two weeks earlier a few isolated mistle thrushes were the only birds to be found there.

In April the mistle thrush begins to build its nest, choosing from preference the edge rather than the depths of the alpine forests. The nest is very similar to that of the blackbird and is usually built in the fork of the trunk or branch of a pine or spruce tree; it is always carefully camouflaged with lichen and protected from the snow by tufted twigs. The eggs are laid shortly after the nest is completed. The author has often seen young thrushes leaving their nest, still unable to fly very well, as early as the middle of May at a height of 6600 ft (2000 m). Losses from the first brood seem to be heavy, aggravated by the systematic pillage of nutcrackers and squirrels who seize the eggs or the fledglings in spite of the vigorous attacks of their parents. It is true, however, that the nutcrackers do not always succeed in winning and sometimes are forced to escape as the author has often witnessed.

In September the thrush has a tendency to assemble in large flocks; they can be seen spreading out over both plains and mountains in search of bilberries, myrtle berries and wild berries of all sorts, and the birds gradually make their way south towards the southern part of France, the Iberian peninsula and Italy. Those birds which remain in the Alps usually descend to the ducts of the valleys and there show a particular preference for mistletoe berries, a source of food which allows them to survive during the winter in spite of the cold and the snow. They are sometimes found together with the black throated thrush from the north, especially on the mountain ash tree, but the mistle thrush is not as gregarious as the former and appears to be independent, even in the gardens where it looks for food in small groups. The mistle thrush is the largest of the European thrushes together with the Siberian thrush, which has a longer beak and which is only found very occasionally in our countries. The mistle thrush does not always remain in the mountains and, at breeding time, it will build its nest just as happily in the plain, where there are small woods or gardens with trees to be found.

The song thrush is distinctly smaller than the mistle thrush and can be distinguished also by its general appearance which is more stocky and russet in colour, the back and top of its head being of a warm brown colour while its throat is fawn and its tail much shorter. Its breast is spotted in the same way as that of the mistle thrush but the spots are smaller. If placed next to each other the song thrush seems to be a smaller model of the mistle thrush with less neutral colouring.

The song thrush is not found at such a high altitude as the mistle thrush and only occasionally goes above 5600 ft (1700 m), although the author has found its nest on two occasions at 7000 ft (2100 m) on the edge of the tree line. Its favourite habitat in the Alps is the spruce forest; it needs a certain humidity and cool ground. Unlike the mistle thrush, it scarcely ever is found in the open, and normally looks for its food in the undergrowth, along forest paths, near streams, in marshy spots or at the edge of glades, always however being near a wood. Extremely shy and furtive by nature it disappears at the least sign of danger uttering a characteristic cry of 'tsic'. The song thrush would be mostly unnoticed if it were not for the song of the male which can be heard at a distance of more than 1500 ft (500 m). The author has heard it very frequently in the Jura in April and May, early in the morning or at nightfall, while he was watching the mating dance of the grouse.

The volume of sound produced is sometimes impressive and always unusual when hundreds of thrushes, perched on the tops of larch or spruce trees, burst into full-throated song with extraordinary energy, the sounds being normally at a very high pitch. The song is very different from the mistle thrush and is made up of various themes comprising two to four repeated syllables, separated by short silences: 'ulip ulip ulip . . . dudi dudi dudi . . . tit tit . . . teretett teretett . . . tilip tilip . . .'. The sound is like a flute being played energetically somewhere in the treetops. Often the song thrush borrows for its song certain themes from other birds and alters them to suit itself, so that there are at times strange concerts to be heard in the forests.

Its nest cannot be confused with that of the mistle thrush or the blackbird. Although its exterior may be similar, it uses more moss and lichen and the inside of the bowl is entirely covered with a layer of mud which has the consistency of cardboard. The eggs are a wonderful pale greenish blue, sometimes speckled black or brown on the smooth, hard surface of the egg and these allow the species to be identified immediately.

In the mountains this nest is most often found hidden at the join of the trunk and branches in the young spruce tree; the author has also found it solidly lodged in the lichen on a pine trunk or even in the depths of a large juniper bush. The nest is never very high in the tree – a maximum of 16–20 ft (5–6 m) – and is occasionally very close to the ground.

The song thrush has a varied diet; it includes many sorts of insects and their larvae, worms, slugs, centipedes and also several types of fruit and wild berries in the autumn. This bird has also the habit of breaking the shells of snails against a stone. It returns faithfully to its territory each year, as is proved by the considerable quantity of debris which is found there.

In September, but particularly in October, it assembles in large flocks and starts to migrate towards the south, stopping here and there in vineyards to gorge itself on grapes. Certain of them, however, have a tendency to spend the winter in the area where they breed, if enough food can be found there. This is not the case in the mountains, however, and the song thrush could not survive there in winter. It therefore descends to the bottom of the valleys, and also spreads through the woods of the plains where the climate is mild, only returning to the higher altitudes at the end of March or April. It is of interest to note that this species which nests in a wide variety of forests and even in gardens at low altitudes becomes exclusively a mountain dweller in the southern regions and in the extreme south of the alpine chain. This is also the case with the mistle thrush, the robin, the dunnock or hedge sparrow, and the tree pipit.

The ring ouzel

Although it is true that spring arrives late in the mountains and that snow can still fall then, covering the large forests which surround the mountains while the plain is already turning green, as soon as March reaches its end, spring begins its mysterious work in the mountains. Almost imperceptible signs announce its arrival: it is perhaps a drop of water falling from a roof, or a fly stretching its wings on a window pane. It may even be those hazy mountain mists which continually hang around the larch trees, giving them a halo . . . It can also take the form of the strange winter cry of the alpine accentor, that intricate warbling song, quietly uttered by the bird whose breast is the colour of rust while it perches on the eaves of an alpine hut, with enormous flakes of snow flurrying around it. And there is this tiny beetle with its wing sheaths of jade struggling desperately to move its legs over the melting snow. It is neither spring nor winter. Something has changed in the air. A new strength of light is penetrating the enormous mountain forests. It is also the time of solitude for the villages at high altitudes . . . Not far from them, on well exposed slopes, snow has given way to earth and the grey grass slowly uncrumples itself, while there are already a few crocuses pushing their way through the old vegetation crushed against the slopes.

This is an area where, on a fine morning, dark brown birds with a lighter coloured band across their breast busy themselves unearthing the juicy grubs. They could easily be taken for blackbirds if it were not for the white breast feathers which contrast with the rest of their plumage, the latter being a little less dark than the plumage of their cousins from the plains. Let us observe more closely these newcomers which are feeding here and there in small groups. Some of them appear darker than others with a crescent of snow white colour across their breast and almost silvery high-lights on the upper part of their wings. Others — the females in all probability — have a less distinct white band and a more greyish appearance, the feathers of the stomach being patched with brown. They have recently returned from North Africa and though they are absorbed in searching for their food these ring ouzels are nevertheless very wild and shy; in approaching a little closer one will see them fly away one after the other to the tops of the nearest larch trees. There they become very excited, wagging their tails and revealing their alarm through their loud cries of 'dack dack dack' interrupted by short pauses.

At the time when their young leave the nest however, towards the end of May or in June, the adults give much louder cries of alarm and sometimes attack the intruder with rapid anguished noises that can almost be described as guttural.

The falls of snow which are so frequent at the end of March often force the ring ouzel to take shelter in the plains. As soon as the sky is clear of clouds, however, it returns to the borders of the high alpine forests and lives in the glades, although they may still be half covered in snow. They also choose the edges of streams, marshy areas, or meadows where the juniper bushes grow. In flight these birds appear very light in colour because of the white fringe on their wings and their stomachs. This is characteristic of the species, which replaces the blackbird in the mountains. Some weeks later, in April, even before the first light of dawn appears and stars are still visible in the sky, the ring ouzel will suddenly utter from the top of a spruce tree two or three loud notes . . . For a few minutes silence falls again. Then another ouzel will awake and take up the well-known, quiet song. It may be only 4.30 in the morning when the first bird replies to its neighbour: before beginning its song it utters a few harsh sounds as if it wished to clear its throat and then suddenly it breaks into a song similar to the sound of a flute, with two or three rhythmical notes, clear and melodious; sometimes a little raucous; at other times more plaintive and monotonous, although extremely poignant when heard in the solitude of the Alps. Soon these loud sounds will be heard all round, uttered more and more frantically, as if the singers wished to compete in expressing their ecstasy. It can happen that dozens of ring ouzels are singing a few hundred yards from each other while the stars are still visible in the sky, turning to saffron before finally disappearing, allowing the dark shapes of the trees to become clearer as dawn approaches . . .

Next the mistle thrush awakes and joins the concert given by the ring ouzels while at the edge of the last conifers, the black grouse, wings spread and tails extended, cluck with rage, beating their wings noisily and dancing over the snow, uttering their ceaseless cooing.

Hidden beneath a shelter of pines, breathing in the perfume of resin, it is possible for the observer to listen ardently to this hymn of life which is offered each springtime in the freshness of the dawn . . .

The black grouse

The black grouse, also called the small peacock or the fork-tailed cock, is certainly one of the finest specimens of alpine birds. Not only its size – that of a domestic chicken in the case of the male – attracts the attention of hunters, but also the beauty of its plumage and its lyre-shaped tail give the black grouse a place in the front rank of the gallinaceous birds of the mountains. In the mating season its wattles become enlarged and look like large fleshy eyebrows which join and give a magnificent orange crown to the bird's head. The splendid dark blue reflections on its throat and crop, together with the white bands on the wings and, more than anything else the strange attitudes which the cock adopts during this nuptual period, make the black grouse one of the jewels of the alpine forest. The female, which is much smaller, is also more modest in appearance and so different from the male that the uneducated observer could easily mistake it for a bird of another species. While the plumage of the cock bird is rather dark brown in colour, that of the hen is more greyish beige and rather dowdy. In fact, when seen from only a short distance away, the plumage of the hen bird is an astonishing blend of fawn and rust colours with wide bands of black and grey. The throat and breast are slightly lighter than the upper parts of the body and are also patched with black, while the white under-feathers of the wings remain concealed when the bird is at rest by long, yellowish median feathers, banded in black. The rust coloured tail is crossed with darker stripes and is only slightly V-shaped when extended, not to be compared with the lyre shape of the male. Although the plumage of the hen is much more modest than that of its male companion, it is nevertheless remarkable because of the subtlety of the colours, the design and the way in which it blends with the mountain background. A bird as large as the hen black grouse would attract much attention if its plumage and habits, which are very discreet, did not help to protect it from the worst of the dangers surrounding it.

It is not always easy to confirm the presence of the black grouse near the upper tree line of the alpine forests. The bird is wild, prudent and endowed with remarkable senses of hearing and sight. It is more skilful than any other bird in hiding amongst the bilberry and myrtle bushes, the juniper trees and the rhododendrons. It seems to prefer ground which is a little damp, slopes facing the north and gullies where from time to time bushes of the green alder or small pines and larches can be found.

In the majority of cases the walker is astonished to see appear at a few paces from himself a large dark bird, emerging from the vegetation with a great deal of noise, then hurtling down the slopes. The bird first beats violently with its wings then, when it has acquired sufficient speed to fly, uses its slightly arched wings to acquire an amazing speed. After flying some 60 yards the black grouse normally stops its flight by spreading its tail and its wings to disappear behind the nearest curtain of protective trees. Sometimes it flies to the top of a conifer some distance away; from that safe position it follows every movement of the intruder, uttering a sharp shrill cry from time to time. When this happens the walker can observe it with the aid of his binoculars and note the shape of the long lyre-shaped tail. If the bird however senses that it is being watched it will take flight again and immediately disappear into the depths of the forest. This is more or less all that will be seen of it! In order to watch the bird more closely and photograph it, it will be necessary to go to the upper parts of the high alpine forests in springtime so as to see the cocks gather together for their mating dances. Such areas are usually situated beyond the last trees; it could be a snowy slope, the top of a gully or a secluded ridge: these are the areas which the bird prefers for its frantic mating parades. A hide built of pine branches is indispensable to witness such parades as the black grouse is extremely vigilant even when carried away by its mating passion. As soon as a human shape is seen, the birds immediately fall silent and limit themselves to their soft cooing noises.

One day in mid-May the author was safely installed and hidden under one of the natural look-outs which he takes care to refurbish every year. It was three o'clock in the morning. A slight trace of light in the east announced the end of night, while a cold wind brushed away the powdery snow from large areas of ground still hidden in shadow. The author was shivering and, at exactly the same moment when the first ring ouzel announced its awakening with two or three silvery notes, followed by a discordant sound. Then there was a strange noise, like a jet of steam escaping with force, which announced the arrival of the first black grouse from the top of the gully 'tschuo uysch! tschuo uysch!'. He heard the noise of several wings and there was no doubt that a second grouse had just landed heavily on the snowy slope. He glanced out through the branches of his hide-out and finally made out a shape which was walking backwards and forwards on the powdery snow making strange movements, followed by violent wing beats. The grouse advanced, retreated, extended its tail then stopped and opened its beak wide to salute the dawn with a cry of 'tschou-uysch!'. The bird extended its neck, lowered its head and uttered sort of loud gurgling noise while the sky turned to violet and the conifers gave out their perfume, the spring stirring beneath the snow . . . Then the male bird circled in the air with convulsive, nervous movements, its wings spread down towards the ground and its tail fully extended. Suddenly it stretched its neck, hooted loudly, beat its wings and moved away a few yards. This time the other cock replied. The two birds became very excited and their hooting became more frequent and more competitive; hissing with rage the two birds approached each other. Finally they were face to face, uttering harsh cries of 'kou krreeeh!'. They hurled themselves towards each other their back feathers raised, tails spread out like fans, under-feathers giving strange reflections in the greyness of the dawn. With redoubled war cries the two birds pecked furiously at each other and also used their claws, while they beat the air with their extended wings. They rolled down the slope tearing

A black grouse during its nuptial period.

Stances adopted by the black grouse during its fights, nuptial period, and scuffles.

feathers from each others necks and also leaving dark stains on the snow. Then, from the forest came the sound of 'cock . . . cock . . . cock . . .'. This sound was made by the hens who were watching from the tops of the larch trees, showing their interest in the strange tournament and maintaining the ardour of the two combatants. Finally one of the adversaries showed signs of exhaustion and retreated, pursued by its rival. A few minutes later the latter regained its 'dancing place' and seemed to be the champion of the area. Nervous and excited, its black form continued to move up and down the slope in the light of the dawn; it was a black patch which became more and more visible against the whiteness of the powdery snow. Then this bird with the forked tail began to sing. Its soft trembling sound vibrated through the morning air and seemed to travel through the entire forest. At times it broke off its song as it jumped up and down, then making cooing noises, it beat its wings noisily and lowered and raised its head energetically. Soon other cries, interrupted with 'jets of steam', echoed from all sides. There must have been a dozen cocks gurgling energetically, each one on the spot it had chosen for itself, each one moving around its own little space ceaselessly coming and going while its throat and whole body were alive with this trembling vibration . . . What an astonishing sight! The birds seemed entirely possessed by some blind force and completely lost in their ecstasy. They seemed to be singing in a choir quite close to each other and carried out some fantastic dance movements, beating their wings from time to time and leaping a few yards into the air . . . Such a ballet was unexpected from these black grouse, puffed up with love beneath their enormous red eyebrows . . . Their loud gurgling provided beautiful and sweet music in the perfumed resinous air and their throats with mar-

vellous dark blue reflections were constantly stretched to their fullest extent . . . Facing the valleys these wild cocks danced! They represented the force of springtime, the space of the snowy slopes and solitude. They represented the noise of the streams freed from the ice and the glowing gold of the mountains. As the light got stronger it seemed to endow their wattles with burning scarlet flames.

A hen appeared from the undergrowth, crossed the snowy surface with quiet clucking noises, moved from one cock to another with its wings lowered, its attitude submissive, its body pressed against the snow, giving clear indications of its intentions. The cocks became increasingly passionate, moved round and round the hen and the author finally witnessed the mating which only lasted for a few seconds. The hen moved away and the dance continued, the movements becoming more and more complex while a second hen appeared to choose its favourite moving from one cock to another, showing herself to be willing or unwilling and thus giving rise to furious combats. This was the way in which the dance terminated, an extraordinary sight.

As the sun appeared the passion of the cocks decreased. The cries became less frequent. One after another the grouse left the arena and flew up to the branches of the nearby larch trees where they began to peck at the young tufts of needles. A pleasant perfume arose from the earth, an anemone slowly opened its mauve petals and the sound of a black restart warbled somewhere in the distance while a cuckoo repeated its two famous notes tirelessly. Slowly silence descended. In the gully which was full of movement only a short while before, there were now only a few feathers the colour of ink to be seen on the snow as evidence of the mating dance.

European nuthatch.

The nuthatch

'Dwit! Dwit! Witt! Wiwitt! Wiwiwitt!'. The spring sun is turning the last patches of snow on the meadows into water and, beneath the big larch where the author likes to sit, there are already ants running to and fro. The anemone bud will open soon; 'Dwit! Dwit! Dwit!'. The liquid notes fall like a cascade from the high branches still bare of needles. Looking up at the tree, where the fine threads of silver are outlined against the blue sky like the cross pieces of a stained glass window, there it is, running across the bark, its head lowered, climbing up or down the tree trunk, tirelessly investigating with its dagger-like beak the smallest pieces of lichen, every nook and cranny in the tree. This is the nuthatch, the acrobatic gymnast without equal ... the tree creeper is only a novice compared with the nuthatch. It never uses its tail as a support like the tree creeper and its powerful claws allow it to climb up and down any conifer trunk, although it is also found on deciduous trees in the plains.

Noisy, restless, constantly indulging in acrobatics, the nuthatch moves over the trunk and the branches of the tree throughout the day, in every season, seeking its food and providing an enlivening influence in every corner of the forest. It can be heard long before it is seen, revealing its squat shape, its black striped head, its white cheeks and throat and its blue back and delicately yellow tinted stomach. The author saw it one day pull out from the bark an earwig, and it also consumes numerous other insects and spiders and beetles. As opposed to the tree creeper, however, the nuthatch also feeds on many different seeds, especially in winter. In the Alps it is particularly fond of certain pine seeds. It looks for them in autumn and knows exactly how to extract them from the cone. When hungry it will also attack nuts, which it skilfully lodges in a crack of the bark in order to be able to penetrate the shell. It chooses a hole in a tree for its nest, being particularly fond of the old homes of the great spotted woodpecker, the green woodpecker and the black woodpecker in the mountains. It has the strange habit of partially blocking up the entrance to the hole with the aid of small pellets of earth which it first sticks together with its saliva. This work is carried out very early in the year, in March or April. The nest itself is made up of small twigs and pieces of bark from the pine tree or the birch, and occasionally, of dry leaves. In the centre of this strange 'bed' the female lays six or seven white eggs speckled with russet, between late May or early June, according to the altitude. The incubation period usually lasts about two weeks. The young grow rather slowly and they only venture outside the hole where they have been born after twenty-five days. The nuthatch, while not being particularly wild, is less inclined to accept the presence of man than is the tree creeper. Like the latter, however, it willingly joins the flocks of tits and goldcrests. Towards the end of March it utters cheerful whistling noises in the depths of the forest, announcing the approach of spring to the inhabitants of the mountains.

The chaffinch

How can one explain the presence of this bird among the alpine species, when it is so common on the plains? Known to all, it would seem almost superfluous to give a description. It is, however, always a little surprising to hear its song on the edge of the high forests at an altitude on occasion of more than 7200 ft (2200 m)! In this connection the author had a strange experience.

One fine spring day he had gone skiing in a particularly remote area of Annivers, called Illgraben. It was a vast area of erosion surrounded by attractive meadows beyond which there were larch and pine woods. The place was isolated and rather difficult to reach at that time of the year, as the melting snow had collected in the gulleys and was rather dangerous for the visitor. It is advisable to follow a well-marked path which takes one first to the foothills of the Illhorn, then leading along the edge of the famous abyss, following the upper tree line of the forest. The author reached the spot and was in the process of looking for a slope free of snow, when he caught the sound of a bird-song, completely new to him. He immediately started to look around for the source and did not have to wait long. The song started again a few moments later. Convinced that he was near some rare bird, the author left his bag and his skis and carefully approached the larch trees which apparently hid the mysterious singer. The strange melody was begun again with extraordinary energy. It was all the more intriguing as its beginning and ensuing rhythm seemed to be typical of the ordinary chaffinch, while from time to time certain phrases used by the tree pipit could be heard. In fact many tree pipits were singing nearby and for a moment the author was rather puzzled. Having located the songster with his binoculars he made a small detour in order to see the bird in a strong light. He was extremely surprised when he recognised, by its wine coloured breast, its dark blue neck and head, its wide white shoulder patches and its greenish crop that he was looking at a chaffinch, the most wide-spread, cosmopolitan of the European birds. The little singer was very excited and paid no attention to the author, so that he could examine the bird at leisure. As with all the males of its species the chaffinch took up its territorial song several times a minute with its head raised, its throat extended and its wings vibrating. The author could check for the first time a fact which certain ornithological books had revealed, namely that the chaffinch does not have its own melody, but is obliged to imitate its relations. The explanation of the extraordinary song which the author had heard that morning was explained by the fact that this chaffinch had installed itself in an area where the tree pipits were particularly numerous and, being the only one of its species amongst them, and probably constantly aware of their song, it quite naturally imitated the sounds of the tree pipits while maintaining its own particular hurried and descending cadence together with the final complicated ending, which is typical of the couplet of the chaffinch. This bird also utters a special cry known as 'rutting' in rainy weather and at breeding times. This cry is a monotonous rolled sound of 'prouy' often uttered for hours at length from the tops of conifers where the bird intends building its nest. The nest, a real masterpiece, is always built by the female. Solidly constructed, it blends perfectly with its background and is made of small roots, dried twigs and moss. The outside is covered with lichen, spider-webs and fragments of bark. Its interior decoration includes fibres of plants, a few feathers and some horse hair.

One striking feature of the chaffinch is the difference in plumage of the two sexes. While the male is brilliantly clad, the female on the contrary appears dull and grey, as its feathers are pale greenish brown and the bands on its wings less marked.

When hatching its eggs, the female is much less visible than its companion who, for this period, constantly guards its territory by uttering its cheerful song at the first signs of day.

Migration is in full swing in October and is completed by mid-November. It covers a very large area but the birds from the north are those who travel widest, covering Europe and flying towards the south-west. Their rallying cry is a harsh 'pink' cry which is heard from afar off. The chaffinches from the Alps probably spend the winter in the south of France and in Spain. Many of them, in particular the males which live on the plains, are non-migratory in western Europe.

A male chaffinch at feeding time.

A green tiger beetle sunning itself in spring.

The cicindelinae (tiger beetles)

It is the end of April and the weather is superb. The path climbs constantly, but gradually following the dorsal spine ridge of the mountain in a very regular way. The last patches of snow are melting into streams of ice-cold water under the strong sun and the pine bark crackles in the silence while eddies of warm air filled with marvellous perfumes drift up the slopes covered with bilberries. An agile beetle crawls across the path; it finally takes flight and lands again some few yards further away. Before the author has taken another three steps however, the tiny creature repeats the same movement and keeps its distance. It thus allowed him to glimpse the beautiful green colours of its wing sheaths, to see how they are spotted with yellow and note how its long metallic legs are well made for racing: this is a green tiger beetle (*Cicindela campestris*). After its next flight the insect unfortunately lands on a patch of snow on the edge of the narrow path. It struggles on the grains of melting ice but becomes slowly overcome by the cold. With the author's help it crosses the last few yards, and once it has regained solid ground it settles on a stone, stretches itself in the sun and proceeds to clean itself.

The tiger beetle opens its wings at intervals, revealing the upper part of its abdomen which sparkles with all the colours of the spectrum like a rare jewel cut by an expert craftsman . . . With its feet, the magnificent beetle carefully brushes its antennae, its back, its sides and then opens and shuts its powerful mandibles; when it has been sufficiently warmed, it crosses the rock in fits and starts, then, suddenly, spreads its wing sheaths and its lower wings which are covered with fine veins and, taking flight, seeks out the sunniest spot on the steep path. Doubtless it has just emerged from its chrysalis after the long nymph stage of its life during the severe winter, when it has been hidden beneath several yards of snow. The metamorphosis takes place in a sort of vertical well dug by the larvae in the hard ground and previously sealed by itself. The larvae of the tiger beetle is very carnivorous and hides in its lair throughout the summer months, seizing its prey as it comes within reach.

At a far higher altitude, on the stretches of sand beneath the streams, or amongst the rocks bordering the dry paths of the meadows lives another species, *Cicindela gallica*, which is similar in appearance and habits to *Cicindela campestris*, although its wing sheaths are decorated in the centre by two transverse bands shaped like hooks. I have observed this insect in the Italian National Park of Gran Paradiso at an altitude of more than 10 000 ft (3000 m)! It is also common in the Alps of the Valais area in Switzerland and in the high alpine areas of France. It only differs from the hybrid *Cicindelae*, which prefer to live in the plains, in very small details. The most important of these is the fine green colour of its wing sheaths; the hybrid has wing sheaths of a more blackish green or bronze colour.

This is not of great importance, as the *Cicindelinae* are the first beetles to appear on the mountain paths as soon as the snows melt. What a pleasure it is to discover them suddenly at one's feet, taking flight at the least sign of danger without ever moving very far off, while the snow melts into streamlets of water on every side. There is a certain sunny charm in such a meeting, in seeing this tiny form of life. These first wing sheaths of the season are as it were a secret sign and the first greeting, however timid, of triumphant spring.

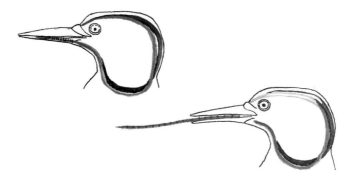

The tongue can be pushed from the beak by a complex mechanism of muscles and ligaments.
The tongue is coated with a sticky secretion which traps insects.

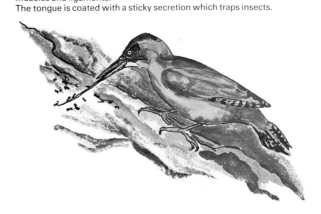

The tree pipit

When the snow is quickly disappearing – when the air is trembling above the silvery slopes and one walks carefully over the unfurling meadows surrounded by warm air, not far from the tree line – a greyish bird can be seen leaving the top branches of a pine tree and fly upwards towards the sky. One can follow the fragile silhouette which, vibrating its wings rapidly, climbs at a steep angle while uttering joyful notes. The bird reaches the limit of its flight and then slows down its descent by spreading its wings and tail, looking like a tiny parachutist. It describes a graceful curve while gliding downwards and continues to throw its loud melody into the immense, blue spaces, a melody which slows down and finishes in a cascade of notes at the moment when the bird regains its original branch. A pair of binoculars will be helpful to trace the small sparrow, slimly built, with red feet, olive coloured feathers and a light speckled breast. There is nothing very striking about the general impression. Its nuptual flight, however, is remarkable and it is this flight which allows the species to be definitely identified. Its song becomes quicker as it flies upwards, gradually dies away during the descent and always finishes with some loud cries of 'tsia tsia tsia'. The pipit is not miserly with its song. It can be seen constantly climbing towards the sky repeating the sounds of its jubilation, and it will almost always return to its original point of departure, in most cases the summit of a tree. Its song would in fact become rather boring in due course if the bird did not accompany it nine times out of ten by its gracious parachute descent. The male uses this method to stake out its territory, whilst the female which is infinitely more discreet, busies itself with building the nest. Using a great deal of care, and cunning worthy of a Sioux Indian, the female normally chooses a small depression in the side of a slope, covers it with moss and dry grass and, embellishing the inside with horse hair, finally lays four or five brownish or greyish eggs there. Well hidden by the vegetation, this nest is all the more difficult to discover as the adults, once the young have been hatched, become even more prudent than normal and hardly ever return directly to the nest. One can see them wait for hours at their favourite places, betraying their alarm by penetrating cries. In order to feed their young, the pipits return to the ground a certain distance away from the nest and then skilfully make their way through the vegetation towards the nest, checking at every moment that they are not being watched. Feeding finally takes place and the adult immediately flies off carrying droppings in its beak.

The green woodpecker

'Kiu kiu kiu kiu kiu kiu kiu ...'. On the edge of the alpine forest it utters this 'brassy laugh', this burst of sound which decreases as it progresses. The larch trees have not yet acquired their delicate greenery and a few last patches of snow still survive in the undergrowth. But the April sun warms the old grass pressed down against the earth, and the air vibrates above the slopes while the crocuses already invade the meadows. The echoing cry rings out again from the forest, drowning the other sounds of the valley ... Then similar cries reply like an echo from some distance away. A few more paces and suddenly one sees flying down from an old larch a rather large green and yellow bird – the woodpecker – which crosses the clearing with a swooping flight and fixes itself to the first tree it finds. It can easily be recognised by its fine plumage, its elongated shape and its vigorous wing beats, which stop completely from time to time. The bird follows this action with a gliding motion through the air, wings pressed against its body ... Its cry rings out again from behind a tree trunk: The green woodpecker is timid but filled with curiosity and will play at hide and seek, peeping out from behind a tree trunk, only to retire again, revealing every now and then its fine red head and its 'moustache' of the same colour, artistically framed in black ... At this distance the last-mentioned detail can only be noticed with the aid of binoculars, but it is a detail of some importance as the female has a completely black 'moustache'. The female also reveals its presence in the forest by repeating the same cries of those of the male, although they are in shorter series and less melodious.

Unlike the great spotted woodpecker and the black woodpecker, the green woodpecker has a vocal display which plays an important rôle when mating or when recreating old relationships; it carries out its drumming action on very rare occasions. The author has never had the opportunity of hearing this drumming, and many other ornithologists are in the same position. Although it spends the greater part of its life in trees, the green woodpecker often seeks out its food on the ground, probably more frequently than do the other species. The observer, however, will scarcely ever have the occasion to surprise the bird, because at the first sign of danger it will immediately fly up to the nearest tree trunk. The author only once succeeded in seeing the bird at work on an ant-hill. The incident took place in springtime at the edge of an alpine forest. The author was hidden under canvas while observing the movements of a pair of nuthatches, when a green woodpecker came down to the heap of needles covering a nest of red ants not far from his hiding place. With a few powerful pecks it pushed aside the needles and then ran its long pink tongue over the ant heap in order to capture the inhabitants . . . From time to time the bird retracted its tongue, all covered with ants and swallowed them with obvious satisfaction. On one other occasion, at 6600 ft (2000 m) in the depths of winter, when the author was returning from a long ski trip, a green woodpecker suddenly left a slope covered with snow as the author was passing and flew so close to him that he at first thought it was injured. Returning to the spot from where the bird had flown however, the author discovered a large hole in the snow and at the bottom of this hole there was an ant heap which had been broken open by the pecks of the hungry bird. Was it the woodpecker which had removed the icy covering in order to reach its favourite food? The author would hesitate to make such a statement; the nutcrackers which are common in this region could have helped with the work. No matter who was responsible, the green woodpecker cannot find life easy at such an altitude, although it can also feed on larvae and wood-eating insects. The hole for its nest is dug in the trunk of a conifer in the mountains; it may be an old pine or larch, the wood of which is soft and cannot resist so well the attacks of that specialised tool, the beak of this bird.

The young make a great deal of noise. When they are fifteen days old they constantly cry for food from the depths of the hole and if one only scratches the hole while passing the young emit a strange sort of loud, rhythmic gurgling noise which seems to have more in common with a concert given by camels than cries made by young birds. The adults feed them regularly every hour and are prudent and careful near the nest. Unless the observer is completely hidden and supplied with a remote control shutter release it will be extremely difficult for him to take pictures of this superb representative of the European woodpecker family.

The red and black ants

It is almost impossible to ignore those tiny creatures. They are to be found everywhere in the forest and even well beyond the tree line. How many picnics have been ruined by the presence of these tiny Hymenoptera (Formicidae ants), how many relaxing afternoons in the grass made intolerable by their bites? And yet, without even considering the extraordinary literature which these insects have inspired from the great naturalists, this world of ants is a fascinating one.

The most common species, a species which one will certainly see as soon as the fine weather begins on almost every forest path, is the red ant, *Formica sanguinea*. This insect is easily recognisable from its large size, its abdomen a blackish brown in colour, banded with shining rings while its thorax, legs and sides of the head are reddish. This is the ant which builds large nests shaped like domes, from pine-needles. They are usually built against an old tree trunk, sometimes even covering it completely. These nests are remarkable constructions and penetrate the ground for more than 3 ft (1 m). They are made up of a quantity of rooms and passages and are most often found in sparse woodlands where air and light can penetrate freely. In areas where man is infrequently seen such ant hills can reach impressive dimensions rising at times to a height of 6 ft (2 m).

Leaning over one of these nests, one will notice on the surface of an enormous collection of pine needles numerous holes from which enter and leave hundreds, even thousands of ants. Towards evening these openings will be carefully sealed with pieces of bark. The same happens when it rains. The stronger the sunlight on the nest the more intense the movement there. It becomes a teeming world of legs, antennae, thoraxes and abdomens, pouring like a living mass over the sides of the ant hill. This ceaseless flow channels itself into paths at the base of the dome which spread out in all directions towards the forest, intersecting the moss and the grass for several yards. If one thinks that a single ant heap can represent hundreds of thousands of inhabitants without including the innumerable larvae hidden in the interior needing constant attention and feeding, one will easily understand that the red ants cover very wide areas in their search for food and play an extremely important rôle in the life of the forest by destroying quantities of harmful insects. Nothing seems to be able to escape from the vice of their powerful mandibles: it can be a caterpillar which has just been attacked by these fearsome hunters, or a beetle or grasshopper; even a butterfly can be found in its death throes or a worm twisting in vain under th

A female green
woodpecker
getting ready to
disgorge some of
its food for its
young.

Tree pipit.

attack of its innumerable enemies. The naturalist Eidmann observed that about 2000 insects were taken into a large nest of red ants every day without including extensive quantities of nectar taken from the green fly.

The red ant does not possess a sting. But, if the surface of the nest is bathed in sunlight while the background remains in shadow, the author suggests dragging a thin stick over the ant hill. It can then be seen how the inhabitants immediately raise themselves on their four hind legs, take up a threatening attitude, open their mandibles, lift the abdomen beneath the thorax and squirt tiny jets of formic acid to a height of 12 or 20 in (30 or 50 cm). These jets are easily visible against the light and if one of them gets into ones eye one will be conscious of a sharp pain. On the other hand the bite of a red ant presents no danger; the author has often put his hands on to a nest full of activity without feeling anything more than a tickling sensation, provided of course that the skin on the hands is healthy and not cut in any way.

Apart from the red ant there is another species, larger in size and shining black, which has the base of its abdomen and its legs as well as the sides of the thorax coloured with reddish brown, and this insect also inhabits the coniferous forests of the mountains up to the edge of the tree line. This is the black ant *Camponotus ligniperdus*. It is one of the largest European ants and the female with its long smokey wings which are much bigger than the abdomen never measures less than about 0.6 in (15–17 mm). This species, however, is less frequently found than the red ant; it does not possess, as does the latter, a poison sac, and only uses its powerful mandibles in the last extremity. Its bite, although harmless for man, nevertheless displays an unusual strength. The *Camponotus ligniperdus* usually lives in tunnels inside tree trunks which are either live or half decomposed, and sometimes it can also be found in the old stumps of larch and pine trees. Small piles of dust often betray the entrance to the nest which is found near the ground while the tunnels and chambers stretch for several yards inside the tree. The colonies of this giant ant, however, never reach the size of those of the red ant and the damage which they cause to our mountain forests is of no significance.

1
A giant ant *(Camponotus herculaneus)* cleaning itself.
2
Red ants attacking a caterpillar of the moth *Bombyx castrensis*.
3
A nest of red ants.

The red squirrel

What a charming forest creature this plumed imp is, which scampers down from the trees just as quickly as it climbs them, jumping from one branch to another with the skill of an acrobat, even leaping into space at times with the lightness of an aeronaut. This furry and very graceful creature, is always ready to show off its skill or nibble a pine cone, revealing between two branches a snow white stomach, a brown back or the face of a tiny faun, constantly looking for some trick to play . . . One will hear its claws scratch against the resinous trunk and see how the red squirrel observes one, how it becomes impatient and reveals its bad temper and alarm by waving its tail and uttering cries of 'douc douc douc', always in a constant hurry. Black beady eyes will be staring from the shadows at the onlooker – an eye which is full of malice.

What would the mountain forests be without this small climber, so similar in colour to the lichens amongst which it lives, that no other existence seems so closely related to the tree, to its seeds, to its bark and even to its roots? Look at the red squirrel as it gnaws the pine cone with its strong incisors, see how it stores the food in a safe place turning its loot in its paws with febrile haste in order to extract the delicious seeds from it. The red squirrel does the same with the cones of the spruce, the white pine and the larch, scattering the ground with hundreds of scales . . . This red squirrel is extremely fond of eggs and fledglings and the author surprised a specimen on one occasion in the process of pirating the nest of a finch. On another occasion he found a red squirrel feeding on young mistle thrushes which were still half naked and it remained unperturbed by the furious attacks of the adults.

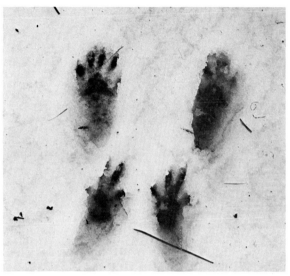

In springtime, when the breeding season begins, the red squirrels chase each other constantly along the tree trunks. They climb up and down at tremendous speed, spiralling around the old trunks, making a noise with their claws which can be heard far off and uttering from time to time a sort of chattering, interspersed with harsh snorting noises. Born surrounded by the perfume of sap and resin, gently cradled by the winds in its nests of moss and twigs, the acrobat would have a joyful life if it had fewer enemies. Unfortunately, the most ferocious of them, the pine marten, pursues the red squirrel from tree to tree, from branch to branch and sometimes even into its nest. The golden eagle also attacks it with impunity. The fox lies in wait with infinite patience and succeeds in leaping onto the red squirrel when the latter ventures on to the ground in search of bilberries and myrtle berries which are its delight. The mountain dweller also succeeds on occasion in shooting the red squirrel in spite of protective laws, so that this graceful creature is never certain of greeting the next dawn without having its delicate fur covered with blood.

1
A squirrel leaping between two pine trees.
2
Squirrel tracks on the melting snow.
3
A squirrel in its summer coat.

The fox

Few wild animals have as important a place in literature as the fox and this fact is not at all surprising, if the frequency of its contacts with man are taken into consideration. These contacts are of course not always the most friendly, as the two adversaries are pitiless in the means which they employ in their merciless struggle against each other.

One only has to think of those silent pursuits through woods and meadows, of those games of hide and seek behind trees and thickets, of those furtive chases along river banks or ditches, of those long waits at the bottom of the earth when it is under attack, of those pretended cases of death, of those false sorties to the edge of the woods or even of those cunning poses at the crossroads right under the nose of the astounded huntsmen. If one considers those cunning manoeuvres against the pack of hounds in pursuit, those unexpected turns, doubling back on the hunters who, paralysed by fear of an accident, are obliged to allow the fox to pass between their legs, one will understand better how this furry, cunning, russet creature with a long muzzle, shining whiskers and oval eyes is a past master in the art of duping its enemy!

Constantly sniffing the air while trotting along, skilful at jumping and swimming, surprisingly light and as supple as an acrobat, hardy, extremely careful, endowed with infinite patience, the fox certainly owes its elite place amongst our indigenous fauna to its highly developed psychic faculties. For many Europeans the fox has become the classic type of the cunning animal. It is certainly cunning to varying degrees, but its case should not be exaggerated. Amongst all our wild mammals it is perhaps the animal which is best capable of adapting to the vicinity of man, while keeping itself remote from them. This faculty is due to its highly developed senses, to its excellent sense of sight and hearing and to its remarkable sense of smell. Everything about the fox indicates intelligence, a certain daring, unbelievable astuteness and all these characteristics are heightened by the sarcastic smile which seems to be created by the line of its black rimmed lips and the intense impression of a bad conscience created by its facial expression. As opposed to many other animals, it has rather irregular habits. The fox is an opportunist and it can be found at no matter what time of day and night both in the mountains and the plains. It sometimes builds its lair well above the tree line and it makes pilgrimages to even greater altitudes. It certainly follows the alpine paths, crosses the highest ridges and even penetrates into the area of snow in search of ptarmigan, mountain hare and the snow vole. The author once found its track at about 11 000 ft (3400 m), and has also seen it warming itself in the sun in the depths of winter; it sets out on its hunt no matter how much snow there is. At such a time, however, the fox rarely appears by day and becomes doubly prudent as it is perhaps aware of the dangers it runs in the deep powdery snow. In spite of its supple regular gait, the fox nevertheless sinks quite deep into the snow and leaves tracks like furrows on the high pasturage. The author often wondered why the fox should climb to such altitudes till one day chance allowed him to discover the reason ... While following the fresh tracks of a mountain hare his skis finally crossed the tracks of a fox. Following the two tracks which kept on mingling, the author was led to the hollow of a rock where the traces of fur from the hare, some drops of blood and the heavy track of the fox who had regained the forest with its victim clearly told the story of what had happened: there had been a drama which had quickly come to an end, in all probability only one of thousands of such incidents taking place each day in the animal kingdom.

The fox, the most circumspect of animals can best be observed in its earth. The observer however must take many precautions and keep a certain distance away, hiding himself completely and never approaching the entrance to the lair, otherwise the adult will move out together with its family the same night. There is nothing more entertaining than a family of fox-cubs playing in front of their earth. The author has often witnessed this charming sight: it usually happens in the late afternoon although it can take place at any time of the day. The small woolly balls with short and pointed tails leave their underground home and come to romp in the sun. The young foxes which are rust or smokey grey in colour, according to their age, are already unruly and full of energy; the author has seen them playing together, biting each other's ears, fighting in groups of two or three, rolling around on the ground and then standing up quickly to leap on imaginary prey or else go stalking along the paths which radiate from the lair as if they were about to surprise a future victim. When the mother returns to the earth, these games quickly stop and the fox cubs rush up to her and disappear in an instant beneath her stomach. If the female notices at this moment one's odour or even catches sight of a person at a great distance she immediately becomes motionless, utters a sort of raucous bark, and this sound immediately sends the young beneath the ground. The female then tries to locate the observer exactly by describing a vast circle around the earth. A vixen who had just brought a marmot to her young which were already quite big, finally became aware of the author's presence because of the noise made by his camera even though it was scarcely audible at a distance of more than 160 ft (50 m). The violent reaction of the vixen was amazing: at the first sign of alarm the young cubs disappeared into the earth then the vixen, while moving away from it, attempted to ascertain from where the noise came while constantly uttering raucous, plaintive barks which were

The fox goes hunting for voles.

Young foxes near their earth.

The citril finch

On the borders of a high alpine forest, near the last larches at the edge of the meadows, there is to be heard during the summer months the constant silvery soft cry of a bird: 'bzih bzeh . . . zizi zeze'. This is certain to be the call of the citril finch also known as the Italian canary. When one hears this slightly nasal sound, of soft and metallic notes, it is impossible not to associate it with the delicate green of the larches or the tufts of the conifer. The sound falls from heaven like drops of crystal and seems closely linked with those furtive shadows which cross the high glades or chase each other amongst the delicate branches impregnated with aromatic perfume.

Through binoculars one can make out a bird the size of a gold finch but with greenish feathers around the neck, grey sides on head and body, yellow on the stomach and crop and a forked tail which is almost black. The bird is a little timid and very alert, constantly on the move and so full of gaiety and energy that it is very difficult to keep it in focus. This bird should not be confused with the siskin which it resembles in size and plumage. The siskin, however, has a stomach which is lighter in colour, sides which are clearly striped with black, while its tail has on its edges large bands of golden yellow, the main factor which will help in distinguishing it from the citril finch. As for the canary sparrow, a charming little bird which is very similar to the previous species in appearance and voice, its presence in the Alps at any altitude is very rare. It will scarcely ever be seen apart perhaps in autumn when it migrates over the alpine ridges on its way towards the south. A curious fact is that the mating performance and the song of the citril finch and the siskin are very similar: both types of bird rise in the air with their tails and wings fully spread and they both flutter around from tree to tree describing curves in their flight through the glades of conifer trees, where they build their nests. The song of the finch, however, is always very varied and perhaps a little softer and more liquid than that of the siskin although there are certain nasal sounds which are common to both species. Finally the siskin nests much sooner than the finch, sometimes in full winter. The siskin seems much more faithful to the spruce forest than the finch and breeds much less frequently and more irregularly than the latter, at least in the mountainous areas of France, Switzerland and Belgium.

Through spending half of its life on the conifer or larch tree, the finch has taken on a little of the colours, and has the greenish tints of their needles on its breast, while on its neck and sides the powder grey colour of the bark is visible; could it also be that its silvery notes are an echo of the melody of the wind in the branches of the tree? It is from the larch or the conifer that its joyous notes rise to the sky and from these trees emerges its cheerful, metallic babble; the bird builds in their branches its tiny nest, a perfect sphere of moss, lichen and hair, and it is here that the bird hatches its young. From these trees it flies constantly after its companion, spreading its gaiety throughout the landscape.

full of hate and wildness. The earth in question was at a height of 7200 ft (2200 m), hidden beneath large rocks and surrounded by pines and larches; the author felt that the mountain foxes were much more mistrustful and wild under such circumstances than their relatives in the plain.

However, the fox remains the hero of numerous fables, legends and amusing stories . . .

As for the author, he has never seen a fox without associating its marvellous fur with the rust colour of the larch needles when they are struck by the autumn sun, or with the glorious halo this sun creates when setting behind the mountains. If ever you happen to come across the fox in the Alps, perhaps you will also associate such a sight with the approach of winter, perhaps you will feel yourself closer to the snow and the first frost, closer to the golden colour of the last grass. Then you will enjoy to the full the wild splendour of the mountain forests, the unchanging beauty of the high meadows and of the crags split by the frost, the eternal silence of those enormous deserted areas where only the stoat and the tiny mountain hare can exist and where the silence is broken only by the fox's cry of hunger or the rasping scream of the ptarmigan . . . .

A brown hare fleeing in the snow.

The brown hare

'Inter quadrupes gloria prima lepus'. Thus wrote the Roman poet Martial about the hare, meaning that amongst all four legged beasts it is the hare which is worthy of the civic crown!

There are few wild mammals who are as skilful as the hare in concealing its presence when near man. But for the round droppings and the innumerable tracks which the brown hare leaves on the snow in winter, it would be considered a rare animal. However in spite of its decrease in numbers recently in several areas due to the hedges being pulled down, to pesticides being showered by the ton over the countryside and to an increase in hunting, the hare nevertheless remains relatively common both on the plains and in the mountains. In the Alps the species is particularly fond of dry slopes, the brushwood of the sub-alpine glade and the upper forests where the sparse trees allow room for the bushes to grow freely, offering the animal numerous places in which to shelter. The brown hare is to be found in the summer months well above the tree line; the author has often seen them on the slopes of south facing valleys which are scattered with boulders and juniper bushes; this was at a height of more than 7870 ft (2400 m). Even in the depths of winter the author has surprised them in their forms in the snow at 8900 ft (2700 m), on occasion as high as 10 000 ft (3000 m), although the forms were built on slopes facing the south. The species can be said to straddle the range of altitude inhabited by the mountain hare and sometimes breeds with the latter giving birth to hybrids which appear to be sterile.

Those mountain hares which spend the entire year in the mountains tend to differ from those of the plains and to create a sub-race which is ecologically speaking more vigorous and possessing powerful muscles, a broader back and ears which are possibly slightly shorter. However, when there are heavy falls of snow they appear less suited than the mountain hare to the rigours of winter and sometimes remain hidden for several days beneath the powdery snow, digging real tunnels along the sides of slopes or ditches. When the storm is over the brown hare waits for the snow to pile up a little or for the sun to harden the top layer before reappearing. It is heavier than the mountain hare and its feet are less covered in fur; it does not have the faculty of spreading its toes like the mountain hare, consequently the brown hare sinks further into the snow; its coat never turns white in winter. When it is disturbed from its form it stands out against the snow and attracts the attention of predators. It is therefore extremely reluctant to leave its shelter. On one occasion the author approached a hare in its form after a recent fall of snow and was less than 6.5 ft (2 m) away before it finally revealed itself. As opposed to the mountain hare, however,

A pair of citril finches feeding their brood.

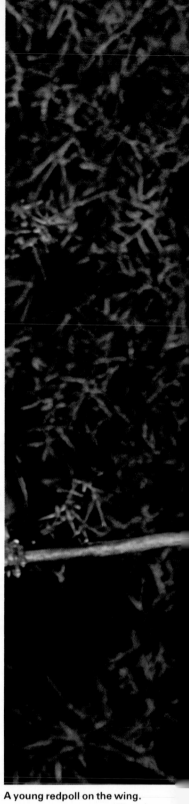

A young redpoll on the wing.

The redpoll replenishes its young.

which never moves very far and often describes large circles around its first form, the brown hare will cover some distance; it dislikes taking shelter in the passages between rocks. In the forest the animal usually escapes by moving up the slope, but if it is surprised in the meadows it attempts to reach as quickly as possible any wooded shelter, and will even go down the slope, taking enormous leaps. It then becomes very vulnerable and the author has on two occasions seen the golden eagle snatch up the hare in its claws and carry it off without any great difficulty. If a goshawk tries to attack a hare it does not always succeed. The brown hare defends itself by lashing out at the bird and tries to reach the shelter of a bush. Too weak to carry off its prey the goshawk will attack it and sometimes finally kills it with powerful blows of its beak on the animal's skull; it will then tear out the heart, liver and lungs of its victim, holding its wings a little lowered and half extended in a characteristic position.

All the characteristics of the brown hare seem to exist in order to help it to escape from the constant ambushes and pursuits of its innumerable enemies, of which man and the fox are the most dangerous. If you feel its powerful, muscular body, you will notice how well it is made for running; its long hind legs allow it to make amazing leaps. It is also very difficult to define exactly the colour of its fur. It is made up of yellow, rust, beige, blackish brown, even grey and beneath the throat, the stomach, and the insides of the legs it is white. Such a wide range of colours blends very well with the ground, old grass, leaves of the undergrowth and dead leaves. The hare which is doubtless aware of this camouflage, makes use of it whenever it settles into a new form.

Although the timidity and under-developed family instinct of the brown hare are proverbial, the animal is nevertheless very cunning and capable of playing many tricks on the huntsman and his dogs. It even displays a certain courage when it is forced to defend its young against attacks from the weasel or members of the crow family. Both the female and male hare, when they are seized by their feet or ears and fatally wounded utter a cry of complaint which is very similar to the crying of a child. Apart from these cries, which are in fact prompted by agony and terror, the hare is normally a silent animal only uttering some nasal grunts, especially during the rutting season.

Usually nocturnal by instinct, the brown hare sometimes creates its form on open ground but more frequently in the bottom of a ditch, furrow, beneath a juniper bush or the low branches of a small pine or some other tree. It can be seen perhaps at dawn or at twilight crossing a field, running along a road or pausing at the edge of a wood before disappearing with a few leaps. The black upper part of its tail allows it to be distinguished from the mountain hare, which has a grey tail in the summer months. The fact that the two species produce hybrids which are sterile explains why they have retained their morphological integrity. After all, the brown hare of Europe is dissimilar from the mountain hare in its structure and the latter represents a true form from the ice age, in the midst of our alpine fauna.

The redpoll

At the limit of the alpine forest where the last larch trees and hundred year old conifers constantly struggle against the violent winds and winter storms, one can see small brownish birds chasing each other continuously in the sky, flying in swooping curves. The weather is superb. It is early June and the constant coming and going of these birds above the first trees of the forest can be seen from far away. Their flight is constantly accompanied by joyful metallic nasal cries, now detached one from the other, now uttered in a series of cascades and prolonged trills: 'trieup, trieup . . . tsche tsche tsche . . . djilili . . . tirrr . . .' These cries sometimes seem to be similar to those of the greenfinch, but at other times more similar to the joyful cries of the siskin. Closely intermingled with these songs, the sound of the torrents freed from ice rises from the depths of the valley. In the distance the summits of the mountains of Anniviers can be seen in all their glory, while at one's feet there are large rocks piled up and half buried in the slopes. The juniper bushes, the climbing willows, the saxifrages of every type, together with the small clusters of catch-fly plants, the carpet of tiny azaleas and the white petals of the dryade cover most of the ground, even clinging to some of the first trees here and there, such as the rhododendron, the dwarf pine, the mountain pine or those larches which have been attacked by the cattle. Those mysterious shapes pass overhead again, but two of them, having described a circular flight above the larches, separate themselves from the group and come to rest on the topmost branches of a young spruce. From a distance of less than 50 ft (15 m) the birds can be seen constantly moving their heads and tails. They could easily be taken for small sparrows which have been lost at this altitude, if it were not for the darker brown colour of their plumage and the fine red feathers of their head. One of them – probably the male – has a splendid bright red breast, an unexpected spot of colour in the decor as it is set off on the bird's throat by a black bib . . . This red colour stretches along the sides and the crop of the bird while its stomach is white. The female appears to have something in her beak and is much more dowdy in colour, with a breast of rust-coloured grey, a large bib and wide brown stripes on her sides. The female flies into the depths of the spruce tree, while the male, like some coloured fruit on the edge of the bush, stands on guard and flutters its wings, constantly turning from one side to the other and spreading out its tail while uttering its gay babble.

After a few moments the female appears unexpectedly from the tree and flies away followed immediately by the male, uttering its metallic cries. The pair soon disappear behind the curtain of old larch trees which are just beginning to reveal a pale green covering. This time the birds could be recognised. They are redpolls, those typical inhabitants of the last trees on the edge of the pasturage, and true descendants of the ice age . . . In the north there exists also a redpoll which is very similar to the one of our mountains, called the northern redpoll. The birds which nest in the Alps, like those of Great Britain, belong to a sub-species which is smaller in size, darker and with more varied colours than the northern race. The latter species has a head marked with a brighter red, a whiter crop and a breast which is of a paler pink in the case of the male. During a journey through Finnish Lapland the author had the pleasure of observing very closely such a bird and its cries were very similar to the redpoll of the Alps. The arctic redpoll is a typical inhabitant of the arctic tundra. This bird is even paler than the northern redpoll and appears well adapted for the snow, with its stomach and crop of pure white and very pale bands across its wings.

After about a quarter of an hour the pair reappear on the top of the bush and the same movements are repeated. The author waits for the birds to leave in order to approach the spruce and see what is hidden there. In the depths of the tufted branches, fixed to the strongest branch at less than 5 ft ($1\frac{1}{2}$ m) from the ground there is a wonderful tiny cup made of roots, lichen and dry twigs, skilfully interwoven. The deep interior is decorated with horse hair, willow leaves and a few white feathers. The nest appears complete, and doubtless eggs will shortly be laid there, a fact which explains the attentive presence of the male near its companion.

The author has also found the nest of the redpoll in the branches of a pine and later in the season on the lower branches of one of the first big larch trees. The reason for this is easy to explain: according to the altitude the larch remains without leaves until the end of May and the redpolls prefer to conceal their first nest in those conifers which do not lose their needles. These charming birds are very trustful of man; the author has had the opportunity on several occasions of watching the young birds being fed, standing less than 6 ft (2 m) away from the nest, without the birds showing any sign of alarm.

A brown hare in its seat.

2

mountainous terrain

from the upper tree-line
to the permanent snows

1
Inhabitants of the alpine heath

The dunnock – the lesser whitethroat – the cuckoo
– the asp – the adder or northern viper.

The dunnock

In May spring begins to gain ground and gradually
frees the gullies of the upper forests from snow. In
one night the succulent morel mushroom pushes its
brown cap through the earth and the petasites develop their plump stems and get ready to flower
again. On the ground among the old grass and lichen
the tunnels made in the winter by the voles can be
traced even now, and the flower of the first liverwort
shyly displays its mauve colour in the undergrowth. A
large bumble bee flies laboriously over the moss and
there are signs that the badger has dug new holes for
its droppings at the edge of the path. The sky suddenly becomes overcast, however, and the scene
changes: snowflakes soon start to flutter in the air
and the earth which was free of snow, turns grey . . .
The walker is obliged to pull out his heavy pullover
from his knapsack together with his windcheater,
since at this altitude the proverb 'Do not cast a clout
until May is out' has particular significance.

These rapid changes in temperature, however, are
of little importance, as are the vagaries of the mountain springtime. In spite of the cold, the snow and the
overcast skies the black grouse, assembled at the
edge of the alpine forest still continue their dances at
dawn, and their soft cooing cries are interrupted by
the noisy beating of their wings and their loud hooting noises. The ring ouzel and the mistle thrush also
continue to utter their eternal flute-like songs from
the top of the larch trees which are still bare of leaves.
If one sits between the roots of an old pine with one's
back solidly resting against its trunk, well wrapped
up, one will silently enjoy this strange morning as the
large flakes of snow fall from the May sky. Suddenly,
very near, a delicious melody breaks out. The bird
cannot be very far off and with a little patience one
will soon find out its whereabouts. The little embroid-
ered phrase with its slightly sharper notes rings out
again while the snowflakes turn the ground whiter

and whiter. Then one might notice above ones head a
small bird which is fluttering lightly through the net-
work of the branches. It seems very similar to a sparrow and rather insignificant in appearance. It has a
pointed thin beak which seems to be similar to that of
a lesser whitethroat and its slate-coloured stomach
also attracts ones attention. Could this be a dunnock?
With a rapid brief flight the bird leaves the pine to
settle on the branch of a young spruce and is in this
way much more in evidence. It twitches its tail spasmodically and its wings have a curious quivering
motion. Suddenly its beak opens, its throat vibrates
above its little round stomach, and its brownish back
arches with the effort it is making: at the same
instance the silvery burst of sound is heard again as it
was a few seconds previously. This time there is no
doubt whatsoever: it is the same, hurried melody of
sharp trembling sounds, but from this distance it
seems weak and quiet. This would explain the fact
that it remained unnoticed until now, lost in the concert given by the other birds.

Except for the time of its mating period, the dunnock leads a very discreet life and passes easily unnoticed. It prefers above all low vegetation like the
branches of juniper and rhododendron bushes or the
tufts of pine trees which grow stunted on the edges
of the alpine forests of conifers. This is where the bird
takes refuge when alarmed and skilfully slips into the
web of branches, disappearing from sight. From this
habit it has acquired the name of 'bush lurker', which
sums up its habits. Its nest can be found, with a little
luck, amongst the bushes or young spruce trees not
very far above ground. The nest looks rather like a
very large cup of green moss, usually placed on the
join of a few small branches. In the centre of the moss
there is a bowl, carpeted with small twigs, roots and
horse hair. The four or five turquoise blue eggs are
together with those of the winchat, amongst the
most beautiful to be found. They are, however, difficult to locate as the dunnock conceals its nest very
cleverly in the tangle of vegetation. The female, when
hatching her eggs, leaves the nest only when in
extreme danger, and takes great care, moreover, to
conceal herself from the intruder.

The lesser whitethroat

On the edges of the alpine forests the last conifers are often interesting trees; they are frequently half destroyed by lightning, and twisted constantly by the icy winds and snow-storms so that they are more like skeletons than living trees. Such is their strength, however, that most of them still push out from their whitened bark young branches covered with green needles. They are not the only trees to struggle against the rigours of winter.

Some young spruces are often damaged by cattle, but the trees would seem, as it were, to attack the meadows with particularly dense branches, and these twisted trees emerge through the bushes of rhododendrons and juniper, together with the climbing pines which resist the avalanches ... It was in these rather special surroundings that one fine June morning the author, while watching the black grouse perform their mating dance, heard for the first time in his life a strange song, a sort of loud beating noise repeated at regular intervals and which for lack of any better expression could be put on paper as 'rutututu-tu!'. Very intrigued, he scanned with his binoculars the pine tree from which came this sort of mechanical trill without, however, spotting anything at all. Tired of the game he was on the point of abandoning it when a tiny grey shape finally deigned to emerge from the vegetation and pass before him twice, settling on a branch for a moment, but in such a furtive way that he had scarcely time to catch a glimpse of it. When the bird was again concealed by a tufted branch the mechanical tune started again. This little sprite was beginning to annoy the author intensely. He wanted to ascertain exactly what it was and started to follow the bird from bush to bush and tree to tree, constantly guided by its strange trill. He was lucky to do so as, at a given moment, when he was much closer to the mysterious songster, he suddenly heard a charming warbling sound, a series of soft melodious sounds, which were succeeded suddenly by the loud trilling. This discovery only intrigued him more and he redoubled his efforts. Finally, during a pause, while the bird was preening itself he succeeded in focusing it for a few moments in his binoculars. It appeared insignificant, greyish in colour, and the size of a small warbler, with a darker colour on its head near the cheeks which contrasted with its white throat. The author was not able to learn any more that day, but one month later when he was in the same area, he made a strange discovery. Just when he was going to conceal himself behind a young spruce, a bird flew out from the tree and almost brushed his face in passing. It was child's play to find the nest: it comprised a sort of light cradle made of dry twigs and roots, well concealed near the ground on one of the branches of the small conifer. The author counted five whitish eggs patched with grey and brown in the nest. In order not to disturb the sitting bird, he returned to his find only ten days later. After concealing himself skilfully, he saw the adult finally appear, with food in its beak, and the author recognised the mysterious songster which had led him from tree to tree for an entire morning. It was the lesser whitethroat. This species is the only warbler capable of nesting at 6600 ft (2000 m) and above. Although it is also found in the plains, it prefers to live on the edges of alpine forests and seems to have a particular affection for dwarf bushes and trunks of small conifers. The lesser whitethroat feeds on insects and spiders and, in autumn, on various wild berries and fruits. It is a migratory bird and leaves either at the end of August or in September in order to spend the winter in the Sudan. It returns towards the end of April or as late as May.

The cuckoo

Although it is in no way an alpine bird, the cuckoo is frequently seen on the upper edges of the forests. It even wanders higher on occasions. The author has heard it sing well above the tree line and twice he has succeeded in discovering a young cuckoo installed in the nest of a black redstart at 7200 ft (2200 m) and 8000 ft (2400 m). Together with the water pipit and the dunnock, it is the bird which serves most frequently as host in the mountains. Of course, everybody knows the cuckoo, or at least the two notes which it utters from the hedges as soon as fine weather begins and which has given the bird its reputation. Very few, however, have succeeded in observing the bird closely at leisure. In fact this strange bird is not at all easy to approach. It is very wild and mistrustful and knows exactly how to conceal itself in the vegetation before uttering its full-throated cry with remarkable power. This difficulty of observation has given rise to numerous legends which still exist nowadays, particularly in the country. Many mountain dwellers are convinced that the cuckoo changes at the end of the summer into a sparrow-hawk. It is easy to understand the origin of this legend: by mid-July the cuckoo has stopped making any sort of cry and the majority of the species have already left in order to return to Equatorial Africa, where they spend the larger part of winter. These departures take place at night and are therefore unnoticed. It is also true that the cuckoo in some ways resembles the sparrow-hawk; it has the same slate-coloured feathers on its back and wings, the same tapering tail and the same breast, finely striped with grey or brown. The russet variety of the cuckoo, peculiar to certain females of the species and called 'Hepatic', has the effect of making the latter similar in appearance to a small kestrel and also leads to confusion. The cuckoo, however, generally flies in a straight horizontal line with rapid wing beats, the wings being held below the body so that it has a characteristic appearance. The wings are longer and more pointed than those of the sparrow-hawk and the tail appears even longer. Also the gurgling mocking laughing cry which it produces at mating time and even more so the two or three loud notes uttered by the male allow the species to be recognised without difficulty. When it sings, the cuckoo adopts a special position: it inflates its throat, lets its wings hang down, opens its beak slightly and leans forward every time it utters its cry, raising and lowering its widely spread tail. When the female is excited she sometimes utters a loud sort of prolonged liquid trill.

It is now known that when a cuckoo has lived in the nest of a black redstart it subsequently prefers to use the same bird as its host and lays eggs of the same colour as those of its host, which are white. A female can lay up to a dozen eggs and leave them in as many nests. Losses are, however, heavy. Does the bird lay its eggs directly in the nest or does it carry them there in its beak? The second hypothesis has not yet been confirmed but it seems very probable as this would partly explain why nests, which have far too narrow entrances to allow a cuckoo to enter, are also used to host the eggs. This is how things normally happen. The female cuckoo has inspected the nest of those sparrows which interest her and is very skilful at choosing the most favourable moment, that is to say the moment when the future adoptive mother has laid some of her eggs. Flying near the nest, which it has already chosen several days previously, the female attracts hostile displays from the small birds around and very often forces the couple which it intends to use as hosts to leave their territory. Its resemblance to the sparrow-hawk is not perhaps fortuitous; in any event the sparrows react strongly and pursue the intruder from a safe distance. The male cuckoo sometimes takes up the task. Profiting from the brief absence of the hosts, the female cuckoo sometimes even goes so far as to remove one of the legitimate eggs before placing her own in the nest. The stolen egg is carried away and eaten although there are some exceptions.

What happens next? The real owner returns to the nest, settles on the eggs as if nothing has happened and proceeds to hatch them. The cuckoo's egg is a little larger than those of the host and it has the facility of developing quicker and hatching generally 24 hours before the others. At this moment the most extraordinary event in the entire history of the cuckoo's life takes place.

This naked fledgeling, blind and almost inert, lying at the bottom of the nest amongst the five or six eggs which are not yet hatched, develops a lot of strength within the next ten hours. It then throws out of the nest everything which comes into contact with its particularly irritable skin; of course this includes the eggs which surround it. If it happens that these eggs are already hatched the young cuckoo does not hesitate to make unbelievable efforts to push, one after the other, its adopted brothers out of the nest in order to remain alone in their place.

This unbelievable behaviour has for a long time been doubted, but it was finally proved for the first time through the patient research of the British ornithologist Chance. After that, the famous bird photographer, Eric Hosking and, more recently, the French film producers F. Bell and G. Vienne have been fortunate enough to film the extraordinary scene of the young cuckoo wedging under its small wings the egg or the small brother in the nest, move towards the edge of the nest laden with its charge and push it over into space. It is most interesting observing the young cuckoo when it has already left the nest and is still being fed by its adoptive parents. The author witnessed such a scene on several occasions beyond the tree line. Usually the cuckoo leaves the nest before it can fly well. It then hides beneath the tufts of the dwarf juniper bushes in the mountains or on the first small trees it comes to. Each time its adoptive parents arrive the young Goliath shakes its wings, opens its beak wide and reveals the strange orange colour of its mouth which probably acts as a stimulant for the parents. The black redstart plunges its head into the depths of this 'chasm' in order to leave there either flies or daddy longlegs, caterpillars and small beetles. The author has even seen the cuckoo being fed by its adoptive parents while the latter were still fluttering in the air; the parents also give the alarm at the least sign of danger as they would do for their own offspring! Sometimes other sparrows from the area come to help in feeding the insatiable cuckoo, which is capable of looking after itself only three weeks approximately after leaving the nest.

If the habits of the cuckoo are now known in detail, there are however still certain problems of instinct and hereditary which are raised by the strange behaviour of this bird and these create heated controversy between ornithologists.

A young lesser whitethroat outside its nest.

A young cuckoo in the nest of a redstart, which comes to bring it food.

Dunnock.

The asp and the adder or northern viper

Skull of a viper.

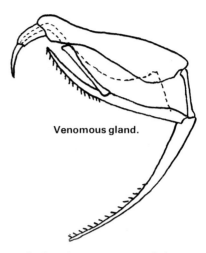

Venomous gland.

Two species of viper inhabit the European mountains and can also be found on the plains: the asp and the adder. Both belong to the family Viperidae and are equipped with poisonous fangs or hooks on each side of the upper jaw. When not in use these hooks lie forward and are concealed in the fleshy parts of the roof of the mouth.

The author will never forget his first capture of one of these snakes, although it took place long ago. While walking he noticed a superb asp coiled against the stem of a juniper bush amongst a pile of stones in the middle of an alpine meadow. At the approach of the author the asp crawled away and then slid into the depths of its refuge with extraordinary grace. The following morning returning to the same spot, armed with a metal box and pincers, the author was surprised again to see the asp stretched out in the sun at exactly the same place as on the previous day. He admired the fine zigzag designs on its back for a moment then, taking great care, he approached the snake which, alarmed, succeeded in escaping into its hole before the author could seize it with his pincers. A little disappointed by this lack of success, the author nevertheless went to work and started to move one by one the stones surrounding the snake's refuge; finally, there only remained the largest stone half buried in the ground amongst the tufts of the junipers. The asp was surely concealed underneath it. After struggling hard the author succeeded in lifting the stone and pushed it away down the slope. There was the snake, in an earth cavity, entirely curled up and partly concealed by roots. It did not attempt to escape and it was easy for the author to seize it with his pincers and then hold it behind its head, very close to the skull, with his thumb and index finger. The asp struggled for a moment, hissing and whipping the author's forearm with its muscular body while it opened and shut its mouth, revealing its terrible fangs. The author had with him a pair of scissors and the idea occurred to him of disarming the reptile by removing its poisonous fangs. With the help of a match he raised the fangs and their supports. At their ends small drops of a transparent yellowish liquid dripped out continuously; the author cut the hooks at their base, taking care not to injure the gums of the reptile; then, proud of his capture, he returned to the village in order to study the snake at leisure. The author then tried to feed his asp with voles, mice and lizards but had no success. Although comfortably lodged in a large box into which plenty of air and sunlight could penetrate, the snake refused all food. The author attributed this refusal to eat initially to the removal of its fangs and to the fact that it was a captive. In fact asps and adders kill their prey by injecting a few drops of poison into them through their fangs. The tiny rodents die very quickly under the influence of the powerful venom. Then the victim, no matter how big it is, is swallowed whole, head first. Only once did the author witness such a spectacle and

could watch the slow progress of the prey as it was swallowed up by the extending mouth of the snake. It was an impressive sight. One always thinks that the vole cannot possibly be absorbed and that the head of the snake is far too small to be able to swallow it whole; however, the body is slowly sucked up by suction from inside the snake and the various bones in the jaws of the asp separate from each other, thanks to the elastic structure of the mouth, so that the opening becomes enormous. Once the prey is completely swallowed it swells up the body of the snake so that its scales separate from each other. The progress of the victim can be easily followed along the body of the snake.

The author on one occasion seized a large asp by its tail as it was trying to slip beneath the stones of a small wall. Having dragged it out of its retreat and held it in space, head down, the author was amazed to see the asp regurgitate a large vole still intact and then a second, rather smaller in size, which had already been partially digested and finally a completely digested third prey. He also captured a snake which had just swallowed a frog which it promptly regurgitated, still alive! The author returns however to his first capture: he naturally thought that the snake's refusal to eat was connected with the operation it had undergone. At the end of the month, seeing that the situation had not improved to any extent and that the asp, following a fast of some length had used up its reserves of fat, the author decided to release it. Moreover, having shown the snake to all his curious acquaintances who wished to examine it without taking any precautions while the author held it, he decided that it was time to put an end to the experiment. His surprise was therefore extreme when the reptile tried to bite him as he was preparing to seize it by its neck and free it from its prison. The author examined the snake's mouth and was amazed to note that in place of the two hooks which he had removed four weeks previously two new fangs, as pointed and as dangerous as the old ones, had replaced them! Having consulted various books on this matter the author discovered that reserve fangs, situated behind those in use period-ically replaced the latter when they were worn out and this took place from time to time, when the old fangs fell out. Unaware of these facts the author had handled the snake for a whole month without taking any precautions not knowing that the asp had been capable of biting him at any moment and perhaps de-spatching him to the next world!

It is rare in nature to see the asp or the adder delib-erately attack man if the latter does not cut off their retreat or seek to attack them. The reverse is in fact true as these two reptiles will always flee as quickly as possible into the first hole if they meet up with man. The author did, however, have the experience when he was crossing the dry bed of a stream, of seeing an asp attack him violently several times. The only plausible explanation of this savage reaction would probably be the following: the asp which seemed to be on the move did not have any shelter or hole into which it could retreat. Believing itself to be in danger, it therefore attempted through its violent attacks to intimidate its adversary and cover its retreat. In such an instance it is wiser to avoid ap-proaching the asp too closely when it is curled up. It is capable of unwinding like a spring and striking from a distance of 12–16 in (30–40 cm). With its head raised and its body arched it hisses and takes up a threatening attitude, looking like a real demon.

If the observer is bitten it is important to find a doctor or pharmacist as quickly as possible as they will inject the victim with an anti-snake serum. One should know that such action is still helpful several hours after the victim has been bitten. Cases of death are relatively infrequent.

The asp only rarely exceeds 24 in (60 cm) in length while the adder can reach 31 in (80 cm) — although such a size is unusual. The colours of the snakes are infinitely varied, ranging from copper red to greyish brown and even to jet black in the case of both species as hybrids are not rare, especially in the mountains. The colours of the snakes appear much brighter after moulting has taken place and the designs on the back are much clearer in the case of males than with females who are often larger and lazier. The two species have a vertical or rather ellip-tical pupil which is capable of becoming quite dilated in the dark. This characteristic distinguishes them definitely from grass snakes which all have a round pupil. In addition, the asp has a nose which is slightly raised and two lines of small scales between the upper lip and the eye whereas the adder has only one line of scales and its nose is rounded. The body of the latter is a little thicker and its tail is always very short. With both species, however, the tail barely repre-sents an eighth or tenth of the length and its point is often coloured red or orange. The author has had the opportunity of seeing an asp at an altitude of 10 000 ft (3000 m) on the Diablons in the Val d'Anniviers and also in the Bec Termin in the region of Mont Pleureur in the Val de Bagnes in Switzerland. A curious fact is that the author has never found an adder in the Swiss Alps in Valais, that is to say on the left bank of the upper Rhône. The asp, which is more of a southern snake, therefore replaces the adder in dry warm valleys and rocky slopes, while the latter prefers relatively humid areas and can be found very far north, sometimes beyond the Arctic Circle. During a journey in Lapland, the author saw numerous adders on the hills surrounding a small lake in Sweden. The two species can be found living to-gether in the Jura, at least in certain areas. The asp can be found up to an altitude of 5000 ft (1500 m), while the adder replaces it above that height in the foothills of the Swiss Alps in Vaudois.

Only one grass snake in the mountains can be con-fused with the asp and adder — the smooth snake (Coronella austriaca). It can be found in dry sunny spots sometimes at an altitude of 6600 ft (2000 m) in Valais. Its size is similar to that of the asp and even bigger on occasion, but its body is slimmer and on its back there is a slightly different design. Its pupil is round and the iris very pale; a blackish or brownish band goes from the nostril to the eye and surrounds the latter continuing behind it and gradually disap-pearing along the neck before reaching dark patches which cover the sides; this band is a typical charac-teristic allowing the observer to distinguish it from the asp, even from a certain distance. In addition the nose is not raised as in the case of the asp and the scales of the smooth snake are smooth and not horny, as is the case with both types of viper. This smooth snake, although perfectly harmless, has an irritable character. When it is seized it tries to bite or violently squeeze one's hand. Rock lizards and young vipers seem to provide its basic diet; the smooth snake captures them by strangling them in its coils.

Head of an adder.

A viper in September before hibernating.

2
Inhabitants of alpine pasturage and mountain lakes

The rock pipit – the common frog – the alpine newt – the hawker dragonfly – the rainbow trout – the arctic charr – the minnow – the wheatear – the stoat – the alpine vole – the common shrew – the viviparous lizard – the alpine salamander – the insects of the alpine meadows and of the high pastures – the alpine marmot – the black redstart – the rock partridge.

A water pipit near its nest.

The rock pipit

In spring the mistle thrush is one of the first to cast its loud modulations above the conifers and the last larch trees. A few weeks later the ring ouzels, returned from Spain or the Atlas Mountains in the Sahara, also break the silence of the dawn with their flute-like song comprising two or three constantly repeated notes. The rock partridges also make the rocks echo with their frantic cries. Even higher, near the vast fields of melting snow and amongst the rocks eaten by lichen and the saxifrages, animal life still finds something on which to thrive, thanks to the bright sunlight . . .

Towards mid-April, when the frost hardens the snow every night and temperatures are often Siberian, a small insignificant bird will attract the atten-tion of the skier: well before sunrise this bird flies up in the sky from a rock facing the glaciers despite the frost and the early hour. There is at first nothing exceptional in the flight of this bird: it leaves the rock as if it had been disturbed, but once it reaches a certain height and spreads its wings it pauses and seems to enter a trance, allowing itself to glide slowly down through the perfectly calm air, while describing an elegant curve, its tail raised to serve as a rudder; almost invariably the bird returns to its point of departure. This graceful descent is an astonishing sight as the tiny aeronaut utters a whole cascade of light notes until the moment its feet touch the ground again. The bird then makes a few hops over its rock, feathers raised, its wings slightly lowered, its tail and crop stuck out in a characteristic attitude. On a nearby rock the female watches this mating parade attentively remaining silent and apparently receiving graciously all the compliments. After a few minutes the male again flies into the freezing air, repeating tirelessly his same song, which becomes softer as the gliding descent nears the ground. It then traces another graceful curve in the air before parachuting

The common frog, the alpine newt and the hawker dragonfly

The author will always recall his extreme surprise when one day he was standing at the side of an alpine marsh at an altitude of 8200ft (2500m). It was still covered in part by piles of melting snow, and streamlets flowed down from all sides of the pasturage into the small amount of water which was still free in the small lake and which stretched to the foot of a slope sheltered from the wind and well-exposed to the sun. Glancing down towards the marsh, the author thought he was dreaming when he saw that on the borders of the marsh there were several frogs which, on his approach, jumped into the icy water. He had noticed that some of them were mating and that in the shallow water near the bank there were already large quantities of eggs floating. Of course spring was making itself felt everywhere, rock pipits were constantly flying up into the sky and gliding down, uttering their acid notes, while there were, indeed, crocuses already above the ground in spite of the snow which was still lying in many areas of the pasturage. From where could these frogs come? How could they risk laying eggs in water which overnight might be covered with ice? On examining them more closely, the author realised that it could not be the edible frog, which normally inhabits the pools of the plain, but a particular species which must be very advanced, fearing neither the ice, the snow nor the altitude. None of them was exactly like the other, but the majority were brownish or yellowish, even orange or grey in certain cases, with more or less dark patches, slightly spotted and with almost black mottling, especially on the thighs. They all had a dark patch on their heads which was clearly visible and well defined. The author saw some of the males pursuing the females while uttering a sort of quiet croaking 'grou grou grou' and he noticed that they did not have external vocal pouches which accounted for the

back to its starting point. One is surprised at finding this bird at such an altitude and in such inhospitable, snowy surroundings, when it seems so fragile that it apparently defies the laws of gravity and pays no attention to the low temperatures ... Where can the rock pipit find its food and necessary warmth for keeping alive? One would be tempted to say that only the flame of love supplies life to this bundle of feathers and that passion raises it into the sky and gives to its flight that intensity which makes the entire body of the bird vibrate while it is singing. What a strange contrast between the Siberian landscape where the rock pipit performs its mating song and the fragile appearance of the bird ... One expects this daring shape to be transfixed to the earth by the cold and yet it quite simply ignores it! It does even better; it flies up into the clear skies, seemingly enjoying this glacial atmosphere and salutes the dawn with its penetrating notes; spreading its wings voluptuously and hopping over the snow as if it were insensible to the cold, it pursues its companion from rock to rock, while all around the snow scintillates in the first rays of the sun.

A pair of brown frogs in a mountain lake.

quiet, guttural sounds. When he had recovered a little from this astonishment the author learnt that evening while looking through various books that it was the common frog which he had seen, a species which also inhabits the plains, but which can create certain local types at high altitude. Of all the frogs, this is the species which is found at the greatest heights. It is less dependent on water than the edible frog and individuals can be found even in the mountains quite a long way from water. The author wondered, however, how these batrachians could survive the winter in the Alps. Doubtless they would live in deep fissures in the earth, sheltered from the frost; but this was only surmise. The author has seen at the edge of the same marsh, when dried up in October, thousands of small frogs recently hatched, but pinned to the earth by the first frost. Some of them had tried to protect themselves from the cold by hiding beneath a plank but they had not escaped the frost, even there. In any event, losses must be extremely heavy at such an altitude, and those individuals which reappear in the springtime are something of a miracle and create a strange enigma.

In all the mountain marshes in springtime a small animal looking like a salamander can usually be seen; this is the alpine newt. During the mating season the male is really superb, with blue sides, decorated with a band of black spots, its stomach bright orangey red and its dorsal spine marked with black and yellow. The female is duller in appearance and has a stomach which is less colourful; both are greyish blue, marked with brown on the upper parts of their bodies. It is always interesting to observe newts while mating. Unlike frogs they have no proper intercourse; the male courts the female by placing itself in front of her, shaking its tail which it holds slightly curved, then releasing its sperm on the mud; this sperm appears as a tiny white tear which the female absorbs through its cloaca, although there is no noticeably sign of her pressing against it. In the plains the period of reproduction appears to end in May, while in the moun-

tains it is longer and lasts sometimes quite late into the summer months. At 8200 ft (2500 m) the adults hardly ever leave the water and the metamorphosis of the young can only take place the following spring.

Also near those alpine marshes which have some vegetation in the summer months the hawker dragonfly, called *Aeschna juncea*, can be found. This superb insect, whose upper wings measure 2 in (50 mm) across, can be seen flying in the Alps in great numbers up to a considerable altitude, even as high as 7200 ft (2200 m). The males fly over those areas of water where there are sedges, horse-tails or rushes; the insects' bodies are either horizontal or arched. They often hover in one place and pursue each other. As soon as the female appears she is immediately seized by one of the males and the pair fly together for some moments just above the grass of the meadows, then settle on a grass stem or a rhododendron and remain there suspended for almost an hour. They should, however, be cautiously approached if one wishes to take close-up photographs as, even during mating, these dragonflies are very easily frightened off. One strange fact which is almost an aberration is that the penis of the male is not found at the end of the abdomen but in a sort of sac or pouch for semen which is found underneath the second segment of the body, very close to the thorax; this is the case with all dragonflies. Before mating, the male has to fill this pouch by bending its abdomen and producing the sperm from the end of the latter. Once its sac is full it will seize a female behind the head while in full flight, by means of appendices at the end of its body; as soon as the couple settle on grass or tall plants, the female also curves its abdomen in order to place its sexual orifice in contact with the penis on the second segment very close to the thorax. This explains the strange position of the insects while they mate. When it is laying eggs the female dragonfly plunges its abdomen into the water and embeds its eggs one after the other in the stem or leaf on which it has settled.

The rainbow trout, the arctic charr and the minnow

Most of the lakes in the Alps and the Pyrenees are inhabited with trout and are particularly attractive for fishermen. These trout belong to two species; the native trout or brook trout which has already been discussed in the chapters describing the rivers and the rainbow trout, of American origin which is extremely voracious and grows very rapidly. The natural reproduction of the latter species is always risky and artificial breeding is therefore necessary. The rainbow trout resembles the brook trout in the shape of its body but it can be immediately distinguished by the absence of red spots, by the purple highlights on its sides and the black patches on its tail. It is of average size, but can occasionally reach a weight of 11–15 lb (5–7 kg) and a length of 27 in (70 cm). A fish which has been acclimatised recently with great success in certain glacier lakes of the Alps and Pyrenees which are frozen nine months out of the twelve is the charr of the Northern Lakes of Canada – *Cristivomer namaycush*. The Arctic charr – *Salvelinus alpinus* also breeds prolifically in certain Pyrenean lakes and can also be found at an altitude of between 7500 and 8000 ft (2300 and 2400 m). In such areas it produces dwarf species well known under the name of 'yellow fish' and is never more than 8 in (20 cm) long. They can also be found in the lakes of Sweden, Norway and Finland, in North America, Greenland and Iceland, in certain lakes of the Alps and throughout the British Isles. The minnow must be known to everyone, as a small, silvery brown fish with a rounded head, inhabiting most of the rivers where trout are to be found and feeding on the eggs of the latter. The minnow can be found also in many alpine lakes sometimes at a height of more than 8200 ft (2500 m). It lives in shoals, especially at the time of spawning. When this takes place, in July or August, the stomach of the male as well as its pectoral and ventral fins take on fine reddish colours while the back and the front part of the body become much darker in colour. The author has often amused himself by bathing his feet in the icy water of the mountain lakes in order to watch the minnows approach in large numbers. They come to nibble at this new kind of 'food', but the slightest movement sends them scuttling away. This small fish provides excellent bait and even if it destroys the eggs of the trout it also acts as their food, so that one factor compensates the other!

The wheatear and the stoat

In the high meadows intersected with outcrops of rock and scree, large patches of snow can still be found in May. Water flows everywhere and the spring anemones open their violet petals in the sun while the lower slopes produce saffron and buttercups. From a deserted hillock a grey and black bird with a pure white crop and base of its tail flies into the sky, uttering some whistled notes mixed with more raucous noises. When it reaches a certain height it spreads its wings, opens its black and white tail wide and glides down towards its point of departure. In the warm wind and blinding light, these clear modulations interrupted by hard crackling noises express the harsh grandeur of these deserted places. When it regains the earth, the small bird indulges in curious bowing movements and bends its body forward only to bring itself upright again immediately; it utters a strange gargling noise while opening and shutting its tail, or lowering and raising it, as if moved by some sudden spasm. This bird is superb with its black cheeks, its white eyebrows, its light coloured breast shaded with fawn. It suddenly flies off rapidly, just clearing the ground. It seems to be a luminous point above the grey background of stones, because of its snow white crop . . . This could be the reason why the wheatear carries the strange name of 'white seat'. One should explain that this popular term describes both the base of the back and the tail, of which the centre and the end are barred with black, which highlight the surprising effect created by the dazzling white feathers revealed when the bird is in flight. The same is true of the female, although the rest of its plumage is rather different from that of the male; it is more brownish on the upper part of the body, more russet on the breast and generally it has a more contrasting appearance. The birds have a rather timid character with a nervous temperament and run over the ground at great speed, weaving their way skilfully through the rocks and escaping into the first hole if there should be any danger. They are particularly fond of settling on top of any projection such as a stone rock, hill or ridge from where they survey their territory and which they use as a starting point for their mating flight.

At nesting time in May or June, depending on the altitude, the couples constantly utter their cry of 'dack dack dack'. These hard short cries ring out abruptly from the meadows, the outcrops of rocks and

A female wheatear in flight.

the last areas of grass. The nest is usually built beneath a large stone, a hole in the ground or a crack in a rock. It is quite big and made of dry grass and roots, decorated in the centre with feathers, horse hair or plant debris. The wheatear, owing to its preference for perching on outcrops of rock or ridges has many enemies in the mountains. The most fearsome of them is the alpine stoat which lives in the same areas. The author once witnessed the following strange event. On a flowery slope beneath which he was sitting, there were two wheatears hovering in the air; soon a water pipit came to join them and hovered together with the others, constantly uttering its cry of alarm. The birds slowly moved down the slope while still hovering and seemed to be following something which was coming from the area where the author sat. Intrigued by their behaviour he looked for the cause of their excitement and finally spotted the supple body of a stoat appearing from behind a stone with a small wheatear in its mouth. The tiny carnivore came straight up to the author a little laden with its prey but full of confidence. The author did not dare to make any movement as he was very curious to see what was about to happen. Less than 6 ft (2 m) away the stoat suddenly became aware of the author's presence, gave a brief squeal and disappeared into the stones. The author used the occasion to seize his camera, which unfortunately was at the bottom of his bag, and when the stoat reappeared it had dropped its burden and made its escape, weaving its way carefully and skilfully between the stones, appearing here and there with unbelievable skill. The author succeeded nevertheless in taking several photographs but because of his slowness in finding his camera he missed the shot of the small animal carrying its victim.

Apart from the stoat which attacks the young while they are still unable to fly and also eats the eggs in their nest, the wheatear has many other enemies: the kestrel is a past master at hovering and raiding the nests and the marten and fox, which often hunt very high up in the mountains in the fine weather, have also to be considered as dangers. In spite of all this, the wheatear is still relatively abundant in the Alps and continues to enliven each springtime with its cries and its flight above the deserted mountain areas.

The stoat is one of the most frequently found carnivorous animals in the mountains, or at least it is the animal who appears most often in full daylight. This does not signify, however, that it can be easily met. On the contrary, to find the animal is always something of a problem and it is usually chance which brings it about, unless the observer finds the spot where the female is raising its young. Even then it is difficult as the mother, if she feels that she is menaced by man, will remove her family elsewhere. In the Alps the nest of the weasel is almost always built beneath a rock, a pile of stones or even in a hole in the ground.

As has been noticed, this wild little creature liked to rob the nests of sparrows and seize the young fledglings – its favourite prey, however, is still the vole; it attacks them ferociously even penetrating their caverns and is particularly fond of the snow vole. The stoat sometimes also attacks the young of the mountain gallanaceous birds. It is not afraid of attacking animals much bigger than itself ... the mountain hare certainly numbers amongst its victims. On a skiing trip the author once discovered a mountain hare which had been killed by a stoat. The poor creature had struggled hard as the scuffles in the snow showed. It had finally succumbed, however, to the sharp teeth of the terrible little carnivore. The neck of the hare had been opened in two places and its blood-spattered fur was a tragic sight. The hare was young and had probably been born late in the season as it appeared particularly thin; perhaps it had been a sick animal, and the stoat had done nothing more than eliminate a creature which was already condemned to death sooner or later by the harsh alpine winter. The sudden appearance of a stoat in a rabbit warren is always surprising. The indefatigable small creature will wriggle between the large blocks of stone, raising its head here and there disappearing into narrow cracks to reappear unexpectedly in a completely different spot from which it stares at you with curiosity, its quick eyes having strange greenish reflections. It will suddenly jump again and continue to appear and disappear, moving

A male alpine newt during the mating season.

Hawker dragonflies mating.

1 Rainbow trout.
2 Young arctic char.
3 Mountain minnows on the shore of a lake
   at a height of 8200 ft (2500 m).

with such strength and suppleness that it is difficult to follow its course and one can only be surprised at the distance the beast covers in a relatively short time . . .

In the Alps above the tree line the stoat is almost always found in its dwarf form; it is not much bigger than the weasel, but much longer. In the summer months, its fur is usually a russet fawn with lighter patches on the upper parts of its body with a white throat and stomach which is sometimes tinted sulphur yellow. The inner surface of its feet and legs are white and its tail almost always ends with a black patch which extends over a third of its legs, a fact which helps in avoiding confusion with the weasel, both in summer and winter. In the cold months, its fur becomes completely white, at least in the Alps. This change of colour does not, however, always correspond with the autumn moult, as one captive animal which had just moulted became white in one week through the rapid depigmentation of the fur. The change from winter to summer fur is on the contrary effected through moulting. The author has seen at the beginning of June at an altitude of 8200 ft (2500 m) a weasel in complete summer fur. The sun had not yet appeared, and the animal which was very excited constantly jumped over the hard snow, describing enormous circles and landing at times on all four feet in order to take off again with greater energy. It passed three times at only a few yards distance from the rock behind which the author was hiding and paid no attention to him. A stoat which the author had trapped in a hole which had no exit and which was near a spring gave a very sharp cry; once it was seized it fought with rage and tried to bite the author, almost suffocating him with the overpowering odour from its anal glands. The pigmy form of the stoat can be found much higher in the mountains than the weasel. The author has observed it in autumn on the ridge of the Bella-Tola at about 10 000 ft (3000 m); it was probably at this altitude looking for its favourite prey, the snow vole.

The stoat has relatively few enemies apart from man who traps it or shoots it. The wild and domestic cat succeeds in overcoming it and the eagle owl and the tawny owl both attack it occasionally in their nocturnal hunts, while the eagle and the goshawk sometimes attack it during the day. On one occasion the author has seen a kestrel give a stoat a hard time in pursuing it ferociously across a meadow, but it failed to seize it as the stoat succeeded at the last moment in hiding beneath a pile of stones. Owing to its small size, its liveliness and its prudence, the stoat usually escapes from its enemies. Its rôle in the mountains as on the plains appears to be the limitation of the number of rodents, and we should be grateful to the stoat for this activity. With its leaps and runs it also enlivens the high stoney deserted areas and offers an unusual sight, while its unexpected appearance always pleases the naturalist.

The alpine vole

This is a strange little beast which is still relatively unknown and holds the record for living at high altitude amongst the alpine mammals as it has been found at more than 13 000 ft (4000 m) on isolated patches of rock amongst the glaciers. The species is also found in forests where rhododendron bushes grow and even at lower altitudes. The author has often observed it in mountain huts and refuges where the snow vole likes to retire in the cold months and appears to be quite tame. In daylight one can often see this little ball of greyish fur crawling quickly over the surface of the ground from one juniper clump to another, to disappear almost immediately. It can also be found in the rough scree of the mountain ridges, where amongst the tufts of the siline plant and the saxifrages it creates tunnels with a round opening, in front of which there is almost always a small pile of pebbles, roots and leaves from the climbing willow. In the fine months, it seems that the snow vole prefers slightly humid northern slopes and streams or springs, rather than slopes which are too sunny and dry. On the other hand in the autumn and later on the author has often seen these creatures running over pebbley slopes which are exposed to the sun. One day in October when some snow had fallen and the author was searching for ptarmigan, he found one snow vole taking a sun bath at the entrance to its hole, well sheltered by a large boulder. This was at a height of 8200 ft (2500 m) in the Anniviers. It was already cold and a bitter wind was blowing strongly. Every time the author made a movement the vole disappeared into its hole, only to emerge a little later to enjoy the sun. It was grey with a long tail, being larger than other similar species living in the mountains. Its long whiskers gave its face an amusing appearance and if it were not for the icy wind, he would have remained longer to observe this little creature. Its traces in the high meadows can be found most frequently in autumn when the first snow falls. Usually the vole does not move very far, only emerging from beneath one rock to hurry towards another. Very often the tracks of a stoat can be found crossing those of a vole and it is not difficult to guess what has taken place under the stars. In fact the alpine vole seems to be one of the favourite preys of the weasel, the fox, the marten, the kestrel and other nocturnal birds. It does not hibernate in winter and moves freely between earth and snow when it burrows tunnels through the flattened vegetation. If walking through the alpine meadows in the early spring as soon as the snow starts to melt one will doubtless see innumerable furrows. These open tunnels are always surrounded with part debris. Sometimes the furrow becomes a tunnel for a few inches and then the ground appears to be swollen up. The snow vole is a strict vegetarian and feeds only on roots, branches and leaves of various alpine plants. It often sets this food out to dry on stones near the entrance to its home.

Arrangement of an insectivore's teeth: the common shrew.

Length of the mandible: 0.3–0.4 in (9–10 mm).
Total length of the skull:
0.7–0.8 in (18.5–20.5 mm).

Arrangement of a rodent's teeth: the alpine vole.

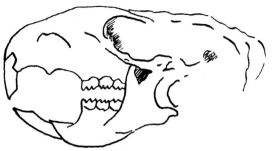

Length of the mandible: 0.6–0.7 in (17–19 mm).
Total length of the skull: 1–1.2 in (27–29 mm).

The common shrew

The common shrew is very similar to the mouse but can be distinguished by its pointed nose and scarcely visible eyes. They belong to those very small mammals which are known only to few people and whose habits are extremely difficult to observe. However, amongst the dozen species living in Europe, the common shrew is indeed the most common. And yet it is hardly ever seen as it dislikes showing itself, is very frightened of the sun and usually crawls around beneath the vegetation or through the tunnels of the vole, or even between the snow and the earth. It is usually found dead on paths, especially in autumn, apparently having no injuries: could this be natural death? It is usually by chance that one comes across a shrew, but a trained ear can nevertheless hear its extremely sharp cries. It often betrays its presence beneath the vegetation by frequent squeals and a sort of curious warbling noise rather similar to that made by a fledgling or a cricket. It is aggressive and kills its companions when kept in captivity, feeding exclusively on animal matter and insects. One wonders how the shrew can survive the long mountain winters as it needs to feed continuously or it will perish after only a few hours. What food can it find in the winter? Driven by hunger does it attack the vole and the yellow necked mouse in their tunnels as has often been claimed? It is certainly very difficult to check on such a statement under natural conditions when there are many feet of snow on the ground. But it is clear that the common shrew remains active throughout the winter. The author has seen a number of them crawling quickly over the frozen snow at 8200 ft (2500 m) on an alpine meadow in Valais. When the author pursued them the tiny creatures disappeared between the snow and the ground at the foot of a rock and he saw nothing more of them. According to Fatio, the common shrew can be found as high up as 6300 ft (1900 m). In the Swiss Alps of Valais however, the species lives at far greater heights. Recently he surprised a young shrew in the process of devouring an owlet moth. This was in a meadow at an altitude of more than 8200 ft (2500 m) and well beyond the tree line. Its fur was of a lighter brown than the adult which is usually rather dark with violet highlights on the upper surfaces, the stomach being greyish white. A fawn band runs along the flanks and separates the upper parts from the lower parts of the body in the case of the adults. The ears are short, sometimes very light in colour and almost entirely concealed in the fur while the tips of the teeth are red. As for the tail, which is medium length and more or less rectangular in form, this does not seem to be a particularly striking characteristic. What is more important is the very mobile nose, evidence of a very developed sense of smell and the constant agitation of this tiny animal who moves speedily in little jumps, its tail held high so that it is not easy to spot it and to follow its movement. All shrews are skilful at hiding in the smallest folds in the ground and of disappearing beneath vegetation or stones. It is interesting to note that a related species in the mountains, the pygmy shrew is a good third smaller than the common shrew and has lighter, more greyish fur, its tail being much longer in proportion to its size. In fact the smallest mammal in the world belongs to the family of the shrew or soricides and is called the Etruscan shrew. Its length does not exceed 2 in (5 cm) and it weighs .07 ozs (2 g). It is only found in the Mediterranean areas of Europe.

A curious fact is that cats, martens and stoats sometimes kill the shrew but do not eat it. Their strong musky smell is probably the reason for this. This odour is produced by two glands which are placed on each side of the body. Certain nocturnal birds of prey however seem to hunt it as their favourite prey.

133

The viviparous lizard

When crossing the mountain meadows, the vegetation becomes more and more sparse. At the foot of the rock outcrops the large leaves of the adenostyle can still be found and, near the streams, the imposing form of the great white thistle. Higher up, however, the juniper bushes grow closer and closer to the ground, the grass becomes shorter and the stems of the flowers lower, and they tend to grow in groups like small cushions. Arctic lichen appears here and there on the terrain and seems to fight for space with the heath, the dwarf azalea and the black camerine. The myrtle has already given way to the marsh bilberry and the last advance guards of the rhododendron are hidden in hollows between the rocks. It is therefore fairly rare to catch sight of a lizard at this altitude. At one's approach the tiny reptile takes refuge immediately beneath a juniper. At first sight the reptile seems a little similar to the grey lizard of the plains, but at an altitude of 8200 ft (2500 m) such a meeting would be extremely unlikely! The tiny creature cannot be hiding very far and can probably be found curled up, well camouflaged beneath the knotty wood of this dwarf juniper. Its brownish back, covered with patches and dark stripes recalls the wall lizard. However, its tail is less pointed and more stumpy than that of the ordinary lizard, while its stomach is a fine orangey red colour, speckled with black, while its head is shorter and its nose rounded. There is no doubt that this species is the male viviparous lizard. In fact the stomach of the female is never so brightly coloured as that of the male and is always yellowish or greyish, sometimes with a few blue scales. This charming little lizard takes the place of the wall lizard in the mountains, as the latter is hardly ever seen above 5600 ft (1700 m). The viviparous lizard is much more resistant than the wall lizard against rapid changes of temperature; it can swim very well and does not hesitate to leap into the water if there is any sign of danger. Unlike the other species, the viviparous lizard produces three to seven young which are perfectly formed and emerge from their eggs as soon as they are laid, measuring at the moment of birth $1\frac{1}{2}$ in (4 cm) in length. This usually takes place in the course of the summer. The young are much darker than the adults and are immediately independant, going their own way and feeding on small insects and larvae of the cricket. An interesting fact is that this species is the only reptile in the world which has penetrated the Arctic Circle, and it is also the only one to be found at altitudes higher than 10 000 ft (3000 m). It lives in the Alps, the Pyrenees, the Cantabrian mountains, the Northern Balkans and the Caucasus, but it can also be found in marshy areas in the plains and in the Jura, and in these types of surroundings in Great Britain and Ireland, where the wall lizard does not exist.

An alpine vole and its tracks.

A female viviparous lizard.

134

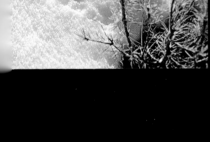

A stoat in its winter coat,
taken by surprise on a scree
slope 7500 ft (2300 m) up, at
the end of March.

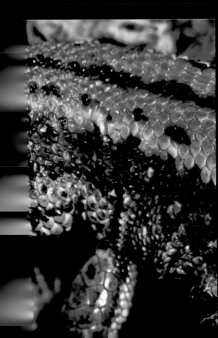

Alpine salamander.

The alpine salamander

This strange little animal is completely black; its body is fat and stocky and it has two rows of tubercles along its back. The skin is shiny, as if covered with lacquer. Two large elongated lumps are found behind the eyes and these are the parotid glands which are very prominent and give a characteristic form to the head. Apart from these, two sorts of furrows run along the length of the body to the tail. The author searched for the black salamander for many years in the Alps of Valais without any success, probably because of the dry climate there. It was only by pure chance that its presence was revealed to him under the following circumstances. He had gone with a friend into the meadows of the Bernese Alps to take a film of peasant life; in particular, the methods they use to make cheese. The sky was sunny at first, but quickly covered over with large clouds in the course of the morning and afternoon; finally an extremely violent storm broke in the region. When his work was finished the author and his friend started their return trip before the rain stopped completely, as two hours of walking separated them from the bridge which they had to cross in order to enter the valley. While climbing the stony path cut into the side of the mountain and running with water, the author noticed a small black creature crawling along the path and he took it at first to be a newt. His surprise was very great when, on examining the creature closely, he recognised it as an alpine salamander. It was the first time he had seen this species and he noticed with interest how clumsily it moved and the shining appear-ance of its body, covered with warts. A hundred yards further on he was even more astonished to come across a second salamander; and before reaching the bridge he saw at least a dozen of these batrachians along the path. One can well imagine his aston-ishment, as he had searched for this species without success for several years. The reason is, however, easily explained; the alpine salamander searches out the most humid areas of mountains. It is, therefore, very localised and is particularly fond of the rocky meadows at the end of the tree line, although it is sometimes found as high as 10 000 ft (3000 m) in the snowy region. In normal weather, it remains con-cealed beneath stones and only emerges at daytime when there have been heavy warm showers of rain. This salamander is an example of special adaptation to the harsh alpine climate. Instead of going into water to mate and lay eggs as does the spotted sala-mander, it gives birth after two or even three years of gestation to two or three young, completely devel-oped and apart from size identical to the adult. The alpine salamander can, therefore, be called vivipa-rous. Its larvae has the surprising faculty of fixing tubes to the walls of the uterus in the mother and these act as suckers which are capable of absorbing the placenta. When they are about to be born these tubes of the larvae are reabsorbed naturally and disappear at birth. This is the strange adaptation of the alpine salamander to the harsh climate of the mountains. It is, in fact, the only amphibious animal capable of living in the areas of permanent snow.

Insects of the alpine meadows and high pastures

In this area, where there is a complete absence of any sort of tall vegetation, the activity of insects is limited to very brief summer periods. Because of this fact their life is more intense and more interesting. Certain insects at this high altitude have a tendency to melanism; many of the species, instead of being brilliantly coloured, are more blackish. A good example is found in a beetle of the family of Carabidae, the *Orinocarabus latreillanus*, found in the Alps of Valais. This insect, unlike its relatives at lower altitudes which are gleaming with colours, has very dark wing-sheaths which are flecked only with tiny violet spots. This melanism, which is also found in certain reptiles like the viper, evidently plays a protective rôle against the cold of the atmosphere, the snow and ultra-violet rays. Another tendency is the reduction or even complete disappearance of wings, particularly notable in the case of certain crickets. Such an example is the *Podisma*, the *Chrysochraon* and some others. This must represent an adaptation to areas where there are strong winds. An incapacity to fly prevents these insects from being carried away by violent gales and provides some sort of a guarantee for their survival. Finally, many insects of these high altitudes are smaller in size than their neighbours living at lower altitudes. This is particularly obvious with butterflies, beetles and winged insects. One should also add the Arthropoda. Certain spiders, in fact, attract the attention of alpine wanderers, as many of them are found even as high as 14 750 ft (4500 m). Centipedes are also numerous in the high alpine areas near the snow line. The butterflies, however, attract the main attention of the tourists in these high pasturages. The fritillaries are by far the most numerous and, together with certain *Zygaenidae*, fly close to the ground, hovering gracefully around the flowers in the sunlight. The most common species is cynthia's fritillary which shows a striking dimorphism between the male and the female. While the latter has the upper parts of the wings coloured orangey beige, crossed with black bands, the male has wings which are partly white with red spots and bands and broad black markings. This fritillary, whose wings measure up to $\frac{3}{4}$ in (20 mm), is found frequently on the high meadows where there are juniper bushes and bilberries. Its caterpillar is spiky, blackish in colour with yellow bands and lives on plantain. These caterpillars sometimes cover the alpine plains in such numbers that it is impossible to sit down in the grass without noticing them.

The author will always recall one unusual experience. He was following a small path at about 8000 ft (2400 m) in the region of Chandolin, when he noticed groups of these caterpillars stuck one against the other on some rocks. On examining them closely, he was surprised to discover that all these caterpillars were being attacked by a tiny parasite called the ichneumon, belonging to the family of Braconidae. In fact, the lower parts of their bodies were fixed to the stones by innumerable tiny cocoons of silk, which completely covered them. Even worse, certain yellowish larvae were in the process of piercing the skin of the wretched caterpillars who were stuck to the rocks, and the former emerged from their victims in order to envelope themselves in their cocoons of silk. An extraordinary drama was taking place under the author's eyes and only nature could explain the reason for it. The caterpillars appeared resigned to their fate, doubtless weakened and half emptied of their substance by these parasitic larvae. The author was even more astounded to see that a second parasite, looking like a small ant, was attacking the cocoons and feeding on them in turn. The interesting fact was that the caterpillars were trying, by twisting and turning, to defend the cocoons which kept them prisoner and contained the larvae which had been growing fat by feeding on them. The wingless second parasite, however, achieved its purpose; the author noticed how, like some tiny pygmy, this insect circled round the furious giants avoiding their mandibles; it then bent its abdomen and thrust its terebra into each small cocoon within reach in order to lay its eggs there. This spectacle had something unbelievable about it; the author noted that the first parasites would, in their turn, serve as feeding ground for the future larvae of the second parasites, which had doubtless been attracted there by the magnitude of the disaster. This would perhaps reestablish a certain balance in the mysterious and inexorable activity of nature.

Another butterfly which is commonly found in the same areas as cynthia's fritillary is the *Mellicta varia*. This species is a little smaller than the former and is only found in the Alps and the Apennines. Both sexes have fawn upper surfaces of the wings, with black markings. Belonging to the same family of nymphalidae, the *Boloria pales* (and its sub-species) is widely found above the tree line in the Alps, the Pyrenees, the Cantabrian mountains, the Carpathian mountains, the Caucasus, Central Asia and the west of

1 | 2
3 | 4
5 | 6

1
The caterpillar of a cynthia's fritillary parasitized by larvae of the Garbage Ichneumons *(Braconidae)* which have woven their cocoons under its belly. A parasite in the second stage is busy laying its eggs in the cocoons.

2
Cynthia's fritillaries mating.

3
A pair of Grisons fritillaries.

4
A female mountain clouded yellow at rest.

5
Shepherd's fritillary.

6
Alpine grayling.

1
De Lesse's Brassy ringlets *(Erebia nivalis)* mating.
2
An idas blue sucking water from the soil.
3
A Scotch burnet just hatching. A cluster of glittering cocoons can be seen stuck to each other.
4
The forester on a purple scabious.
5
Psodos alpinata (little moth).
6
A caterpillar of a Lackey moth: *(Malacosoma castrensis).*

China. It is similar to the *Mellicta varia*, but the reddish brown or violet markings on the underneath of its wings allow it to be identified easily.

The family of Pieridae is also well represented in the alpine area. The author has already described in the section devoted to sub-alpine insects the *Colias palaeno*, the Arctic species which is widely found in the cold and marshy areas of Scandinavia and Finland at low altitudes. The ice age, however, drove this insect to the south and, when the glaciers had retreated, this butterfly did not only return to its northern homeland but remained in the Alps, introducing a new typical wood-alpine element into the existing fauna. The mountain clouded yellow butterfly – *Colias phicomone* – which resembles the former in that the underparts of the wings are suffused with dark grey, is a very common species found on the alpine meadows; this insect, which has colours rather more subdued than those of the other varieties of *Colias*, already shows signs of melanism, guaranteeing the creature a better absorption of the rays of the sun when it closes its wings. Another form of the family Pieridae found amongst the high Alps and the Pyrenees, the *Pontia callidice* flies extremely rapidly over the grassy slopes and the screes near the glaciers up to a height of 10 000 ft (3000 m) and more. They are very rarely found below the tree line. The same is also true of another butterfly strictly limited to the Alps, the alpine grayling – *Oeneis glacialis*. This butterfly is a brownish yellow, and its rear wings have a blackish appearance, with lighter patches and white veins. Its caterpillar lives on the winter fescue for two years before completing its metamorphosis in July of the third year. Numerous forms of *Erebia* inhabit the pasturages, the rocky screes and the moraines; they are difficult to differentiate and the author limits himself to noting a few of the most typical types. The *Erebia nivalis* is localised in the Swiss and Austrian Alps and often flies a little lower than *Erebia cassioides*. *Erebia pluto* is limited to the Alps, being found up to 8900 ft (2700 m), and its companion *Erebia gorge* rises to 10 000 ft (3000 m). Finally, the 'large black butterfly of Berne' – *Erebia pandrose* – flies over the pasturages and the rocky slopes of the Pyrenees and the Alps, although it is also found at low altitudes in Scandinavia and Finland. There can also be seen flying over the flowers of the high meadows a great number of that small grayling, *Coenonympha gardetta*, which has on its rear wings a series of well developed 'eyes' in black with white pupils.

The various forms of *Erebia* are often to be found along the mountain paths or near the streams as they like the humidity. The 'little blues', charming little butterflies, sometimes keep them company. Some of these 'little blues' are found both on the plains and at high altitudes; for example the *Vacciniina optilete* and *Cupido minimus*, the latter being found almost throughout the whole of Europe. The idas blue is found along the sides of the valleys up to 6600 ft (2000 m) and above. But some species appear only in the meadows of the Pyrenees, the Alps and the Balkans. This is true of the glandon blue and a few others. The alpine argus flies up to an altitude of

8500 ft (2600 m) and is also found in Sweden and Norway. It is, however, absent from the Balkans. The Hespeviidne, also of small size with rapid flight, are found not only on the flowers of the meadows but also, together with the graylings and the *Erebia*, near patches of mud on warm days in July and August. Certain species can only live in the high mountains at the alpine level; this is particularly true of the dusky grizzled skipper. Another closely related species, the alpine grizzled skipper, lives not only at great heights amongst the mountain peaks of the Pyrenees and the Alps as high as the Gross Glockner and the Julian Alps, but can also still be found in the mountain ranges of Scandinavia between Dovre and the North Cape, as well as beyond the Arctic Circle. Other species, generally fawn in appearance with wide brown borders to their wings, such as the silver spotted skipper or the large skipper, also inhabit the mountain pasturages up to 8200 ft (2500 m), but can also be found elsewhere, as the silver spotted skipper is found throughout Europe from sea level up to the North Cape. The zygaenidae are also very numerous, inhabiting the high Alpine and Pyrenean meadows up to the snow line. The most widely distributed species which the author has found at heights of 10 000 ft (3000 m) is the *Zygaena exulans*. The caterpillar of this small butterfly, clumsy in flight, can sometimes be found in such large numbers on the short grass of the mountain tops that it is not unusual to find some ten to twenty shining cocoons pressed one against the other, often stuck on two levels, on the same stone. The beautiful statices whose wings are green or metallic blue and which also belong to the family Zygaenidae, gather honey from the flowers of the centaury and scabious well above the tree line. The Arctiidae are also well represented in the mountains. The *Parasemia plantaginas*, found everywhere in the sub-alpine zone, sometimes flies in the high pasturages up to a height of 8200 ft (2500 m). The *Endrosa aurita*, whose caterpillar eats the lichen on certain rocks, flies over the valleys of lower altitudes, but from 6600 ft (2000 m) and above the veins of its wings, which are normally yellow, develop thick blackish ridges and produce the ramosa form. At even higher altitudes, towards 8200 ft (2500 m), the size becomes smaller and the yellow on its wings turns very pale, while the darker ridges of the veins remain well developed; this is the form called Pallens.

Another species, one which is endemic in the high mountains of the Alps – the *Arctia flavia* – is quite large in size and has on its upper wings black and white marbled markings. There can certainly be seen in all the meadows of the alpine zone the fine caterpillars of the *Malacosoma castrensis*. When young these caterpillars live in colonies inside loose silk nests. As they grow bigger they become independent and feed on numerous short plants. Their blue, reddish or brown stripes, with fawn hairs allow them to be easily recognised. The caterpillar of the *Malacosoma alpicola* is very similar to the previously described creature and also lives in colonies, usually on the climbing willow. Finally the *Noctua* and the *Phalaena* can also be found in these high alpine meadows.

The cold and humidity of night in the mountain forces these butterflies, which are normally found either at twilight or even at night, to live their life in full sunlight. This is the case with numerous of the *Noctua* and of a small black *Phalaena* which has a

Tiger moth (*Arctia flavia*): actual size.

Peak white moth (*Pontia callidice*): actual size.

Testediolum glacialis: magnification 9x.

orange patch on each of its wings; the *Psodos alpinsta* – and this also applies to the *Crocota lutearia*, a charming moth with ochre-yellow wings which can be found flying in large numbers over the heather and bilberries surrounding the alpine forests. In the mountains, near stretches of water or on sandbanks at the sides of streams, one will not fail to see small greyish butterflies in large numbers, together with the little blues and the Hesperiidae. They belong to the genus *Titania*. The most widely found species is the *Titania phrygialis*. The micro-lepidoptera of the high mountains are innumerable; amongst them the *Pyralis* or bee-moth has an important place.

Almost half of the beetles belong to that enormous family Carabidae. These insects generally hide beneath stones, cushions of moss or small plants, even concealing themselves in the cracks of rocks. They are of great importance to entomologists as some of them, like *Testediolum glacialis* live at high altitudes near the glaciers. The author has already mentioned the melanism of the dark coloured *Orinocarabus latreillanus* native of the Alps of the Valais. The Scarabaeidae are also well represented on the high pasturages; the *Geotrupes vernalis alpinus*, which has very smooth wing-sheaths and is smaller than its relatives of lower altitudes is not at all rare and can be found near cow droppings. This is also the case with *Aphodius fossor*, entirely black in colour and *Aphodius alpinus*, which has a black thorax but reddish wing-sheaths. The Staphylinidae can also be found at very high altitudes. The author was very surprised to find one day the common *Staphylinus caesarus* at an altitude of more than 8500 ft (2600 m) hidden in the crack of a rock. Perhaps, however, it had only been carried up to that altitude by strong winds.

With certain crickets living at high altitudes one notices that the wings are either completely absent or only exist as tiny flaps which would not be strong enough to allow the insects to fly. This is a protection to stop them from being carried to extreme altitudes by strong winds – ever present in the high mountains – which would be fatal for them.

The most common of the crickets is a species found in the mountains and the forests of the Alps – *Podisma pedestris* – which can be found as high as 10 000 ft (3000 m) in the dry mountains of the south. The female is brown and rust, decorated with a yellow band and can reach a length of just over 1 in

(30 mm). At a slightly lower altitude, where dwarf bushes and bilberries grow, there is another closely related species – *Podisma alpina*. This insect is green with black bands. The male has a slightly hairy body and is always much smaller than the female; it is rarely longer than $\frac{2}{3}$ in (17 mm) and its rear legs are marked at the base with violet-red spots. Another species which is of Siberian–Alpine origin can be frequently found, particularly in the high meadows between 6600 and 10 000 ft (2000 and 3000 m). This is the Siberian cricket – *Aeropus sibiricus* – which has a characteristic appearance, in that the male has a sort of swelling underneath the front legs which allows the insect to be identified immediately. Its antennae are also enlarged at their ends. This strange creature still has very close relations in the vast steppes of Central Asia. It can be considered a typical 'Tertiary Alpine' species. Huge numbers of other grasshoppers and tiny crickets also inhabit the grass and scree at these high levels. To mention only a few, there are the *Chrysochraon*, the *Chorthippus*, and the *Stenobothrus*, amongst which can also be found more familiar species from the southern Alps, such as the interesting *Anonconotus alpinus*, an inhabitant of the rhododendron zone and which is also without wings, like the *Podisma*.

Bumble bees are also frequently found at high altitudes. The *Bombus terrestris*, which has an abdomen stripped in black, yellow and white, is found everywhere both on the plains and on certain mountain slopes at more than 9200 ft (2800 m). The *Bombus alpinus*, a species of Arctic origin, with a black thorax and a rust coloured abdomen, can be found at more than 10 000 ft (3000 m) and builds its nest well beneath the ground, sometimes using the old tunnels of the snow vole. Many other insects inhabit these high alpine meadows but it would be of no interest to add further names to the list. We have seen that their origins are very complex: as certain boreo-alpine species have followed the retreat of the ice both towards the extreme north and to the highest European mountains, others combine Asiatic with indigenous or even western and Pyrenean antecedents. Such abundance and diverse adaptations to harsh conditions of life must not, however, allow us to forget that several species are very vulnerable, and that we must treat this world of small fauna with discretion, and respect.

A pair of crickets *(Podisma pedestris)* **(above).**

Cricket *(Podisma alpina).*

The alpine marmot

Its name alone is sufficient to evoke an entire world; a world of stones and short grass, of the chirruping of crickets flying from beneath your feet, a world of freshly dug hillocks of earth on the mountain slopes, created by mysterious subterranean creatures who live in shadowy burrows . . .

Suddenly, at a turn in the path, a strident whistle makes one jump. A marmot, alarmed, is giving vent to its feelings. With its front feet spread wide, its head bent forward, its body arched by the effort of each cry, it opens its mouth and uses its throat to the full, its back arched a little; finally, exhausted by its efforts, it takes up its original position, half sitting, and gradually its cries subside. Other marmots, however, have taken up the challenge and now there are whistles everywhere over the flowery slope. Suddenly this deafening concert gives way to complete silence, broken only a few seconds later by cries which have an intense feeling of panic about them. What is happening? The entire colony has just disappeared beneath the ground. There is just cause however, as at this moment a shadow flickers over the meadows and two large brown wings, a little curved at their ends, appear in the sky; it is a golden eagle. The bird of prey has missed its victim and slows down its flight. Making use of the rising currents of air, it regains height, while slowly exploring methodically its hunting area, describing wide circles. Today however the tiny colony of marmots is safe as the guards have been efficient. The eagle was unable to take them by surprise and will go elsewhere to hunt.

However, events do not always take this course: The author has seen on two occasions the eagle capture a marmot. Generally, it spies its prey from far off and takes it by surprise, by flying very rapidly from one side of the mountain to the other to seize with its terrible claws the rash creature which has strayed too far from its hole. Very often, the eagle seizes its victim without even touching the ground. The marmot dies very quickly, its skull pierced by the huge claws of the bird of prey, a fact which is confirmed by the majority of the skulls found in or near the eagle's eyrie. The bird normally seizes young animals, but also attacks adults in the summer months. This sympathetic rodent also has other enemies, such as the fox, which attacks particularly often in spring from mid-March to the end of April when the marmot emerges from hibernation and pierces the snow which covers its hole. The author has often seen a fox sitting near a hole in the early morning, patiently waiting for these small creatures to poke out their noses. In summer, also the fox hunts through the colonies of marmots, seeking to capture those young animals who still lack experience. When this occurs the adults set up an endless concert of complaining cries.

The young animals are always darker in colour than the adults and the colouring of the latter changes considerably from one individual to another and from one region to another. In general the fur of the head, the back and the side is greyish brown turning paler towards the end of the body, while the sides, the stomach and the legs are much lighter, sometimes beige or even cream coloured. The author has seen, however, certain marmots which are russet, while others have been completely pale fawn. There are also certain individuals which are slate grey. The tail is brown and rather tufted, turning darker towards the end; it is usually fairly short.

In those regions where hunting is allowed, the marmot usually shows signs of extreme prudence. is suspicious, careful, even timid, uttering whistling cries and disappearing into its hole at the least sign of danger. In territories where it is protected, however the marmot becomes trusting and shows disarming

Alpine marmot. Below lies Lake Silvaplana.

1
Dor beetle (*Geotrupes vernalis alpinus*).
2
Rose chafer (*Aphodius alpinus*).
3
Violet ground beetle (*Carabus hortensis*)
which resembles the *Orinocarabus
latreillanus* in appearance.

The black redstart

In the high alpine pasturage, amongst the scree and the rocks, where only the dwarf juniper bush and every sort of lichen are to be found in the enormous stony deserted areas, one will sometimes see a small bird, coloured like soot and rust, appear in the summer months to examine you while hopping up and down, wagging its tail! Then a strange chirping, a series of sharp notes interspersed with grating noises rather like the sound of breaking glass will be heard; this is the sound of the black redstart.

How can we explain the presence of this bird in such a desolate area when it is normally found on the plains near villages and farms, or in ruined buildings and old walls? It is surprising to find it at such a high altitude in such harsh surroundings little suited, it would seem, for its fragile appearance, its small size and the food on which it normally lives. In fact, this bird which greets one so formally, hopping from rock to rock while bowing a thousand times, poses something of a puzzle. The black redstart moves with such skill and with such rapid beats of its wings that only its russet tail is visible. This bird looks like a tiny orange flame moving through the grey background of the rocks like some miracle, breaking the monotony of the harsh surroundings. If one is to stand still, the bird will approach to within a few yards and one will be inspected carefully while it constantly makes its bows and wags its tail. Soon, however, a new arrival will oblige it to return to its normal activities! You will then see this little bird throwing itself into the pursuit of its adversary, and the two will circle in the sky, face to face, wings vibrating, tails spread out, expressing their rage with loud gurgling noises. Suddenly the two redstarts will separate and retire to their respective rocks. These aerial battles, this aggressive and violent behaviour, is part of the nuptial activities of the species. The males confront each other on their return from the southern countries of Europe and the north of Africa, in order to gain possession of a territory which represents for them their essential domain, in which each couple will raise its family. This small soot coloured bird, with its russet tail and, in the case of the male, its wings striped with white, will build its nest among the rocks, in some crack or cavity there. The answer to the puzzle is now established; the black redstart was originally a bird of the rocks, a typical species localised in the mountains. Gradually, however, it has become used to the presence of man, and to buildings which he has created, so that the walls of houses have finally replaced the high outcrops of rock in the Alps for this bird. That is why we are always a little surprised to see it fly well above the meadows up to the level of the high moraine. The black redstart has found surroundings in walls created artificially by man which suited it and it has become so well adapted that we forget the primitive origins of the little bird — the lonely Alps where are to be found the harsh rocks and scree.

confidence towards man. It becomes completely used to his presence. In many alpine areas in Switzerland, the marmot provides great attraction for the tourist; its curiosity, greediness and above all its innocent yet artful appearance are very attractive characteristics. The author has spent many amusing hours studying these creatures. There is nothing more disarming than to see a marmot appear slowly from its hole; it first shows its nose then, having sniffed the air in every direction, it reveals its head, waits a few moments and then, having carefully examined the surroundings emerges, its body half raised and front paws stretched out, while its back feet remain curled beneath its body. This typical position shows their prudence and vigilance. The alpine marmot is one of the few alpine mammals which like the sun, and it is essentially a creature which is active by day. More than anything it adores to stretch out on large granite rocks and warm itself for hours in the sunlight, particularly if the sky is partially covered and the sun only appears from time to time. If, on the other hand, the sun-rays are too strong, the marmot retires to its home. The species, which is typical of the alpine meadows, likes to burrow and digs numerous holes and tunnels in the ground. Certain of these can reach a length of 65 ft (20 m) although, in general, they are between 13 and 26 ft (4 and 8 m). Towards the middle of September the marmot, which has accumulated large reserves of fat during the warm weather, prepares its winter home and brings in pieces of grass for its nest. At the beginning of October it falls into deep hibernation and succeeds in remaining alive for more than six months, by slowly drawing on these reserves. The grass used inside the hole is not eaten during the winter but is only used as bed and as an insulating agent.

A partridge in flight.

The rock partridge

Although the mountain fauna does not now seem to be severely threatened by the dangers of our civilisation thanks to the creation of more and more nature reserves and national parks — the ibex is in the process of reappearing in its ancient domains in the Alps while the pyrenean brown bear, due to this protection, has a change of survival — there still exists a bird which has been recently subjected to catastrophic destruction and has become extremely rare during the last ten years! What has become of the rock partridge, which was once so common? Where is this agile bird hiding? Formerly, in spring, it could be heard each morning uttering its cry of 'pi-ti-je' along the rocky slopes? This bird, with its black neck feathers, its white throat, its soft grey, almost blue plumage, its fawn sides striped with darker, russet feathers, its coral circles around the eyes, and its red beak and feet used to be the joy of the hunter and the naturalist. The rock partridge, the monarch of the alpine gallinaceous creatures, runs the danger of becoming nothing more than a memory of our past.

How can we explain this amazing disappearance of a species which only fifteen years ago was commonly found on all those alpine slopes where the sun shone! This spectacular decrease is particularly obvious in those areas of the Swiss Alps where tourism has replaced former pastoral activity. It would seem that hunting and poaching cannot be held responsible and that we must seek elsewhere the real causes of this sad phenomenon. Could it be linked to the profound changes which have taken place in the last ten years throughout the Alps? The pressures of tourism have been felt more and more, ruining both the old pastoral economy and the ecological system of the traditional mountain way of life. The fields of rye and corn have been abandoned one after the other and the sound of threshing is now nothing more than a memory. The small watermills have fallen into ruins and innumerable bake-houses have become disused for ever. There is an even more serious fact — cattle are becoming less and less frequent in the mountains and many meadows are neither ploughed nor watered, while numerous barns remain empty in the winter.

What connection, you may ask, is there between all these facts and the rock partridge? It is precisely this: During the heavy snowfalls these barns, filled with hay or straw offer excellent shelter for the partridge. It can find there an excellent source of food at high altitudes and in this way succeeds in surviving during the cold weather and obtaining protection from such predators as the eagle, the marten and the fox.

There are of course other reasons for the rarity of the species; parasitical diseases, the indiscriminate use of pesticides and the severe long winters such as occurred in 1962–3 have also played their part in destroying the partridge. But, amongst all these possible reasons, the most significant and that which doubtless would be responsible for the disappearance of the species, at least in the mountains would appear to be the abandonment of certain crop by our mountain dwellers. We must therefore be rather pessimistic as to the future of the rock partridge in the Alps. This is all the more so because this fine bird originates in Asia and lives in our mountains only in the western areas, and as it is in no way a descendant of the ice age like the black grouse and the ptarmigan it is not well adapted to the severity of the alpine winter.

Black redstart.

The beautiful rock partridge warms itself in the October sun.

3
Inhabitants of the scree, rocks and snow level

The rock thrush – the alpine chough – the chough – the alpine accentor – the snow finch – the chamois – the ptarmigan – the mountain hare – the dotterel – the wall creeper.

The rock thrush

On the 24th of May, in magnificent weather, the author again returned to the high pasturages and the first rocky outcrops of the foothills. There were still vast areas of snow here and there. In the strong sun they were, however, melting and formed in the hollow of the slopes streams which chattered noisily as they flowed towards the nearest torrent. At the author's feet could be seen black and gold lichen amongst which was growing the tiny carpet of dwarf azaleas. Their pink buds were almost ready to bloom. There were also other dwarf shrubs which had survived the long winter and were stubborn enough to exist in this desolate terrain, recalling the tundra of the Arctic north: the author saw the woody stems of the marsh bilberry, the tough leaves of the night-shade, the spiky leaves of heather all intermingled with the large dark patches of tiny juniper. All these plants were scattered thinly over the slope, while on the rocks the pink tufts of the furry primula and several types of saxifrage succeeded in growing in the cracks.

Blinded by the light and buffeted by the constant wind, the author had just taken a rest in the heart of this enormous kingdom when he suddenly heard a clear melodious song burst forth from somewhere in the heavens. Raising his eyes, the author finally spotted high up in the sky a rust-coloured bird, its wings spread in a triangle, apparently hovering in one spot. It was, however, in fact slowly rising with its tail

spread but without making any movement of its wings as it was carried upwards by the current of air, uttering its exquisite flute-like song. What a marvellous sight! Like a small flame, the unfamiliar shape continued its ascent. From time to time the beautiful bird rested for a little while, its wings and tail fully extended, while continuing its song, but it would then beat its wings and continue its ascent in triumph. Hearing this bird amongst these desolate surroundings of bilberries and snow, in the pure cold air of the mountains, the melody seemed to 'stab' the heart. How could one fail to react in this way in the vast loneliness of the Alps? The song, however, drew to a close and the bird began its gliding descent; the author watched as the bird described a graceful descending curve and returned to its familiar rocks. In a prudent and timid way the bird kept its distance . . . only through his binoculars could the author admire the orange colour of its breast and tail, the light blue of its back and head, the brown of its wings and the pure white of its crop: this was a male rock thrush.

A few moments earlier the bird had been performing its beautiful nuptial flight and the author searched, alas in vain, for the female, which is much more modest in colouring, its feathers being fawn, speckled with brown, gray and russet. It was pure chance which helped him to discover, a few weeks later, the nest of this bird, well concealed beneath a juniper bush amongst some rocks. The male rock thrush is certainly one of the jewels of our mountains and probably the most richly coloured alpine bird. The female, on the contrary, recalls a young black red-start, although its larger size, its squat shape, and its rather short tail allow it to be identified from the latter. The rock thrush is very timid and wild so that it is difficult to observe, especially as the bird normally lives in extremely wild surroundings where its rather dull plumage, in spite of the subtlety of the colours found in it, allows it to pass completely unnoticed. When disturbed, the rock thrush utters a cry of 'dak-dak' rather similar to the cry of the wheatear. Its call to its mate is a soft plaintive whistle somewhat similar to that of a bullfinch. The species is normally found in southern areas and loves the sun and warmth, the sun-warmed rocks and rocky meadows well above the tree line. It does not fear to venture at times up to an altitude of 9200 ft (2800 m). It is, however, often seen at much lower altitudes in the areas of hills where there are vineyards, provided that it can find rocky outcrops or steep rock faces with crevices where it can build its nest, away from the wild, harsh areas of scree.

The alpine chough

From the balcony of a mountain chalet, one looks down into the valley. There are still some patches of snow in the hollows in the fields near the village but the crocus is already invading the slopes where the pale grass has been crushed to the ground. In the mild air, one senses the astonishment of nature which suddenly becomes revealed after the long winter.

One suddenly hears a loud strident cry breaking the silence and sees thirty or so black birds gliding gracefully just above the slopes seeking a rising current of air. Soon they succeed in finding such a current and rise in slow spirals above the gray background of the larch trees and above the inky abyss. Their wings and tails are spread wide, looking like glistening fragments of metal in the blinding light and they constantly circle round each other, wheeling in the air, rising without any movement of their wings. They finally almost disappear in the clouds, climbing through the calm air, becoming nothing more than small black specks twisting in the immense blue space of the heavens. Suddenly, like a mist which clears, the flock of birds ends its circling movement and the black shapes, wings pressed close to their bodies, dive obliquely towards the earth from where they have started their flight. They seem almost like a hail of pebbles hurtling from the sky, moving in a few seconds from a height of 13 000 ft (4000 m) or more to the fields in the depths of the valley. As if attracted by some powerful lover, the birds fly just above the surface of the slope again, opening their wings together, so as to slow down their flight and allow them to settle on the grass over which they solemnly walk. The rear guard of the flock continues to keep a watchful eye on the others who have already reached the ground. From their yellow beaks, their jet-black plumage, their acrobatic flight and their loud cries you have immediately recognised that these are choughs, the famous little crows of the Alps which are always to be found near winter sport resorts, flying through the mountain skies.

To some extent these birds are for the mountains what the gulls are for the sea. They are masters of aerial acrobatics at high speed and their happy cries, a sort of cry-pitched loud rattle, together with their yellow beaks allow them to be easily distinguished from the other members of the dark-plumaged members of the crow family. The adults have coral-red feet, as opposed to the young which have blackish feet and a paler yellow beak during the first year of life. The chough is a typical inhabitant of the higher rocky cliffs of the mountains. Extremely sociable and gregarious by nature, it often nests in small colonies in suitable areas such as the crevices and depressions of inaccessible rock faces. Thanks to its speed in flight, this bird can in one day move from one area to a completely different one, moving in a few minutes from one altitude to another, varying by several thousand feet.

In winter the chough will assemble in large flocks near the winter resorts, or the towns and villages of the alpine valleys where they seek to survive by searching for food which has become scarce elsewhere. Their dark shapes can be seen flying over the streets filled with skiers, constantly examining the streets and paths in order to pick up litter of all sorts, or even settle on balconies to collect the crumbs which visitors may have left there. They become tame, although remaining prudent and utter their cries of alarm if a cat appears or if one of their number is shot. Towards three o'clock in the afternoon the choughs again gather together in large flocks — sometimes comprising several thousands — above the roofs where they have spent the morning. It is extremely interesting to watch them rise in ever ascending circles until they reach a great height. They will then return to their communal sleeping quarters, usually some rocky outcrop which serves as a shelter for the night and to which they become extremely attached during the winter months as they repeat the same operation described here every day at more or less the same time. This sort of winter migration is dictated first and foremost by the need for food. The alpine chough is very eclectic with regard to its diet; in spring and summer it eats many types of insects, worms and snails while in autumn fruit of every type become its favourite provender. When winter arrives, however, it will consume anything which it finds. The chough does not distain to eat the flesh of animals killed by falls of rock or snow and the author on one occasion surprised a number of them in the process of consuming the entrails of a large chamois, while succeeding in keeping at bay, thanks to their large numbers, two big ravens which were vainly trying to gain control of the carcass!

An alpine chough stopping in mid-flight.

The chough

The path leading to the high pasturage is rough, and only through endless twists and turns does it take one gradually to the foot of the high cliffs eroded by ice and wind. A marmot repeats its whistling cries, and a herd of chamois leave the slopes here which are now bathed in blinding light. At ones feet small crickets are seen making their escape while chirruping loudly. What can the bird be, however, which is making so much noise amongst the rocks uttering a cry of 'jiar! jiar! jiar!'? The cries have something similar to those of a jackdaw, but at such an altitude it could certainly not be such a bird, and even less an alpine chough whose loud whistling cries are known to you! These are metallic, nasal sounds of 'jiar! jiar!' The cries can be heard now further away, echoing through the surrounding rocks ... finally two black birds fly from the high rock face rising in spirals, with wings spread wide as if they were suspended in the blue sky. At such a distance the shape is very similar to that of the alpine chough; the wings however appear a little longer and wider, while the feathers seem separated from each other at the end of the wings; the tail is shorter. Suddenly the two birds close their wings and hurtle dizzily towards the ground, stopping their flight suddenly only a few feet away from the earth and settling gracefully on the sloping ground. They walk solemnly up and down over the grass, pecking at grasshoppers or beetles from time to time. It is immediately apparent that their beaks are much longer than is the case with the alpine chough and they are coral-red as are their feet; on their feathers can be seen a bluish green or even purple sheen. These details make it possible to recognise the species – it is the chough. The bird, which is the closest relation to the alpine chough, is becoming rarer in the Alps for reasons which are still obscure, while the latter has been more and more frequently found during the last ten years. The habits of the chough and the alpine chough are very similar except that the former lives in isolation at breeding times, practically never nesting in colonies, at least at high altitudes. Apart from its special cries which allows it to be recognised from far off and the fact that it is diminishing in number, the chough can be distinguished from its cousin by another factor: it is as much at home in certain areas of the Alps at a height of more than 6600 ft (2000 m) as on the seaside cliffs of the Brittany coast where, for example, a large colony has been established at Cap Sizun! The species inhabits rock faces wherever they are and even on occasion lives in ruins or in the holes in the walls of old castles. This is particularly the case in the Grisons area. It is a fortunate chance to find the chough in the Alps, especially as it is more timid than the alpine chough and keeps away from man, spending the night in communal sleeping areas which are inaccessible, apart from the period when mating takes place.

The alpine accentor

In those areas where there are constant winds and mists, where there is no soil, no tree, hardly any moss and only few blades of grass, there, at the heart of this kingdom of stone and silence can be heard at times a loud, melodious voice. And one will only see a large timid bird resembling a sparrow hopping over the ground amongst the lichens and the occasional blade of grass, fluttering its tail. On looking at the bird more closely, it will be seen that it has a delicate pointed beak, russet touches on the sides of its body, white borders to its wings, thin greyish stripes on its tail and a dull brown appearance to the rest of the plumage: such is the appearance of the alpine accentor. This bird chooses desolate areas as others prefer more inhabited regions; it would seem that the alpine accentor needs this chaotic rocky terrain, these stony deserts eroded by ice, these golden and rust coloured lichens and this dazzling sunlight. Here, in the immense solitude of the rocky spaces the accentor really feels at home. It is here that in springtime this bird utters its loud, bold cry; it is here that its mating passion causes it to rise in the sky like a lark; it is here that it shakes its wings, displays its tail, displays its breast to the light and returns to rest on its rock after a few moments of flight ... When it stands without moving on its rock, like some grey spot, lost in its surroundings, the bird seems to be beyond time and space. Silence again reigns supreme in the mountains and there is only a yellow flower to relieve the monotony of the stones where everything seems very close to eternity.

Suddenly, the bird's song breaks out again, loud and cheerful, as two shapes fly away into the sky, pursuing each other in rapid flight, while throwing into the abyss their hoarse cries, 'drui! drui! diriwi! duri! diriwi!' It is difficult to separate these cries from the stony desert, the mounds of catch-fly plants, the last stretches of grass. There is, in these cries, the melody of the rocks, the lichens, the brittle grass, the melody of the wind and the clouds blending with that more intense melody of the tiny gentians growing at the edge of the snow ... the song of the accentor seems a little unpolished, recalling the song of the lark, but although it may be a simple expression of joy it is all the more moving in the harsh surroundings of the mountains. No other song reflects so well the wild atmosphere and the gentle desolation of the high pasturage. There the chatter of the stream blends with the noise of falls of stones and the general calm is only occasionally disturbed by the cry of an alpine chough or the whistling of a marmot! The alpine accentor is so well suited to its rocky existence that it seems to have taken on the colours of its surroundings, the colours of the earth and the rocks. Doubtless this bird would pass largely unnoticed if it were not for its song. The author has often discovered its nest built either in a crack of a rock or beneath a large stone in an outcrop. They were found at varying altitudes, sometimes higher than 10000 ft (3000 m)! The nest is made of dry grass, moss, and lichens and the interior, which is quite deep, is decorated with feathers or hair. In winter heavy falls of snow force the accentor to descend to the foothills or even into the villages where it becomes tame, spending the very cold nights in barns feeding off crumbs which are left on balconies. Mountain dwellers know the bird well and use it as a sort of barometer; not without reason, incidentally, as its appearance near man is almost always followed by heavy snowfalls.

An alpine chough in winter.

Alpine accentor.

A male rock thrush with its young.

The snow finch

Once again the author is climbing up one of those steep valleys in the Umbrintzes, filling his lungs with pure mountain air. Surrounding the rocky scree through which he is climbing, there are on every side fissured rocks, high cliffs, and immense black boulders lying chaotically over the steep slope; chaos seems to reign supreme here and water from the snows runs down over the old lichen-covered granite on every side. In the smallest cracks in the rock there clings miraculously either a tuft of moss or strange tiny flowers; there are tufts of catch-fly and saxifrages; tiny cushions of pink and white *androsaces*, delicate corollae of *Ranunculus glacialis*, blue gentian and tufts of *linaria* which seek to hold back the loose stones in the gully.

A few grey and white feathers together with some brown droppings which the author finds on his path show him that he has already entered the realm of the snow partridge. Today, however, he is looking for another bird and continues his climb. Two black and white birds fly from a nearby rock face and circle over the author's head, uttering plaintive cries; these are the snow finches! The presence of the author in this place seems to intrigue them greatly. They fly backwards and forwards over his head continuously uttering their nasal cries, while they are sometimes carried upwards on currents of air, by stretching their broad wings, and at other times fly from one rock to another like great twin-coloured butterflies. The sight is fascinating and extremely beautiful. One of the birds settles on a boulder quite close to the author and its cries and rattling noises become more intense. Doubtless the author is near the nest, as this would explain the bird's agitation! The bird has the appearance and size of a large sparrow, its head being grey, its beak and throat black (in autumn the beak is yellow with only its point black) and its back brownish, while its breast is pale. As soon as it lands on the boulder, the snow finch seems to merge into the background. The large white and black patches of its wings and tails, which are clearly visible in flight, are reduced to a thin white stripe which is itself bordered by the dark outline of the large wings and the median tail feathers, giving to the bird's plumage a general drab appearance which blends well with the rocks and lichens amongst which it spends the greater part of its life. As soon as the snow finch flies into the air, however, its marvellous striped appearance creates an extraordinary effect! At the end of summer, when these birds collect together in large flocks and circle continuously near the high rock faces, they seem to be flakes of hoar-frost caught up in the wind, or the first snow flakes of an early autumn. The mountains are their true home, the mountains with their ice and moraine, their rocks and sparse grass and their long silences. There, at the heart of these deserts of stone, in some secret crevice, well sheltered from the wind, the snow finch builds its nest. It raises its young there and animates the wild solitude with its presence and cries. Its flight has inherited from the ice something of its whiteness and it is possibly only the snow finch, together with the ptarmigan, which enliven the greyness of the mountain scree.

The chamois

Few wild animals have aroused as much passion in the heart of the hunter as this noble antelope with its highly strung movements, its incomparable sense of smell and its extreme prudence. The rôle which the chamois has played and still plays in the life of the mountain dweller is extremely important. All those who have observed this animal from afar or at close range know how difficult it is to take by surprise a herd of chamois. In spite of a thousand precautions, some of the animals always succeed in detecting one's presence. Even carefully concealed behind a rocky ridge, one will still remain at the mercy of every change of wind. How many careful approaches have been doomed to failure through the noise of stone or even the brief reflection from the camera in the sunlight. It is true that in our national parks or reserves certain of these creatures seem much tamer than elsewhere; however, they still keep their distance with regard to man and will never display the same confidence as the ibex.

The shape of the horns of the chamois, curved back into a hook, allow it to be distinguished immediately from the female of the ibex and even from any other related species, i.e. the species *rupicaprini*. The chamois combines grace with strength, shapeliness and agility with robustness. The latter is revealed in the powerful muscles of its body and its legs which are capable of extraordinary movements. It is very well adapted to the demands of its habitat and is much more resistant to the rigours of winter than is the roe-deer. Unlike the ibex, the chamois avoids the sun and, in the warm months, seeks out the coolness of the snow fields or slopes facing north. In winter, its magnificent black fur, to which is added a thick level of down, protects it from even the most severe cold. The author has seen during an extremely cold January how the animal sought out the shade when a weak glimmer of sunlight reached the sparsely wooded ridge where it was seeking with great difficulty the little food that was available.

One November day, the author was making as rapid progress as possible through the high pasturage of Anniviers, searching for the mountain hare. Some snow had fallen on the previous day and numerous traces quickly lead him to the form of the hare. One specimen, almost entirely white, relied on its camouflage and lay close to the ground, its ears pressed down against its back, allowing the author to approach within a few yards. Suddenly, the animal bounded down the slope, while the author, with the aid of his automatic camera, succeeded in taking a dozen shots, one after the other. A little later, the fresh tracks of the hare led him to the top of a hillock. From there, to his great surprise, he could see at a distance of less than 650 ft (200 m) a splendid herd of chamois. The animals had not yet noticed him and he quickly hid behind the first rock he found. It was impossible to approach any closer from any direction. His shadow on the snow even at that distance would have quickly alarmed them and the only solution was to wait patiently. Towards eleven o'clock the troop moved north, very slowly, into a depression which the author knew well. He immediately profited from this new situation; keeping down-wind from the animals, he succeeded in getting to within 230 ft (70 m) of the herd. There were about fifteen females with their young, some young adults and a large male which was guarding the herd jealously. Many of the animals were lying down and chewing peacefully while others indulged in playful frolics, scratching the powdery snow in their search for some vegetation; others were pushing against each other energetically. The author had never seen such fine black winter coats, so warm in contrast to the snow which was on all sides, dazzling in its brightness, and he had never enjoyed so much this splendid sight in the vast white desert, fresh and silent: the freshness seemed to be the pure breath of the mountain.

The large male was a splendid specimen, with its long mane floating from its withers to its crop, its white face and cheeks standing out clearly against the black body, as they were bordered by a black band which extended from the nostrils to the ears, circling its fine fierce eyes. Its black horns, although they were not very large, were thicker and different to those of the female, as they seemed much more curled. The male was in the process of rubbing his horns against a small twisted larch. By doing this he was marking out his territory; in the rutting season, which reaches its climax in November, two special glands which are placed behind the horns secrete a sebaceous liquid which has a strong smell and allows the large males to announce their presence to any possible rivals. The attitudes adopted by the males in this period reveal their sexual excitement. Presently, the male which the author was observing from behind a rock, having rubbed its horns against the bush for some time, sniffed the place which had recently been occupied by a female. Then the male opened its mouth, drew back its lips a little, put out its tongue and stretched its front legs forward in an attitude of great satisfaction. It sniffed the odours reaching its nostrils with delight and its shape again changed; its mane stood up on end and it seemed that the animal was wearing a large great-coat: finally the beast gave a soft bleat, rasping and tremulous which, however, echoed strangely in the silence and expressed his desires quite clearly. He then approached the first female who rose, then squatted down and urinated. Was the author going to witness the action of mating? Unfortunately no! The male advanced a few paces but the female walked off and the same action as had previously taken place were repeated, the beast drawing back its lips, pushing out its tongue and raising its mane to its maximum.

If another male approaches the area and comes too close to the group, the master of the territory will not hesitate to chase him off and this gives rise to headlong pursuit through the snow. The animals hurtle at full speed down steep slopes, overcoming every obstacle. The author has seen some of these animals literally jump into space, making enormous leaps. They are so hardy, however, and agile, that they always seem to land on their feet. Occasionally two males of the same strength join in battle. Although such battles are rare, they become extremely fierce and sometimes only end with serious injuries on both sides; very often the furious males try to strike each other under the stomach with their horns and one of the adversaries will retire with his abdomen pierced; when this happens the animal will die after some days of terrible suffering.

The chamois spend the greater part of the winter in the forest and sometimes descend right into the valleys, driven by hunger. They will eat anything at such times, tearing at the bushes of juniper and rhododendron and scratching at the thick snow for hours in order to reach some sparse vegetation. Sometimes they will attack even the bark of the trees beneath which they sometimes remain trapped for several days on end. The weakest and oldest will perish. Others will be crushed by avalanches. At the end of winter those animals which have survived all these tribulations will greedily fall on the first spring shoots which appear. The animals are very thin and still carry their thick winter coat, but this soon becomes discoloured and takes on some pinkish tinges.

In May and June moulting takes place and large tufts of hair remain attached to rocks and bushes. At the beginning of July most of the chamois have developed their summer coat which is much shorter and more or less russet in colour, although sometimes it can be pale greyish fawn. The legs remain darker as does the dorsal stripe. From mid-May at high altitudes and a little sooner at lower altitudes pregnant females retire to isolated spots, often beneath bushes, in order to give birth to a single offspring; twin births are very rare. The author has twice witnessed birth taking place. The mother first shows signs of agitation and lies down and gets up constantly; after this birth takes place very quickly and the newly-born animal is licked by the mother for a considerable time, and it starts to take milk as soon as it has strength to do so. Less than four hours later the young creature is standing firmly on its legs which are often much longer than those of the young ibex; it is already capable of following its mother for short distances. Another three days and it will be able to escape from man although it still keeps close to its mother who sometimes takes it very far from its birthplace and defends it bravely against attacks by the eagle.

The Pyrenean chamois is only a geographical variation of the alpine chamois. It is a little smaller than the latter and its horns are more slender. Its coat is always lighter in colour and the animal seems more at home on bare slopes than in the forest.

A snow finch in October.

A chamois in November
at rutting time.

A buck sniffing
the odours of
a female.

The alpine ptarmigan

As a true relic of the ice age, the presence of the ptarmigan in the Alps and the Pyrenees can only be explained by the retreat of the great ice age glaciers. Instead of returning to the north, together with the reindeer and the musk ox, certain of these birds found in these mountains a climate which was suitable and so inhabited them. They have remained up to the present as if they were living on Arctic islands surrounded by the temperate zone.

The ptarmigan is consequently a bird which lives throughout the year at the highest altitude. Not only is it admirably adapted to the cold but, even in summer, this bird seems to have a sense of nostalgia for its original homeland. To observe the ptarmigan one must be very patient, cross desolate areas, climb steep gullies, wander at length through rough stony ground or over slopes with sparse vegetation which recall the tundra of the north. For the person who loves solitude and needs to return to wild nature, however, the search for the ptarmigan in the vast deserted areas of the mountains can be one of the most exciting adventures in the world. The searcher finds himself amongst the mossy stones covered with lichens and saxifrage; he will derive great pleasure from the flight of the snow finch, the harsh cry of the accentor, the joyful whistle of the chough. He will be cold, hungry and tired; his heart will beat fast and he will be short of breath as he will have to climb hard until he finds the first feathers left by the birds amongst the rocks, or its droppings near the cushions of moss, or, finally, the tracks it will leave on the melting snow. Suddenly, a miracle will occur! The bird which has been invisible, coloured as it is like the rocks and the lichens, will suddenly spread two white wings and, with a loud rasping cry, will fly away from under his feet.

Then the searcher will know that all his efforts have been worthwhile. The ptarmigan, instead of spreading its wings and flying away from the slope, may well settle in front of him and walk with hurried or slow steps depending on whether it is alarmed or feels confident. Sometimes it is so trusting that the observer can walk right up to it and study this small grey or beige coloured bird which walks before him, tail raised, like a living piece of the landscape.

This bird, which still surprises the naturalist, moults three times every year and, like the mountain hare, becomes completely white in November, apart from its tail which remains black throughout the year. When the bird is at rest, the dark tail is more or less completely hidden by its caudal, white feathers. The male ptarmigan also has a black band from its beak to the eye, extending a little beyond the latter. In spite of this black patch, however, the bird blends so well with its background in winter that one must have very keen sight in order to spot it through the binoculars when surveying the high, snowy slopes which it chooses as its habitat.

In mid-April, at the same time as the mountain hare and the stoat start to moult, the immaculate plumage of the ptarmigan becomes marked with brownish feathers, while the wattles of the male become red; the female acquires beige coloured feathers mottled with black. This spring moult starts at the head and the neck and develops through the breast, the sides and the caudal feathers, finishing with the back and a part of the wings. Towards the end of May or in mid-June, according to the altitude, the bird will acquire its nuptial plumage and will then, in the case of the male, have dark brown feathers over the upper surfaces of the body while the stomach remains white; the female will be more russet in colour and moults more rapidly than its companion. Both sexes will keep throughout the summer the greater part of their wings covered in white feathers. At the approach of an enemy or when it is at rest, the ptarmigan in its summer costume will take great care to conceal the lighter parts of its plumage. The feathers at the base of the wings, those of the back and the stomach in the case of the female completely conceal the white wings; the male will crouch down on the ground, to conceal its white stomach. In summer the bird will only take flight when forced to do so and then it will suddenly spread its white wings

The mountain hare of the Alps

while uttering its wild, guttural, rasping cry. The layman is always greatly surprised by such an event.

In September the ptarmigan moults again and becomes much greyer on its upper areas, more pronounced in the case of the male, while the area covered by the white stomach feathers increases in size. The thread-like feathers which cover the feet of the bird as far as its claws thicken and remain white. This autumn plumage lasts for only a short time and as soon as the first frosts arrive the 'snow partridge' becomes progressively whiter. Towards the end of October or in mid-November most of the ptarmigan and hares in the Alps will have regained their immaculate winter coats.

In winter the ptarmigan lives in small groups and will spend the night beneath the powdery snow, digging out with its claws a sort of shelter in which it is completely protected from the wind and extreme cold of the high altitudes where it lives. In order to avoid its principal enemy — the fox — at this time of the year, the ptarmigan lands directly on the lower slopes and disappears beneath the snow in a few moments; it will only reappear at dawn the following day if the storm has ended.

In the early morning the solitary skier may witness a rare sight: one after the other small white balls pierce the powdery snow and suddenly appear on the vast snowfields which had appeared absolutely empty; they immediately start to move and, to obtain their food, search the ridges which had been swept clear of snow by the wind. Thanks to their extremely strong constitution and their capacity to store in their crops large quantities of grass, lichen and leaves from bushes, the ptarmigan can remain throughout the year in the mountains at an altitude where no other bird could survive. This is a true miracle of nature, a perfect adaptation not only to the severe alpine climate, but also, when one thinks of the four annual moults of this bird, to the appearance or disappearance of snow in the mountains.

The mountain hare, together with the ptarmigan, are the animals which the author knows best, having hunted them for several years and subsequently photographed and filmed them to his heart's content. Having studied the hare in the vast desolate spaces which it chooses for its habitat during the greater part of the year, the author has been able to make a close study of its ways of life and its extraordinary shyness. He admits that without the numerous tracks left by the mountain hare on the fresh snow during its nightly wanderings, it would have been impossible for him to track it down in the majority of cases. Even with the tracks to help him he still needed to interpret the criss-cross of the marks and understand its way of life in order to find its home on the enormous stony slopes which it chooses as its favourite habitat. The author is not really sure what interests him most about this strange animal; would it be its skilful knowledge of camouflage, its astonishing adaptation to the cold and snow, the changes in colour of its fur from season to season, or its special shyness which allows it to avoid man with a skill which is worthy of great admiration? Doubtless it is a combination of all these gifts.

If one wishes to search for the hare, one must leave behind the town and the village and that civilisation which is gradually poisoning us. One must also leave the well-trodden paths and set out across country beyond the last large trees and reach those desolate regions where the rocks, the wind and the silence share the immense space between themselves. When this is done, however, the lungs breathe in fresh air, the blood is cleared of the miasma of the plain, the muscles become supple again and everything seems to find its original beauty and inner significance.

Nothing can be more exhilarating than the discovery of this small mountain hare, which, at the end of the ice age, retired both to the Arctic north, its true origin, and to the alpine heights where it remained as if on some Arctic island, surrounded by the temperate zone. Other species, also of nordic origin, took the same action and retired to our mountains; such as the ptarmigan, the redpoll, the tengmalm's owl, which is so warmly covered that it can withstand the most severe cold, and the pygmy owl, smallest of the nocturnal birds of prey, together with many others.

One October morning, the author was striding over the first pasturages of Anniviers. The weather was superb; it had snowed the previous day and the author found innumerable tracks of wild animals. He spotted the regular marks of the fox in search of the vole, the tracks of the claws of a black grouse which had left the trees in order to reach the foothills and the supple double tracks of the beech marten amongst the snow-covered stones. There were many small tracks made by the accentor hopping over the slopes and innumerable tracks of the hare in the powdery snow which was already sparkling around the juniper bushes and the occasional rocks found along the slope. Most of these tracks, however, disappeared into the trees and in order to observe them more closely the author had to climb higher. Stopping on a small outcrop, he scanned the white spaces of snow before the sunlight made such an operation blinding. On the foothills tracks of the hare had already become so rare that it was possible to judge whether the animal had remained in the open spaces or retired to the shelter of a rock. This preparatory work is important; it allows the observer to save precious time and avoid spending hours walking over the treacherous snow. He suddenly saw a single set of tracks climbing from the forest towards the hollow of a small valley facing south. There the hare circled several times on the right side of the valley where there were numerous boulders and rocky outcrops. From where he stood it was impossible for the author to locate the form of the hare, as the tracks went back on themselves several times amongst the large rocks. One thing, however, could be said: the animal was not very far away, as the higher areas of the valley were empty of any tracks. Encouraged by these signs, the author reached the spot twenty minutes later. He avoided following the tracks too closely as this would arouse the suspicions of the animal, but made a detour in order to arrive above the spot where he thought it would be. All efforts to track down the animal were, however, in vain. Sometimes the hare remained crouching on the snow, its eyes half closed, in full sunlight, usually near some natural depression in the ground where it can take refuge at the least sign of danger. In this grey and white background, however, where the light had become blinding, it was no easy task to find the animal, especially as the author's shadow could have alarmed it. If it was an adult hare, its fur would be almost white by the end of October and the animal would take care to flatten its ears against its back and shut its eyes so that it would blend perfectly with its background. If, on the other hand, it was a young creature, the animal would be moulting and would have a greyish appearance, its head being beige. The author has seen young hares still completely brown in the middle of November as they always moult later than the adults. This autumn moulting, however, does vary according to regions, altitude, and weather. It can also vary from one individual to another and lasts for a shorter time than the spring moult.

Temperature influences the autumn and spring moult of the mountain hare and also affects the colour of its fur in summer, but experiments carried out by Russian physiologists have shown that other facets also influence this change in colour, in particular the increase or decrease in the periods of daylight. By exposing a number of captive mountain hares to artificial light for eighteen hours each day, the Russians succeeded in causing the spring moult to begin in January. The problem is therefore extremely complex and far from being fully understood, as during the spring moult, the colouring of the fur seems to be closely linked with the appearance of certain hormones in the organism.

Let us, however, return to our story. Thanks to the detour which the author had made, he was able to dominate the right side of the valley where the animal had built its form. Scanning the tracks with his binoculars, the author established that this mountain hare had chosen his resting place for the day with great care; not only had it retraced its steps several times as if to conceal its tracks, but the presence of numerous stones all over the slope provided several possible hiding places. For a time the author searched in vain. The hare must certainly have chosen a large stone and would leave its retreat only at the last moment. Generally speaking, the rocks which it chooses provide two exits and the animal would only leave its hiding place at the last moment when the author would be very close. The thicker the snow, the more reluctant the hare will be to leave. Sometimes the hare refuses to leave its shelter, either because the form has only one entrance or because a marmot's hole has allowed it to disappear beneath the ground. The mountain hare, which never digs a refuge, often uses the hole of the marmot when it is wounded or closely pursued by dogs, or frightened by man. The young often do this by instinct and find a form close to such a hole to which they retire when alarmed. If there is thick, fresh snow and strong sunlight, the mountain hare has a tendency to hide beneath stones rather than leap into the open air. This is a habit which is often fickle as poachers, on skis or snowshoes, can capture it by hand without difficulty as the animal is trapped in a crack or hollow of an easily accessible rock. When the animal is dragged out of its hiding place by its back legs, it utters plaintive cries which sound something like those of a child. It tries to bite its attacker and wriggles and defends itself with great energy. Its magnificent winter coat dazzlingly white apart from the end of its ears which remain black comes out when given the slightest tug, a fact which often saves the animal from the claws or teeth of carnivorous animals like the stone marten or the fox.

Carrying his camera with a telephoto lens, the author decided to approach the hare's tracks, forcing the animal to leave its shelter. The snow was not very thick and he felt certain that he would see the animal leap out of its form when he was quite close to it. On occasions the author has approached to within a few feet of the mountain hare as it remained crouched on the ground, relying on its extraordinary camouflage for protection. However, after a fresh fall of snow, becomes more prudent, especially if its fur has ne

A female
ptarmigan
running in
the fresh
snow during
winter.

A male
during the
spring moult
(May).

An alpine
ptarmigan
in its
September
plumage.

completely moulted. The author slowly descended the slope which was more difficult than he had expected, as the powdery snow concealed holes in the ground into which he sometimes put his feet, almost losing his balance. It was essential for him to survey constantly the area around him, from which the animal could leap at any moment. After a few more steps, two brown ears suddenly appeared from behind a rock less than 20 ft (6 m) away; they were twitching and betrayed the alarm of the hare; the author just had time to focus his telephoto lens when a greyish body suddenly hurtled out onto the snow as if from a catapult.

The mountain hare in full moult escaped up the slope with enormous leaps, using every fold of the terrain and the occasional boulder to conceal itself from the author's sight. The entire event only took a few seconds, but the author succeeded in taking several pictures of the animal in full flight thanks to an automatic spring which allowed the camera to take a dozen shots in rapid succession. After such nervous tension the author felt a great sense of relief. He sat down on a large boulder facing the marvellous scenery and took a few moments' rest. The sun was high overhead, the snow was starting to melt and a wonderful silence surrounded him, while the blinding light made it essential to wear sun-glasses. Two choughs flew overhead while several snow finches appeared over a neighbouring ridge; the larches at the edge of the first meadows seem to encircle the mountain with colours of yellow and gold.

There was no point in pursuing the hare. The author knew by experience that it would not go very far away, especially as its fur was still brownish in parts so that its legs stood out against the snow and could betray its presence to its enemies in the sky, the golden eagle and the goshawk. It would be better to wait until the animal settled down. Thanks to its fresh tracks, he would be able to find it again without any difficulty. This proved to be the case and he tracked down the animal twice during the afternoon, although, as it was already aware of his presence, it left its form each time while the author was a certain distance away. This, however, was of no great importance as at the end of the day when he returned to the village, he was delighted with his day's work.

The movements of the mountain hare when seen for the first time are always quite astonishing. The long back legs push the body along with great speed and, while moving forward, frame the front legs while these are leaving the ground. At this moment all four legs are clear of the snow. At the end of the move-

ment the rear legs, when they touch the powdery snow, are still in front of the front legs. Because of the length of its back legs, which are of great advantage when climbing, the mountain hare always tries to escape uphill. No other animal of the Alps leaves such characteristic tracks on the fresh snow. These tracks can also vary in appearance according to their freshness, the condition of the snow, the weather or the speed of the animal. When it is moving normally and going about its business under the starry sky, the mountain hare leaves two parallel tracks on the snow, having the shape of small slippers. These prints, which are those of the back legs, can never be confused with those which follow them closely. The front feet are smaller, closer together and always leave their imprints on the snow behind those of the back legs, one being a little further forward than the other.

It is, consequently, always possible with the help of binoculars to establish even at a great distance, whether the animal which you are following is climbing or descending the slope. Moreover, due to the thick tufts of hair which surround the pads of its feet, the mountain hare can cross any type of deep snow without sinking in very far.

Weighing only half as much as its larger cousin, the brown hare of Europe, it seems much better suited than the latter to the harsh climate of our mountains and the author has often surprised it at night searching for its food no matter what the weather was like. In addition its front paws have toes which are able to spread out like snow shoes, thus enabling it to cross the powdery snow easily. During severe storms the brown hare is obliged to dig tunnels beneath the snow in order to reach its food and protect itself from the cold, and from its numerous enemies. It appears, therefore, to suffer many disadvantages in comparison to the mountain hare although the author has seen the brown hare on occasions, in the depths of winter, at a height of 9200 ft (2800 m) – an exceptional altitude for the species in the winter months!

In winter the majority of mountain hares leave the high pasturage and the foothills in order to seek shelter on the wooded escarpments, where the low branches of the pine trees give it sure shelter. If compelled to do so, the mountain hare digs an ill-defined hole in the snow and hides there during the day. But as soon as the snow has piled up, its tracks can again be seen on those ridges blown clear of snow where rtain of them go regularly each night to search for arce nourishment. The author has seen the moun-in hare at this time of year scratch away at the ow with its paws, to discover the tufts of dwarf nipers which it eats down to their roots. Moreover, illow trees attract them and they even eat the bark id sometimes complete branches. This meagre od, nevertheless, seems to be enough to enable the ountain hare to survive all the rigours of winter ithout great harm. As soon as the fine weather turns some of them are to be found on the south cing slopes well above the last trees. The author on e occasion disturbed them from their forms at) 500 ft (3200 m) in January. That was a record! thers, on the contrary, descend during the winter to e depths of the valleys to a height of less than)00 ft (1000 m) and live near villages, crossing icy reams and wandering through the copses of alders id larch trees, and areas of fallow land, in search of eds which the snow may have left exposed there. ertain of them never return to the desolate ridges, it live permanently in the depths of the forest cover-g the north and northwest slopes of the Alps. In immer the mountain hare, like the ptarmigan, main-ins a certain longing for the ice and cold, as it ways seeks out shady copses, damp scree and eas near glaciers, sometimes wandering well yond the limits of vegetation to a height of almost 3 000 ft (4000 m)!

The spring moult begins in April. Dark coloured air, which is either brown or beige, progressively vers the head, the neck, shoulders, back and finally e sides and thighs of the animal, finishing with the et, the ears and the tail. This moult lasts much nger than the autumn moult and the author has en in mid-June at a height of 8900 ft (2700 m), a ountain hare which was still half white.

Bad weather can hold back the spring moult and e sun hastens it, as very often in April and May the uthor has seen through his binoculars hares spread it in the full sunlight in front of their forms, trying to asten the fall of the winter fur.

The mountain hare is much more widely dis-ibuted than the common European brown hare and ometimes breeds with the latter. In fact, in many re-ons, particularly in the meadows of Anniviers in the alais the two species live together. The author once w in the middle of winter a hare with a very pale at whose morphological characteristics where omewhere between those of the alpine mountain are and the common brown hare. These hybrids are erile and cannot therefore produce a new species.

The dotterel

One fine autumn morning the author left the village, crossed the forest and the first meadows to reach the nearest ridge. As he reached the summit a bird which he had not noticed before left the short grass almost at his feet, uttering a plaintive cry. He followed it with his eyes and saw to his great surprise that it settled not far away. With its wings only slightly folded the bird immediately merged with the background, and the author understood why it had escaped his notice a few moments previously. The bird remained motionless and seemed to be the size of a thrush, but with longer legs, a rounded head and its neck set low in its chest. It observed the author with curiosity while the latter studied it through his binoculars. The back and wings of the bird were entirely covered with a kind of blackish scale on a background of coffee coloured feathers. The top of its head was also speck-led and there was a wide yellowish eyebrow extend-ing towards the bottom of the neck, separated from the greyish cheeks by a black line. Its breast was pale brown and the general effect was neutral, a fact which allowed the bird to blend so well with its back-ground. It settled down onto the ground and became almost invisible amongst the grass and the lichen. The author thought he was dreaming, but the bird was still there within the field of his binoculars, and the author's curiosity increased. He had never seen this bird previously and wondered what it could be doing there so high in the mountains where it had come from and what made it so confident. It had something about it similar to a small wader and this intrigued the author greatly. He took out his camera and approached the bird slowly. Less than 30 ft (10 m) away the bird was still motionless and the author's surprise grew . . . The noise of the shutter did not frighten it until, when he finally approached too closely, it rose, reluctantly, took a few paces, turned to look at the author again, and hopped further away, only to stop again, start off once more and finally disappear behind the nearest rock. Such confidence and familiarity was really most disarming! Its walk and shape reminded the author of a small plover which he had once seen on the banks of the Haute Rhône. Of course this bird was much bigger and walked more slowly, while its behaviour and plumage were different. It must, however, be some sort of a plover but which sort? The author did not know, but was determined to find out. Taking endless precau-tions, he approached the rock behind which the bird

The progressive spring moult of a mountain hare from April to June. In summer, its fur becomes reddish-brown in colour.

A mountain hare in its seat: winter coat.

A dotterel in autumn during
its crossing of the Alps.

The wall creeper

This is the rare bird of our rocks, the born climber and
the bird which is found at the highest altitude in the
Alps. (Doctor J. Burnier of Geneva has observed it at
13 304 ft (4055 m) at Bernina in the Grisons.) The
bird is not only a unique species of its kind, but is con-
fined to the high rock faces of Europe and Asia. It
seems to have been specially created for the part and
everything is unusual about it, not least its scientific
name of *Tichodroma*, which derives from the Greek
'teikos' (well) and 'droma' (running rapidly). Its fluttering flight recalls a large moth rather than a bird.

The rocks seem to have been created for the wall
creeper rather than the reverse. It should also be
noted that not any ordinary rock face is acceptable to
the bird, only the true, high, mountain rock face, that
strange fantasy of rock and ice, suspended like some
lost paradise between the abyss of the lower snows
and the blue sky. It is there, amongst the granite
crags which jut into the sky, amongst the fissured
rocks, trickling with water, that the wall creeper feels
itself at home.

There you will see this bird, running up and down
the rocks, like a little mouse; with its grey and black
spot, lost against the immense rock wall. Suddenly
the bird flies away from the stones, its broad wings
half open, fluttering for a moment above empty
space, revealing the beautiful carmine red, speckled
with pearls, which decorates its wings. Seen from
above this sudden burst of fire, against the greyness
of the rocks, creates an extraordinary effect. It is all
the more surprising as nothing about the humble bird
seen a few moments earlier leads one to expect the
blossoming of colour and startling beauty. The wall
creeper suddenly closes its fan and again merges
with the rocks, disappearing into its background. It
needs a very skilled eye to follow this bird and spot
the grey patch, looking like a piece of moving lichen
as it starts its ceaseless climbing again. Observing it
through binoculars, it can be seen how it squeezes
into narrow cracks, crosses the smoothest rock faces
with ease and hangs on the most frightening vertical

had hidden, and walked round it with his telephoto
lens in his hand. However, he could see nothing. Suddenly, a slight rustle of wings behind him, followed by
a soft tremulous cry, announced the disaster which
had taken place. He had scarcely enough time to turn
and see the bird fly over the slope with movements
which were both graceful and powerful, then disappear in the first fold in the terrain. The author knew he
would never see this small wader again in the Alps
and sought the bird in vain for the rest of the day.
When he returned to the village, an ornithological
book threw some light on his rare encounter: it was a
dotterel. From the book the author discovered that
this bird nests in the high tundra of Scotland, Scandinavia, Lapland, the north of Russia and Central
Asia. The dotterel, when migrating in autumn, likes to
rest for a while on the grassy high alpine meadows
and the specimen which the author had photographed on that memorable day was without any
doubt a bird of passage. The European dotterel
spends the winter in the south-east of the Mediterranean region, in the vicinity of the Red Sea and on
the coast of the Persian Gulf.

or even overhanging surfaces, acting like an acrobat and constantly using its long claws, while it opens and shuts its wings rapidly, as if driven by some nervous impulse. While moving in this way, the bird sometimes shows something of its red fan, speckled with pearl-like white spots, which stands out against the slate-grey wing feathers.

Very timid by nature, the wall creeper normally builds its nest in inaccessible crevices, if possible near a waterfall or a stream, between 2000 and 9200 ft (600 and 2800 m). If it is not disturbed it remains faithful to the site of its choice. This excellent climber announces its presence in the spring by strange whistling cries which sound almost human. The melodious sound, uttered loudly in this harsh, rocky landscape of the mountains is all the more pleasant to hear, as it often accompanies the rock climber during his ascent, encouraging him to persevere. With its long, slightly curved beak, the wall creeper constantly explores crevices, mossy cracks and every unevenness in the rocks, feeding on the insects and larvae which are hidden there. Always suspended between heaven and earth, constantly buffetted by the wind, repulsed by the ice, this bird with carmine, pearl-speckled grey wings still continues with its teasing, whistling cry and its constant climbing in search of food. In winter it often descends to the plains, where it explores not only the rock faces of the alpine foot-hills, but also the walls of old towers and castles.

A male wall creeper
bringing butterflies to its brood.

165

3
endangered species

A European brown bear
caught unawares by the photographer.

1
Endangered and extinct species of the Alps and Pyrenees

The brown bear – the wolf – the wild cat – the bearded vulture – the otter – the eagle owl – the peregrine falcon – the griffon vulture – the Egyptian vulture – the lynx – the mouflon or wild sheep – the ibex or wild goat.

The brown bear

The fauna of the Alps, although extremely rich in variety even today, cannot be compared, unfortunately, with what it was only two centuries ago. Several large carnivorous animals, which formerly played an important part have now totally disappeared from our mountains, following the advance of civilisation and the improvement in guns. The first of these large carnivorous animals, the least dangerous and certainly the most sympathetic is the brown bear, which, for practical purposes, has ceased to exist in the Alps. At present, even in the Pyrenees, there are not more than 50 specimens, between 150 – 180 in the Abruzzi, and a few isolated specimens which survive in the Trentino, in Italy. A century ago, the bear was regarded as the classic mountain animal, and the one which caught the imagination of our ancestors, inspiring many stories, legends and myths. It would appear that in Switzerland a few bears existed, somehow or other, in Grisons and Valais, until the beginning of this century. Tschudi, in his important book on the Alps writes, 'In 1830, it was still not unusual to see the bear descend from the mountains of Anniviers and Herens in order to visit the hillside vineyards and enjoy the grapes. In 1834, a bear entered a vineyard near Sierre. A young man who was there to frighten away the birds was rash enough, to fire a charge of lead-shot at it and fortunate enough (!) to kill the animal'. It was in fact in Grisons, and particularly in lower Engadine, in the Scarl and the forests of Ofnen that the bears found their last shelter, as well as in the Pyrenees. In the French Alps, the last appearance of the animal was recorded at the end of September, 1937, in the hamlet of

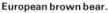

European brown bear.

168

Château, to the north-west of St Martin, in Vercors, Drôme. According to Couturier, the two ranges of Vercors and Basse Maurienne sheltered the two related races of the Alps. The last capture, which dated from 13 August 1921, was a very old female, shot near Mongeois ridge, not far from Montgellafrey, in the Savoy. Her skull is kept at the museum of Grenoble. The majority of the French bears live in the Basse Pyrenees, in the valleys of Saint-Engrâce, Vert-d'Arette, Lourdios and Lauzom, with the largest number living in the valleys of Aspe and Ossau.

The brown bear, one of the most typical animals of the Pyrenees, raises serious problems for the directors of the national park there. Pierre Chimits writes in the French Forestry Review of 1971 that, 'hate for the bear is traditional and the mountain-dweller desires its death. The bear is held responsible for the direct and indirect damage inflicted on flocks of sheep and herds of cattle. It is therefore difficult to plan co-existence between shepherds responsible for large flocks and a wild animal which attacks sheep and even cows.' At present the survival of the bear in the Pyrenees seems threatened. This is due both to its low breeding rate and to the poison used by shepherds, in spite of large indemnities offered for any damage caused.

The author will return to this important problem in connection with the Pyrenean National Park. Having visited the reserve of the Pic du Midi of Ossau, together with a friend, several years previously, the author was amazed to hear one of the keepers inform him that he had not seen a bear for fifteen years! This gives ample proof of how the animal has become nocturnal, fearful, and very discreet, carefully avoiding man, thanks to its highly developed senses of smell and hearing. The tourist has little chance of seeing this animal, which wanders a great deal and feeds mainly on roots, wild fruits and berries, insects, mice, frogs, honey when it is to be found and the occasional sheep. At present the park is trying to introduce the alpine marmot into its territory, hoping to interest the bear in this new type of prey.

The author considers such a plan to be highly praiseworthy. He cannot, however, understand how a large carnivorous animal, which has become nocturnal and very timid, will succeed in capturing marmots which love the daylight and the sun. Perhaps the bear would break open the burrows of the marmot? This appears unlikely. On the other hand the creation of marshes for frogs, and plantations of apple trees and chestnut trees would certainly offer welcome food to the bear.

The wolf

At the same time as the bear was gradually disappearing in the Alps, the wolf which was ravaging the flocks of sheep was also slowly dying out. This animal seems to have existed for quite a long time in the alpine valleys. The last wolf in these parts was killed in Engadine in 1821, and the penultimate in Valais at Guercet in the region of Martigny in 1869. A further wolf was killed above Ayer in the valley of Anniviers in about 1870. The penultimate capture made in Switzerland was at Irana at Monte Ceneri in the Ticino in 1872. Finally, in 1946 and 1947, wolves killed a number of sheep of the Meretschi regions, in the valleys of Tourtemagne and Anniviers in Valais. The slaughter attracted a great deal of press publicity and hunts were organised in a military fashion in the enormous wild forests of the above regions — but all to no avail. The 'monster' of Valais continued to attack and kill both goats and sheep until one day when a poacher, who believed he had killed the fox feeding off a calf in front of his barn was surprised, after firing, to discover that he had killed a wolf! It was a fine male specimen, aged between 18 to 19 months, weighing 80 lb (36 kg). This incident, which took place on 27 November 1947, brought to an end the extremely complicated affair known as the 'wild beasts' of Valais.

The author well remembers taking part in one of these hunts. With two other companions from the village of Chandolin, he climbed to one of the crests of the Illhorn after three sheep had been killed during the night. One of the sheep was discovered headless amongst the rocks, its flanks stripped and the vertebrae of its neck completely crushed. A light fall of snow made it possible to track the 'monster' for a distance up to 8200 ft (2500 m) and the author took several photographs of its tracks, still unaware that the attacker had been a wolf. Unfortunately, the day was very sunny, and the light covering of snow melted quickly so that it was impossible to discover anything further that day.

Although still present in Spain, the wolf no longer

European wolf.

exists in the Pyrenees and its attacks become more and more infrequent. There appears to be, however, a certain number in France. Robert Hainard describes in his book *The Wild Mammals of Europe* how a young wolf was killed by huntsmen during the winter of 1945–6 at Hauteroche in the region of Flavigny-sur-Ozerain, in the Côte-d'Or. In the winter of 1963, after a period of intense and persistent cold, a wolf appeared at Sologne, near Bourges, 93 miles (150 km) from Paris. The photographer, François Merlet, succeeded in photographing the animal as it emerged from a thicket after several nights of heavy snow, and a temperature which could be described as Siberian. Extremely prudent and discreet by nature, the wolf is for the European a sort of fabulous beast in which he has difficulty in believing ... Hainard states, it is one of the least known of our fauna, whose habits deserve greater study, as this would probably lead us to some surprising discoveries. The wolf is very cunning and savage; it is strong enough to carry off a sheep without any effort and it is capable of pursuing its prey for hours on end.

The origins of this animal are in the steppes more than in the forest. It is active mainly at night and is capable of covering immense distances, without any signs of exhaustion, during a single night. In winter wolves band together for hunting. When driven by hunger, they approach villages, but they only attack man when they are threatened or are desparate with hunger.

The wild cat

Are there still wild cats in the Alps? The question is often asked and it is difficult to give a positive reply. The majority of books dealing with European fauna treat this animal as extinct in the Alps. The few remaining wild cats in Switzerland exist in the dark forests of Jura. The author had the pleasure of tracking one of them, following a fresh fall of snow in April of 1953, in the woods of Risoux, not far from the French frontier, when he was trying to photograph the mating dances of the capercaillie. The tracks left on the melting snow by the wild cat were similar to those of the domestic cat, but they were much bigger and wider especially in the case of the adult male. We must here point out that the wild cat is a completely distinct species from the domestic cat, as the latter descends directly from the African species. The exact origin of other members of the cat family inhabiting Europe, Asia and Africa is, however, not at all clear. The wild cat is heavier than the domestic cat, varying between 9 and 17½ lb (4 and 8 kg). Certain males, however, can be heavier. The species must not be confused with the domestic cat which has become wild. In fact these domestic 'wild cats' can be found very far from any human habitation, but their size is always smaller and their weight less than the true wild cat. The tail of the true wild cat is very characteristic; it is generally shorter than that of the domestic cat. Moreover, it is much thicker, very furry, with seven or eight blackish bands, the last band being wider and darker than the others, completely covering the end of the tail. At present it is impossible to state categorically that the species has completely disappeared from the great alpine forests. There are for example, in Valais enormous wooded areas which are little known and which still have no roads through

them. The wild cat is a creature of the twilight and is very discreet in its habits, apart from those of the mating period, so that it is highly probable that they have escaped notice. One fact seems to confirm this theory: Robert Hainard in his excellent book *The Wild Mammals of Europe* quotes the following: 'A Wild Cat was apparently shot near Vex, in the valley of Hérens in 1941 and was recognised as such by a zoologist, Klapkai, from Zurich who had previously seen some 300 or 400 specimens in the Carpathians.' This is encouraging as it does not totally eschew the possibility of certain wild cats still existing in areas of the Alps, although the species has no preference for the mountains; indeed it seems to prefer the oak forest and dry brushwood of the plains. Some re-introductions of this animal were made in Switzerland a few years ago, particularly in the reserve of the Augsmatthorn near Interlaken where four specimens were released. Recently some wild cats have also been released in the Jura. The species is still relatively common in certain forests in the foothills of the Pyrenees. But it is in the Côte-d'Or that the wild cat is most frequently found in France, although its numbers would seem to have decreased in recent years. They are also found in Lorraine, in Auvergne, and in Languedoc.

The wild cat is first and foremost a forest animal, extremely wild and prudent in its habits and consequently difficult to observe. It usually lives in a hole amongst the rocks, the hollow of a tree, a crevice in the ground, the hole of a badger, or in the undergrowth and hunts rabbits and small rodents. It also attacks birds' nests, either on the ground or in trees. The main part of its diet consists of small mammals like the vole which it helps to keep under control by preying on them. The wild cat likes to stretch itself in the sun, lying on a rock or a tree branch for its siesta. It seems to spend the greater part of its life half asleep and only becomes active at twilight. Much remains to be discovered about the relationship between the badger and the wild cat. Cohabitation is not excluded, but still it needs to be proved.

Wild cat
and its tracks in the fresh snow.

171

Head of a bearded vulture.

The bearded vulture or lammergeier

Amongst those birds of prey which formerly lived in the Alps we must particularly regret the disappearance of a very great bird, the bearded vulture. The wing span of this bird was almost 10 ft (3 m) judging from specimens found in Switzerland and its appearance was similar in some respects to both the eagle and the vulture. This magnificent gliding bird fed basically on dead animals and could not survive the fierce war waged against it by huntsmen, especially those seeking rare trophies.

It disappeared from the Alps about sixty years ago. In Switzerland the last specimen died from poisoning in 1886 near Viège in Valais.

This was the canton where the species was still found in the first half of the 19th century, as was the case also in Grisons and the Bernese Oberland. The last specimens of this bird were killed in neighbouring countries in 1906 in Austria, in about 1910 in Savoy, and in 1913 in the Italian valley of Aosta. If appearances have been noted since then it has only been a case of young specimens coming from other mountain ranges; this happened in 1957 when a specimen flew over Loèche-les-Bains which was noted by Willy Thönen. Another ornithologist made a similar observation near Glaris and, some years later in the Bernese Oberland. Elsewhere in Europe there are a few pairs of bearded vultures existing on both sides of the Pyrenees; there are also some specimens in Corsica where great efforts are made to ensure the birds' survival; and a few living in Sardinia and in some areas of Spain. In the Balkans it has become rare, only existing in Macedonia and in Greece, where it is a threatened species. The areas where it is most frequently found at present are in Asia, especially in the Central Mountains of the continent and in the Himalayas.

Robert Hainard, the well-known animal painter and engraver, has observed at length the bearded vulture in the Pyrenees and gives an excellent description of it in his book *Hunting with a Pencil*. He describes it thus: 'Birds of prey are generally elegant but sober in colouring. The bearded vulture, however, gleams with distinction. Contrasting with its back, the wings and the tail are dark and each feather from the smallest tectrices to the great quill feathers is white at the base, gradually changing to black towards the ends. The rest of the body is of a whitish yellow colour which brightens at the throat into a flaming orange. As with all the great gliding birds, the triple folded wing exceeds the rest of the body in length. When the wings are closed, the bird appears to be carrying at his sides its shield and sword; (the sword is represented by the long primary wing feathers which cross over above the enormous oval tail) . . .'

The most striking factor about this colossus of European bird life is its very long shape, its large body and powerful neck, surmounted by a head which is relatively small and shaped like the head of a lance. The feathers on its head are paler in colour than the rest of the plumage, sometimes being almost white, and it is decorated with a wide blackish band which starts from the centre of the skull and completely circles the eye to end beneath the beak with a strange beard of bristles which point forwards, giving the bird a very characteristic appearance and giving it its name. This beard partly covers its large heavily curved beak, and is grey or beige, overlaid with a shining bluish surface. The eye is astonishing, having a pale yellow iris circled with a bright red membrane and this, in turn, is surrounded with bluish or black skin. The scarlet membrane is only a part of the sclerotic of the eye which has been exposed more than is normally the case. The claws are heavily covered with feathers but the feet are less powerful and less heavily armed than those of the eagle. The young bearded vulture differs from the adult by having brownish plumage, mottled with pale patches; the under part of its body becomes gradually paler and paler until it is five years old, but the orange colour only appears at the age of six or seven years, when it is adult.

In Greece near Delphi, the author saw for the first time in his life the immense shape of the bearded vulture and he will never forget the power, majesty and grace of the bird, one of the finest gliders in the world. It would be impossible to confuse it with the other vultures; the wings are long and tapered while the tail is large and wedge-shaped. The bird appears much more graceful than one would believe possible from its size. The bearded vulture lives alone in the moun tainous regions of Europe and only utters its harsh cry at breeding time. Its nest is always built on inaccessible rock faces, protected by a vertical drop. It is made of dead branches and intertwined roots, and the inside is lined with wool, pieces of bark and hairs. Its egg, which is a dirty white colour or on occasions even rust coloured — there are often two of them — is laid very early in spring, between February and March, and the young is covered with down at birth. It seems particularly slow to develop and only starts to fly after three months, usually towards the end of June or in July. The bearded vulture feeds largely on the bones of large mammals, and it knows very well how to extract the marrow by letting the bones drop from a certain height onto the rocks, from where it acquires its Spanish name of 'bone breaker'. It seems to take the same action with tortoises in order to break their shells, but it will also live off carrion, and enjoys the placenta from lambs; doubtless it occasionally also seizes small vertebrate animals and birds while they are still clumsy in flight.

The bearded vulture can be placed at the head of the alimentary chain and represents the summit of a complete system of fauna; its disappearance would be regrettable. Strict protective measures must be taken in Europe and elsewhere for the benefit of this extraordinary bird, which is perfectly harmless and a great scavenger, if its extinction is to be avoided.

Recently its reintroduction into the Alps has been seriously considered. The famous ornithologist, Paul Géroudet from Geneva, has, with the support of the Swiss Association for the Protection of Nature (LSPN), formed an international work study group with French and Italian colleagues to examine this possibility. The first experimental station is planned to be in the Haute-Savoie, thanks to the initiative of the engineer responsible for the lakes, forests and wild life areas for that district. In Switzerland they are considering Valais, an area where the bearded vulture would only need to return to its ancient domain, and perhaps also the Alps of the Vaudois; in Italy the national park of Gran Paradiso in the valley of Aosta is being considered. The bearded vulture needs mountainous regions with high rocky escarpments, at an altitude of between 3300 and 6600 ft (1000 and 2000 m). This experiment is of great interest to the author and he considers it highly desirable! It would return to its native home one of the most remarkable specimens of alpine fauna. The people of the mountains, especially hunters, would then be obliged to become interested in this reintroduction. In order to assure the success of the experiment, the bearded vulture, like the ibex, must be completely protected. It would need to be artificially fed, that is to say, carcases would have to be supplied in certain well determined places, if only to ensure the permanent presence of the bird in the chosen sector. The experiment is already being carried out in the Pyrenees and in Corsica during certain times of the year. The difficulties appear in no way insurmountable and, perhaps in the not too distant future, it will be possible to see the immense shape of the bearded vulture gliding through alpine skies again.

A European otter about to dive into the river.

The European otter

Although it is in no way a typical mammal of the Alps, the otter formerly inhabited most of the rivers and streams of the mountains where trout were to be found. Without being particularly common, this remarkable animal, related to the marten, but very well adapted to life in the water, formerly covered a very large area of Europe, and was found in the Alps well above the tree line, but to an altitude of 8200 ft (2500 m). At the end of the century, its numbers had already been diminished to such an extent in Germany, Belgium, and Switzerland that its extinction was forecast. The otter has always been hunted by fishermen who considered it their most dangerous competitor, and trapped in all seasons, hunted for its fur and even poisoned, so that the species has probably only survived thanks to its keenly developed instincts, especially its excellent sense of hearing, the prudence of its way of life, and its timidity.

Certain measures of protection have recently been taken, now it is almost too late, in Switzerland and Germany. But the increasing pollution of rivers, the use of every type of pesticide and the continuous destruction of marshes and humid areas for the benefit of industrial and urban development, and finally the damming of rivers have all delivered a mortal blow to the otter. There are even worse contributory causes: certain areas of the Alps which were formerly almost unpopulated are now crowded with noisy tourists and entire valleys have been submerged beneath artificial lakes, while numerous fast-flowing streams have been reduced to innocent trickles! Everywhere, both on the plains and in the mountains, the essential habitat for the otter has been gradually eroded. Calm, natural banks of streams are now a rare phenomenon. One must travel very far to find rivers which have their banks intact, with abundant wild vegetation. Man has spoiled some of the finest corners of the globe and protection for nature is today only the concern of a few dreamers, although it is now an agonising world problem.

The otter was a symbol of abundant life, depending on freedom. It needed for its life unpolluted rivers, and stretches of water which had not been domesticated by the greatest predator of all time. Its demands were very modest but questionable compared with those of fishermen, although it is true that the fish was the largest item in its daily fare. Shall we ever see otters again in Switzerland and France in the future? The species is certainly disappearing in several areas of Europe; it is already extremely rare in Germany. This is an additional reason for providing complete protection of the animal. It is, of course, the natural areas which must be protected from the deprivations of man first and foremost and that is becoming more difficult.

The habits of the otter are still relatively unknown. It is said to have no fixed home apart from the period when it raises its young, and is a wanderer by nature, but this may only be because it is constantly disturbed or cannot find enough food. Like the marten it prefers the night and the twilight, except in those completely undisturbed regions, where apparently it likes to stretch out in the sun during the day. Its fur is very soft and compact, being a rust brown on its back and greyish brown over the rest of its body and it would appear to be waterproof. It seems more mischievous and good humoured than other related species, always attracting great attention from the public in zoos.

In spite of its natural timidity, it is easily tamed and becomes attached to its master, giving signs of real intelligence. Moreover, thanks to the webbing which connects the toes of its feet and its very powerful thick conical tail, it is an extraordinary skilful swimmer and can remain beneath the water for six or seven minutes at a time. Its dwelling almost always possesses one entrance beneath the water as well as a small ventilation hole well concealed by vegetation. The otter, however, can also adapt natural holes on river banks for its home and, in large marshes, can live without any dwelling place. Its long whiskers play an important part in its underwater hunting. Like the marten, it leaves its droppings, which are full of fish bones, in certain fixed places. It often utters its soft, high-pitched whistling cry, somewhat similar to that of a bird; it does, however, also make growling and harsh mewing noises which are protracted when it is annoyed.

The eagle owl

Night birds have always fascinated the author. Doubtless there are several reasons for this, but the most important is the sense of mystery surrounding their lives. They do nothing in full daylight and everything about them seems unusual. To begin with, they have marvellous plumage, in which the range of grey, beige, brown and black colours create a subtle, harmonious total effect. Then there are the large eyes, circled with gold or fiery red, and its pupils which are capable of dilating or contracting according to the time of day or night and the strength of the light. Finally there are their plaintive cries, interspersed with periods of silence, creating a strange sort of enchantment for the listener, when they are heard in the silence of the shadows. Of all these night voices the cry of the eagle owl certainly creates the most impressive effect. The male repeats the cry about every ten seconds, sometimes for hours on end when it is excited, its echoing syllables 'whoo-augh', lowering the sound on the second syllable; the female replies from time to time, at a higher pitch with a cry of 'Whoo-oo-augh . . . Whoo-oo-augh.' Heard at dusk, or a little before dawn, in the utter solitude of the mountains, this cry, although not very loud, becomes poignant and even has an element of grandeur about it. It expresses the wildness of the deep gorges, and the snowy forests, still undisturbed by man. The cries mingle with the noise of the torrents at the foot of those tall cliffs where the eagle owl seeks shelter from ever encroaching civilisation, still possible in the Alps.

The eagle owl has fallen a victim to the high voltage wires, the cable railways, the intensive exploitation of the forests and the enormous pressures of tourism; it has become rare throughout Europe in spite of being protected in many countries, unfortunately a little too late to be of great help. The disappearance of this species would be a great pity especially as it plays a part in the biological balance of fauna in the mountains.

In spite of its size, this giant among nocturnal birds is not easy to spot. Only its cries, uttered from the end of winter onwards, especially in February and March betray its presence and allow couples to be located. The eagle owl spends the day dozing and remains immobile for long periods, sheltered by a rock or bush. Its nocturnal activity makes it difficult to observe, as does its rarity. The author's encounters with the eagle owl can be counted on his fingers! To

174

A peregrine falcon in mid-air.

The peregrine falcon

The author was installed on a rocky promontory covered with bilberries. The trunk of an old larch served as a support and, leaning on it, he could look down to the right and the left, with the impression that he was suspended between heaven and earth. The feeling of dominating such a wild, tormented landscape was deliciously heady. What was even more enchanting was the thought that no one would disturb him there for the whole afternoon. The weather was fine and the March sun was almost warm: from time to time pieces of ice or loose stones fell away from the cliff faces. The author listened to the noise they made hurtling down the gullies, enjoying all the more the patch of green where he had installed himself in complete safety. Suddenly some long, drawn-out plaintive cries rose from the abyss. What could they be? Almost at the same moment two grey shapes, with curved wings, pointed at their ends, dived swiftly into the abyss towards the author's promontory. As they flew closer the two birds, which were of differing sizes, closed their wings, making them more like two shells from a gun than birds. An outcrop of rock hid them from sight. The author expected them to reappear on the other side of the rocky spur but nothing happened: he could only hear their strident cries, to which there were other, harsher sounds in reply: 'Gaieh, gaieh . . . graieh, graieh, graieh!'

The two birds-of-prey had probably landed on a rocky crest or ledge some 150ft (50m) below the spot where the author was standing, but it was impossible for him to see them. With a little patience however, he would see them again when they continued their nuptial flight and could then study them at leisure. Certain details which the author had spotted during their brief appearance, together with their plaintive cries had already indicated what the birds were. From their size, a little larger than a pigeon, their slate-coloured heads and necks, their pale throats and cheeks, above which was a wide black moustache and from their long, triangular wings, first stretched out like a cross-bow, then pressed to their sides while plunging into the abyss the author recognised that they were peregrine falcons. As with the sparrow-hawk and the goshawk the

gether with a guide he visited a nest at Lötschental in Valais, and noted that around the nest there were the remains of a black grouse, feathers of a ptarmigan and the paw of a mountain hare. A pellet regurgitated by the adult bird which he also found that day contained numerous bones and hairs of small mammals, the claw of a small grouse and the skull of a garden dormouse. It is known that the eagle owl also occasionally kills young marmots and weasels, stoats, young foxes, crows and other nocturnal birds of prey.

The following encounter is the one the author remembers best. Towards the end of November he rose very early, before dawn, in the hope of photographing some white hares, as it had snowed the previous day and he hoped to find their forms without too much difficulty. While still some distance away from the last larch trees he noticed a large shadow moving over the snow. Astonished, he looked up and saw two vast silvery wings in the sky: an eagle owl in flight! Its shape moved smoothly and silently in the moonlight. It was a rare and unfortunately short-lived experience as the bird soon disappeared into the icy dawn. Doubtless, the 'eagle of the night' had noticed the author hunting and, possibly interested by his presence, had left his rocky vantage point in the hope of surprising a vole or a hare. Whatever the reason, the author will never forget that brief apparition in the moonlight!

A griffon vulture in soaring flight.

male was a good third smaller than the female. The male suddenly reappeared, but it was alone. Its companion was doubtles preparing the depression in the earth or gravel where the eggs would be laid. Using the rising air currents, the magnificent bird-of-prey spread its wings and rose in spirals, quickly gaining height. Had the author been seen? From time to time the bird hastened its ascent with a few rapid beats of its wings. Its shape, seen against the sky, seemed different to its first appearance and was much easier to observe. The author could make out the grey bands on its breast and wings, the dark stripes on its tail and the almost pure white of its throat, bordered with black. Compared with the kestrel, the peregrine falcon in flight appeared larger, with longer, wider wings and a shorter tail. It created an impression of controlled strength lacking in the former, and its mastery of space is such that it can rise almost vertically or dive straight downwards at a speed of more than 60 miles per hour. Together with the alpine swift, it is one of the fastest birds in the world. It almost always attacks its prey while in flight and lands on it like a meteor, seizing the prey from behind with its back claws; sometimes it even kills its prey with the impact of its attack. Its acceleration, together with the skill of its movements, have always earned it high esteem from falconers.

Unfortunately, the robbing of nests, traps, poisoning and sterilisation caused by the accumulation of pesticides absorbed by these birds from their prey have reduced the numbers of peregrine falcons to such a point during recent years that they are nearly extinct. One couple exists in Belgium and, in order to prevent their nest being robbed, young ornithologists have guarded it day and night until the young could fly. Less than 200 birds exist in France, while in Britain their numbers have been reduced by ninety per cent in six years! The situation is hardly better in Switzerland. A victim of 'progress' and civilisation, the noble falcon, formerly a favourite of kings, will soon be condemned to extinction in Europe unless every step is taken to give it complete protection and agricultural pesticides are prohibited from use.

The griffon vulture and the egyptian vulture

This enormous bird of prey, which builds its nest more often in France than at the foot of the Central and Western Pyrenees, and which makes rare appearances in the Alps, always arouses vivid memories for the author. Together with his family, he visited the region of the Col de l'Aubisque at the end of June 1962 in order to add some pictures of the griffon vulture and the egyptian vulture to his photographic collection. Soon, after settling in at the local hotel, he was told that a ram had died in a sheep-fold in the neighbourhood and immediately made his way there. He was shown the animal, already full of maggots, and when a price had been agreed the shepherd put the body of the sheep into a canvas bag. The bag was loaded onto a donkey and the little procession made the way to a quiet spot which the author had spotted the previous day. He then found a hiding place in a thick bush, and set up his tripod and camera, fitted with a 600-millimetre telephoto lens, the most powerful available at that time. The body of the ram lay a little lower down on a rock, at a distance of 65 ft (20 m), stinking unbearably. A picture of the griffon vulture would be worth this price, however. The author waited until evening without any success, but was not discouraged, as he was determined to achieve success. At dawn the following day he returned to his hiding place. The weather was rather dull and the light poor, but occasionally the sun appeared through the clouds. Towards mid-day the author suddenly saw a dark shadow crossing the ground and a little later a griffon vulture landed a

177

short distance away from the ram. It looked enormous, although, judging from its dark plumage, it was not yet fully grown. The author did not dare move, even to shift the telephoto lens, and he could only hope that the bird would approach the carcase and come within range. This the bird eventually did, hopping clumsily over the ground. As it was extremely careful, it kept a watchful eye on the end of the camera, which protruded a little beyond the bush, and moved to the far side of the ram, so that the author could only see its neck and back. Reaching the carcase, it tore off a large piece of flesh, crawling with maggots, spread its wings and departed abruptly. The author had only taken a few pictures and was not satisfied with this brief appearance. While reflecting on this, however, he saw an enormous adult suddenly settle on a spur of rock a few feet away from the ram. Its plumage was coffee in colour, very different from the first vulture; it also had a collar of light feathers at the base of its neck, and two circles of naked flesh could just be seen, pink and blue in colour. Its entire neck was covered in fine, closely knit, greyish white down. Its head seemed small for such a large body but it was increased in size by its thick beak, rather square in shape and curved at the end, yellowish brown in colour with a wide band of grey wax at its base. Perched on the rock, the great bird looked like a hunchback wearing a monk's habit. Its S-shaped neck emerged gracefully from its collar and the general effect was not unattractive, although its greyish blue feet were more like those of a chicken than a bird of prey, as the claws were insignificant, compared with the powerful talons of the eagle. The author expected the bird to attack the carcase at any moment, but nothing of the sort happened. After carefully examining the ram, the vulture suddenly spread its vast wings and the author saw nothing more of it that day. Perhaps the carcase was too rotten and had repulsed the vulture? The experiment had to be started again somewhere else.

Fortunately, two lambs had recently died and the author bought them quite cheaply. He then chose a steep slope near a sheep-fold. The author now carried the two carcases down the slope and tied the horns of the two sheep with wire to iron bars which they fixed in the ground, so that the vultures could not drag the food which had been supplied into the ravine. This work completed, they returned happily to the hotel. The author promised himself an astonishing spectacle the following day. After four days of waiting in the shepherd's hut, however, he had to confess to being disappointed. Saturday, on the first day after leaving the carcases, several vultures circled majestically over the victims. The same thing happened on the succeeding day. None of them decided to land and the author wracked his brains to find the reason. It was obvious that something had aroused their mistrust. The two victims were 50 ft (15 m) away from the shepherd's hut and the large birds could hardly see the author, as the telephoto lens occupied almost the entire space in the window of the hut and did not stick out in any way. Nevertheless, the author enjoyed the fine sight of the large birds in flight. Although the griffon vulture

A griffon vulture perched over the remains of a ram.

An Egyptian vulture at its meal.

seems clumsy when on the ground, its silhouette in the sky is magnificent. It is very different from that of the eagle and seems much bigger, with wider wings, the feathers being more separated at their ends, and it has a very short, almost rectangular tail; the neck is largely hidden by the collar of feathers and only the small head and the powerful beak are visible. This enormous gliding bird uses the rising currents of warm air with great skill and gives a grandeur to the pyrenean valleys which is not easily forgotten.

On the fifth day, the author's wife accompanied him to the hut and followed him quickly inside. Having waited for a little time she then opened the door and left, slowly following the path by which they had arrived. Thanks to this simple action the author on that day had the good fortune to achieve his ambition! His companion had scarcely disappeared behind the shoulder of the mountain when, to the author's great surprise, a griffon vulture settled a few feet from one of the lambs. It then approached the carcase at full speed, lifting its feet in a curious way holding them in the air with nervous movements, as if it wished to push aside an imaginary rival. Soon however, other vultures dived onto the carcase from the sky. The largest of them, with their wings spread wide open kept the weaker individuals at bay, making a sort of strange growling noise. Very rapidly a sort of hierarchy was established. One of the vultures then gave several pecks at the stomach of the lamb which almost immediately burst open. This was the signal for a general onslaught and several birds hurled themselves at the greenish entrails, beating their wings, uttering loud cries, chasing each other and losing feathers. In a few minutes, about fifteen vultures surrounded the carcase, the weakest of them patiently waiting their turn a short distance away. Then the author witnessed some impressive scenes. A raven, looking like a pygmy amongst the giants, was bold enough to peck the tail of a large vulture busily feeding on the inside of the lamb. Furious, the

vulture turned quickly and the raven seized the opportunity to snatch away the pieces of entrails which the vulture still held in its beak. Another vulture was busy with the anus of the lamb. It plunged its neck inside, going so deep that the collar of feathers acted as an emergency brake. Other birds also plunged their long naked necks into the interior of the carcase and worked so efficiently that after half an hour all that remained of the carcase was a little wool and a polished skeleton! The author had unfortunately used up all his films; leaving his cine-camera inside the hut, he quietly opened the door and appeared outside, certain that the vultures would immediately take flight.

What happened next amazed him. The large beige birds stared for several minutes, remaining motionless and stupefied; had they lost control to such an extent that they had forgotten the meaning of prudence? Was it because they were sated with flesh? Finally, one of them opened its broad wings and flew regretfully away from the lamb, crossing the ravine, where he was followed by its companions who flew off one after the other with slow ponderous movements of their wings. The author bitterly regretted his hurried action, although he took in every detail of the magnificent sight.

The author ran back to the hotel to fetch new films and returned to his hiding place in the hut an hour later, hoping to see the vultures return. A black kite was flying over the remains of the carcases and two ravens were carrying off pieces of skin and wool. Finally the author saw appearing in the sky a pair of black and white wings; he immediately recognised the bird to be an egyptian vulture. The shape of this small vulture is strangely similar in flight to that of the bearded vulture but it is only half as big and the contrast between its white feathers and the black of its wings is so typical that there is no problem in recognising this bird. When it is young, however, the egyptian vulture has dark coloured plumage and can be taken at a distance for a young bearded vulture, only its size giving rise to any doubts. The small vulture settled gracefully near the remains of the second lamb and busied itself with the entrails so that the author could observe the bird at leisure. The most striking feature of this bird is the naked folded skin on its head and throat which is a bright yellowy orange colour and contrasts with the white collar surrounding it and with the thin pointed, hooked beak. On the ground it walks less clumsily than the griffon vulture although it still waddles a little from side to side. It can also take flight more easily and uses the slightest currents of rising air to describe elegant spirals above the Pyrenean valleys, where there are still a few of the species to be found. Formerly it nested along the alpine range as far as the Drôme and even the Salève, near Geneva. But it finally disappeared towards the end of the 19th century. They are still to be found in the alpine foothills and in the Causses, but their numbers are constantly decreasing. This is a pity, as the egyptian vulture is a great scavenger; the author has seen a bird near Delphi gorging itself every morning with human excrement. Everything seems acceptable as food and the bird is a past master at cleaning up remains of animals and rubbish of every kind, including small animals which have been crushed on the roads.

The lynx

To his great regret, the author has only seen this feline animal behind the bars of a cage in a zoo but, nevertheless, he could still admire it as a marvellous animal. At first sight, the lynx seems similar to a very large cat; it is short in the body, long in the leg, and the general impression is one of stockiness, of controlled strength and gentle calm masking the power of its muscles. One notices first of all its large pointed ears, very white inside and terminating in a tuft of black hairs, then its strange whiskers framing its greyish face covered in darker stripes; the whiskers are thicker in the male and longer in winter than in summer. Finally, one notices the eyes which are pale gold or bronze surrounded with pure white. The throat and the chin are also white.

Its fur is soft, velvety, yellowish grey and paler in winter, marked with darker round patches on the sides and on the outer sections of the feet, although these patches are almost absent on the back. The female is always smaller than the male and the summer coat is much more rust and beige than is the winter coat.

The lynx normally lives in the forests; in the Alps it always seeks out wooded hills intersected with rocky outcrops which give it a natural shelter for its young.

The animal is very shy and prefers the night or the twilight, although it is also active during the day. It prefers to stalk its prey and lives alone except during the mating period. The lynx is skilful at climbing and its leaps are remarkable. During the mating season the male utters loud howls which finish with a sort of quiet growling. Extinct in the Alps since the beginning of this century, the presence of the lynx would nevertheless be very desirable, especially in the reserves and parks where there is much large game. These reserves are lacking in natural predators and the lynx would act as a regulator, helping to prevent epidemics more efficiently than the activities of the keepers. Conclusive experiments have been made in this regard in Poland in areas where there are many deer. The lynx, in the course of several years, has been responsible for a strict natural selection amongst the deer. Instead of declining in number and becoming degenerate, the latter has produced much stronger specimens with magnificent horns.

The last lynx killed in Switzerland in 1894, was at the Weissthorpass, to the southwest of the Simplon. Robert Hainard, in his book on the Mammals of Europe writes, 'In 1909, a lynx was seen unsuccessfully chasing chamois on the Valais slopes of the Simplon.' On the 17th of February 1970, the State Council of the Canton of Unterwalden in Switzerland, studied a report by the Forest Engineer, Léo Lienert, which emphasised that the lynx was not dangerous to man and that its introduction would cost nothing to the Canton. Several organisations for the protection of nature guaranteed to pay any costs for damages caused by the species, and so the Council decided to re-introduce the lynx on a trial basis into Obwalden. Lienert was given the task of setting up the experiment and four couples were eventually released into the forests of the reserve of the Melchtal. Reaction against the experiment was very strong in the Swiss press and the local hunters were loud in voicing their indignation, although they were later proved wrong. The reintroduction of the lynx three years ago in Obwalden has not given rise to any problems. In the autumn of 1972 a couple were released in Grisons on the edge of the national park in an attempt to establish a certain natural balance amongst the deer which had become too numerous. It is known that the lynx is responsible for deer moving from one place to another and prevents them from staying too long in one spot and consequently causing considerable damage. Damage to trees is in inverse proportion to the presence of the lynx which concentrates its attacks on the female and the young.

Further reintroductions of the lynx would be desirable in different parts of the Swiss and French Alps, in particular the reserves of Aletschwald, Mont Pleureur, in the free Federal zones of Entremont and Ferret and doubtless too in the French National Park of the Pyrenees. In France the lynx occasionally still makes a rare appearance in the Pyrenees, coming from the Spanish side, but it is impossible to decide if they belong to the boreal species. Pierre Chimits, Director of the National Park of the West Pyrenees, makes the following comment in the French Forestry Review of 1971. 'A lynx was killed at Lurieu in the high valley of Ossau in 1957.' He does not, however, explain whether the lynx belonged to the Spanish species or the boreal species (*Lynx lynx*). The same author also states that the only irrefutable presence of the boreal species in the Pyrenees was reported in 1962 by the discovery of a skeleton of a large lynx (*Lynx lynx*) which was authenticated by the museum and which is still in its collection. The animal was found in a grotto between Aspe and Ossau and its death dated from two to ten years previously. Pierre Chimits adds, 'It is true that the lynx, which is a carnivorous and mainly nocturnal forest animal, is very distrustful and difficult to observe, even in certain European reserves where it is relatively common.' It is therefore highly probable that a certain number of lynx exist in the Pyrenees.

In connection with these two species of lynx the author quotes Paul Schauenberg, Keeper of the Museum of Natural History in Geneva, and a specialist in feline animals who writes in *Realm of the Animals*, Chapter 8: 'The Spanish lynx, wrongly considered as a distinctive species, is in fact a local breed, whose skull does not differ from that of the other types of lynx. This breed is found mostly in Eastern Europe and the Middle East. Its fur is beige-grey in winter, becoming more rust coloured in summer. The body is completely speckled with black patches which are elongated and irregular in form. The size, shape and number of patches varies enormously. It is consequently dangerous, if not totally wrong, to consider the Spanish lynx as a different species from the common lynx of Europe.'

The last specimens of lynx killed in the high Alps were in Queyras in 1907 and 1909. In 1913 above St Paul d'Ubaye a forest guard spotted a lynx watching marmots. Since then, however, there has been no record of any observation in the French Alps.

Lynx.

The mouflon or wild sheep

This wild sheep, a native of Corsica and Sardinia, was almost exterminated through hunting and poaching. The last specimens living in Corsica were saved just before they finally disappeared, thanks to the creation of the Bavella Reserve.

Subsequently the mouflon was reintroduced successfully into several regions of France, particularly in the Massif Central, in the Mercantour Reserve in 1957, in the Vosges at Donon in 1954, in the Pyrenees (the Reserve of the Pic du Midi d'Ossau) and finally in the Reserve of Bauges in Savoy in 1954–5, where the author observed for the first time, in October, specimens of the mouflon living in complete freedom.

The author was struck by the wildness, agility and grace of these animals. They are fine reddish brown with a pale patch like a saddle set at the rear of the back in the case of the male and armed with splendid well developed horns curled in spirals. It has been proved that the wild sheep introduced into France have not only withstood the new climate but have also benefitted from more abundant food than was available in their native country. The majority of animals in the French reserves have increased in weight in comparison with the wild sheep of Corsica. The female is usually without horns which, if they exist, are short and almost straight. In winter the coat becomes much thicker and takes on a blackish brown colour, while the saddle becomes whiter. The hair becomes much longer and underneath it there is a thick flock. The animal's cry of alarm is a sort of short hoot repeated two or three times.

The introduction of wild sheep into mountains of medium height has been completely justified particularly in the southern regions like Mercantour and Cevennes, (it should not be forgotten that originally the wild sheep was a forest animal) but its introduction amongst typically alpine animals would seem to be a mistake. Above a certain altitude the ibex and the chamois are better suited to take the place of the mouflon and the latter only disturbs a balance which is already difficult to maintain. Moreover, the mouflon has difficulty in surviving hard winters, unless it can descend to lower mountains and live on dry or stony slopes. Fossils of wild sheep have of course been found in England, Germany, and in France dating from the ice age; by introducing these animals throughout Europe man is probably only restoring the animal to its original habitat. However, the animal is not typically alpine and its presence in the high mountains can hardly be justified.

The mating season for the mouflon begins in October. The author had the opportunity of watching, in the region of Bauges, a violent combat between two males. The antagonists, having stopped 50 ft (15 m) apart, stared at each other for a long time, with their heads lowered; then they hurtled towards each other and clashed with their heads. The impact was of unbelievable violence and the animals gave each other such a hard blow that the author will remember it for a very long time. Then the sheep spotted the author and immediately separated.

182

Lynx.

A wild sheep in winter.

Male ibexes
in April
in the Gran
Paradiso
reserve.

The alpine ibex or wild goat

With its large curved horns, its faun-like face, the golden irises of its eyes, its short beard beneath the chin, and its body which is more robust than that of the chamois, the alpine ibex seems to have been created especially for the mountains. They form its natural background and the animal seems at ease on the edge of every abyss, moving easily over the most difficult terrain. It displays such trust in man that this factor has almost caused its destruction. Everything about the ibex seems somewhat archaic and patriarchal. First its shape, which one finds drawn by prehistoric artists on many rock faces, then its powerful muscles, its aristocratic ways and the almost theatrical care it takes to place itself on certain ridges or escarpments from which it can dominate the entire valley.

The female is rather different and much more modest; it is also less trusting, but is perhaps even more supple than the male. From a distance the female could be mistaken for a wild goat, as it has shorter horns, is of smaller size, and has a coat which is either grey or coffee coloured, blending perfectly with the rocks. The female spends almost the entire year away from the males, often at different altitudes; only in the mating season, between December and January do the males and females join each other. Heavy falls of snow often prevent the animals from coming together and several females are not fertilised, so that the development of a colony reflects this difficulty.

At the beginning of December the author was climbing a track well known to the forest guards in the Reserve of Mont Pleureur in Valais. There was very little snow and fortunately the ground was largely unfrozen. A clash of horns hitting each other aroused the author's curiosity but the rocks surrounding him echoed the sound and made it difficult for him to trace the whereabouts of the two antagonists. Finally, at a turn in the path, he arrived at the scene: less than 165 ft (50 m) away down the slope two fine large males, in their chocolate brown winter coat, were fighting fiercely. They appeared equal in size and strength. Raised on their rear legs they were pushing against each other furiously with their heads, horns intertwined. The sounds echoed in the silence, then the beasts separated, backed away a little, snorted noisily, and flung themselves at each other again with all their strength. The noise of their horns meeting, amplified by the cavities inside them and by the special acoustics of the area, could be heard for miles.

It was the first time that the author had seen such a furious combat. How long had it lasted? He could not hazard a guess and was curious to see which of the males would be victorious. The animals took no notice of him. The slope where the struggle took place was a sort of promontory on a crest and there was a distinct possibility that one of the adversaries might lose his balance and fall into space. Nothing of the sort happened, however! The animals seemed to be equally matched and continued to attack each other energetically without giving an inch of ground; the noise of their horns clashing was repeated at regular intervals in the cold December air and the solitude of the mountains. A trickle of blood now ran down the nose of one of the males, while the other had lost several pieces from its left horn, but the combat continued as fiercely as ever. The animals were beside themselves, panting and furious and seemed to want to give ever more violent blows, driven by ever increasing aggression. Suddenly after a particularly violent clash, the two rivals, either exhausted, or perhaps just stunned, stopped the fight. There was neither winner nor loser.

The large goats separated without attempting to pursue each other; one of them starting to browse while the other, who seemed exhausted, licked his wounds on bended knees. Its eyes were almost closed and its head was lowered. Judging from its enormous horns, it must have been the master of the area; he had remained master, but at what a price! Evening fell quickly and everything grew quiet... The clash of horns a few minutes earlier had given way to complete silence; all seemed to be in order on the mountain.

This powerful mountain goat, whose superb horns are a desirable trophy had become almost completely extinct in the Alps in the 19th century. In 1820 there were only a dozen or so specimens in the Royal Reserves of Piedmont and Gran Paradiso. There have been many discussions on the reason for the disappearance of the ibex in the Alps, while the chamois has managed to survive in areas where protective measures were practically non-existent. Those, however, who understand the trusting nature of the ibex, their laziness and phlegmatic character, together with the confidence they have in their own strength, can understand the reasons. The animals were almost exterminated by guns as soon as these were perfected, placing them at the mercy of poachers. If one thinks that this noble creature, reduced to a few hundred specimens in Italy after the last war, was reintroduced into the Swiss Alps very successfully 50 years ago, one can only rejoice and congratulate all those who through their devotion — and the author is thinking in particular of the forest guards — have contributed to the success of this magnificent repopulation.

A curious fact is that the huntsmen themselves took a large part in this operation, helped of course by the authorities. At present the most successful colonies are in Valais in the free zone of Mont Pleureur, in the mountains of Albirz and in the National Park of Grisons; they have also been successful in the Canton of Berne, at Augsmatthorn. After the creation of the famous National Park of Vanoise in Savoy, the

Ibex.

2 month old male.   6 months   2 years   3 years   6th year   12th year.

The rings on the horn serve to delimit the yearly segments. The nodes do not bear any direct relationship to the annual growth segments, as there can be 1, 2 or even 3 on each segment.

A herd of ibexes fleeing on a firn in July.

ibex, assured of complete protection, has flourished extremely well, especially in the valley of Chavière, the valley of Leisse and near the springs of Isère, not far from the Italian frontier, bordering the Gran Paradiso.

In recent years the ibex has become a type of symbol for all nature needing preservation. Attempts have been made to reintroduce the animal in the alpine range. Males and females have constantly been taken from flourishing colonies by forestry guards, and then released in areas which appear particularly favourable. In Valais, for example, numerous attempts at reintroduction have been made outside the Reserve of Mont Pleureur, in the most favourable lateral valleys. At present there are reckoned to be more than 2000 ibex in Switzerland and more than 4000 in the National Park of Gran Paradiso in Italy, which is one of the finest mountain parks in the world. These figures alone show what great progress has been made, despite the initial difficulties. All the ibex living at present in France, Switzerland, Austria, and Germany come originally from a common source – the few remaining ibex which still lived in the mountain range of the Gran Paradiso in 1821.

The ibex, whose trust in man has been even more developed in the reserves, gives great pleasure to tourists and photographers. Certain of the more spectacular large males allow you to approach them during their siesta up to a distance of less than 30 ft (10 m); sometimes one has to clap ones hands in order to make them get up, although this does not stop them from moving very rapidly and nimbly when they finally decide to take their leave. It is however amongst rocks that they show their talent for climbing and, in spite of their weight – certain males weigh more than about 2 cwt (100 kg) – they are so surefooted that one can only admire them.

When surprised by man, the ibex gives a short whistle through its nostrils while energetically emptying its lungs of air. This whistling noise, which is rather unexpected from a mammal, expresses its uneasiness and is a way of giving the alarm. Roger Heim, describing the ibex writes, 'Man controls the destiny of this mammal, one of the most marvellous in Europe. The species only needs to return to its ancient domains in order to flourish. To do this it needs complete protection.'

Female ibexes followed by a fawn
on a sheer rock wall in November.

A mother chamois and her
fawn in November.

2
The national mountain parks

Whether one likes it or not, the national parks of the mountains will play an ever-increasing rôle in our 'leisure civilisation.' Not only do they constitute an interesting development in man's attitude towards his environment, but their ecological and biological aims have been widened to include cultural and economic plans which can have a far-reaching effect on a social level. This last observation is particularly true of the French national parks which have their own particular statutes and which are carrying out in their border zones certain original experiments. These take the form of an economic development of regions which are usually desolate, either by significantly improving agricultural life, or by creating a certain style of accommodation suitable for the country, ranging from camping sites to extremely comfortable hotels; sometimes even by building individual cottages which provide the city dweller with the best possible means of making contact with nature.

The prime objective of the national parks is to reconcile modern man, overworked and overstressed, with nature. The parks must therefore fill this need, this desire for nature which can be felt throughout the world as our surroundings deteriorate, as pure air, unpolluted water, silence, wild animals and certain natural beauty become more and more difficult to find. This desire becomes more and more important as comfort, leisure and longer holidays become avail-

able to everyone. However, this new form of tourism – for it is a form of tourism – poses certain problems and one is justified in asking if certain sanctuaries in the Alps and elsewhere will not suffer seriously from this desire and if this leisure civilisation does not in fact present grave threats in those areas which should be preserved at any costs? One only needs to look at what is happening in the Swiss National Park of Grisons. This reserve certainly has marked paths for visitors but it does not possess any 'pre-park'. From year to year, tourists interested in wild life have become more and more numerous so that in the summer months they present serious problems for the directors of this Swiss park. An influx of visitors would, however, be very pleasing for the directors of the French national parks which are set up to receive many visitors.

The creation of numerous parks and vast reserves has become a more urgent need than ever before in the world. To retain their value however such creations must not fall prey to cunning speculators. Even apart from the latter our mountains are already seriously threatened. The Alps and the Pyrenees, to take but two examples, have already been infiltrated to their very depths. Is this good or bad? Should one rejoice or become alarmed at such a development? The problem is extremely complex and involves vast areas ... The rapid rise of our civilisation has made wild, natural species more and more difficult to find. But, parallel with this, life in great urban centres becomes more and more of a nightmare, creating anguish in the hearts of citizens who can only support their present existence by avoiding it, at first in their dreams, then transforming their dreams into reality by turning again to nature. This is where the peripheral zones of the parks could play a useful rôle: they could provide welcome relief for man with his overtaxed nerves so that he can leave the congestion of the town and the highway and become a new being, attentive, respectful, and relaxed, with his eyes, thought, and soul aware of the most marvellous and exciting history in the world, which has existed since the beginning: the marvellous history of nature.

Let the national parks and reserves be encouraged to play their part in educating the public, putting at their disposal a whole new world, so that they may at all times treat the fauna and flora properly and have due regard for rural areas and traditions. The author believes this to be one of the main objectives of the parks. Even if such an objective is reached one day, however, something even more important should never be forgotten, as explained by Robert Hainard in his book, *Expansion and Nature*. 'If, for the conservationists, this creation of reserves is a means of forgetting the problems of civilisation, avoiding any conflict with new developments, then the whole scheme is nothing but a great illusion!'

Let us now list rapidly the main mountain parks of France, Switzerland and Italy. The most famous in France is without any doubt the National Park of Vanoise, the first of its kind to be created, on the 6th of July 1963. Stretching over 130 470 acres (52 800 hectares), it borders in part the Italian National Park of Gran Paradiso. Both parks are complementary. Amongst the numerous species living in the Vanoise Park, the ibex is the most interesting as, at the time of its creation, only thirty of these animals existed there

In January 1971 about 200 animals were counted, mainly in the valleys of Chavière and Leisse. At present the herd has increased by another 50 so that there is every sign that the survival of the ibex in Vanoise is more or less assured.

The second national park in France was created by a decree on the 23rd of March 1967. This decree authorised the formation of the national park of the Western Pyrenees. The park itself covers an area of 111 200 acres (45 000 hectares) to which can be added in the east the 5680 acres (2300 hectares) of the Reserve of Néouville. It includes the mountainous regions of the Atlantic Pyrenees and the High Pyrenees and follows the Spanish frontier continuously for 68 miles (110 m), from the high valley of Aspe in the west to the high valley of Aure in the east. The peripheral zone is enormous and covers 87 communes, that is, an area of 617 750 acres (250 000 hectares). The large fauna of this park is unique in western Europe and it was in urgent need of complete protection. This is the area, in fact, inhabited by the last bears in France, about which the author has already written. Unfortunately, the survival of this remarkable carnivorous animal, sympathetic but timid by nature, cannot be guaranteed as poison is a grave threat to the species. There are also numerous wild goats which numbered 2000 in 1970. Mention must also be made of a small insect-eating mammal, unique of its type in Europe, the famous pyrenean desman (*Myogale pyrenaïca*). The only other related species lives in the east of Russia. This exclusively Pyrenean animal is the size of a mole. It has a long trumpet-shaped nose and is nocturnal and aquatic by nature, living in the trout streams in the lower peripheral area of the park. The birds of the park are also extremely interesting. The Pyrenees still have the last five or six couples of the bearded vultures in France, about 30 nesting pairs of the griffon vulture and a small vulture with black and white wings called the egyptian vulture, which is still rather rare.

The monk vulture, which is even larger than the griffon vulture, makes only sporadic appearances in the Pyrenees, coming from the Spanish side. Finally the capercaillie, in its particular form (*Tetrao urogallus aquitanicus*) is still relatively common in the forests of the high valleys of the Pyrenean Park. These few examples will help to understand the great importance which lay behind the urgent creation of the National Park of the Pyrenees – the protection of such rare and original fauna, almost unique in Western Europe.

Let us also mention the National Park of the Cévennes, covering 207 570 acres (84 000 hectares), with a peripheral zone of 568 350 acres (230 000 hectares) which was created by statute in September 1970. Amongst other species which had been reintroduced there we must mention the corsican wild sheep or mouflon which has flourished there. Finally the National Park of Mercantour which covers a wonderful mountain area marked by the action of glaciers and famous for its rock paintings, particularly at Mount Bégo. It is situated between the Alps and the Mediterranean, between Provence and Piedmont and borders the Italian Reserve of Valdieri Entraque. The park is reckoned to have between 3000 and 4000 chamois, numerous ibex which continually cross the frontier and many mountain sheep

Pyrenean desman.

which were successfully introduced some twelve years ago.

Switzerland has only one national park but many federal reserves. The park is in the lower Engadine on both sides of the road along the ridge of the Fuorn. The Swiss National Park had very modest beginnings and was subsequently enlarged thanks to successive annexations. At present it covers an area of about 42 000 acres (170 sq km). Its existence is guaranteed by the Confederation. The first ibex were introduced there in 1920. They have since increased rather slowly, preferring to move to the reserve of Piz Albris which was specially created for them and where they are to be found at present in large numbers. Roe-deer, on the other hand, are rare in the park itself and only number about thirty, while the chamois neither decreases nor increases in number, totalling about 1300 according to a census made in 1968. The chief problem of the Swiss National Park is, however, the problem of their red deer. This animal had disappeared from the Engadine when the park was created, but then it returned spontaneously from the east. Profiting from the abundance of food available on the meadows of the park, the red deer has subsequently multiplied in a spectacular way to such a point that it inflicts considerable damage on the forests. Moreover, in place of the natural balance of species existing when the park was created there has now developed serious imbalance due to the large amount of red deer, which have a tendency to drive away even the chamois and the ibex. There is consequently an urgent need to limit the number of red deer. It should be noted, however, that the red deer of the Swiss National Park spend more than half of their time outside its boundaries, only entering the park at the beginning of the fine weather and leaving again at the first fall of snow. The problem, therefore, is one of migration. In order to reduce the numbers of animals living in the park it has been necessary to kill a certain amount of them recently near the limits of the park when the deer begin their autumn migration. One must also wonder if the absence of natural enemies,

◁ Topmost vegetation: lichened rocks. Natural habitat of the ptarmigan, the mountain hare and the marmot.

The capercaillies have left their trails in the powdery snow. ▷

like the lynx and the wolf, does not play a part in this problem of over-population? An experiment should be carried out in this connection. A pair of lynx was in fact released near the park in 1972 but other couples should also be released there, not so much to establish a balance in nature, but at least to avoid an over-population of large deer, as this would at least limit the damage they cause. It is known that the lynx forces the deer to keep on the move and that it chooses the hind and the fawn from preference as its prey. Conclusive proof has been drawn of such behaviour, particularly in Poland. There would be no reason therefore for not trying such an experiment in the Swiss National Park of Grisons.

Without any doubt the Italian National Park of Gran Paradiso in the valley of Aosta is one of the most beautiful mountain parks in the world. It occupies the mountain range of the Gran Paradiso, that is to say, the left side of the valley of Cogne, the right side of the valley of Rhême, the Valasavaranche and the right side of the upper valley of Orco. This covers 160 620 acres (65 000 hectares) but, bearing in mind the relief of the country, covers an actual surface of nearly 494 200 acres (200 000 hectares). Chamois are very numerous there (between 7000 and 8000) but the Gran Paradiso is famous above all for its ibex, saved from extermination at the last moment by King Emmanuel II of Italy. This stock has been used to re-populate most of the other mountains in the Alps, in particular the Grisons, the

Reserve of Augsmatthorn in the Canton of Berne and the area of Mont Pleureur in the Valais. Apart from the chamois and ibex, the marmot and a few pairs of eagles, mention should also be made of the presence in the Gran Paradiso of certain descendants from the ice age, such as the mountain hare and the ptarmigan.

The National Park of Stelvio in the Alto-Adige covers a total area of 237 200 acres (96 000 hectares) and was created in 1935. It covers the ranges of Stelvio, Ortler, and the Cevedale. A few brown bears wander over its territory, coming from the west part of Trentino. This park also has numerous chamois, deer, marmots, and eagles.

Finally the National Park of Abruzzi was created in 1923 to guarantee the protection of the neuman chamois (*Rupicapra r. ornata*) and the altobello bear (*Ursus arctos marsicanus*) and the ibex. This park covers a surface of 178 050 acres (29 160 hectares). It covers a part of the Apennines which has a typical glacial relief. This fine mountain region is heavily wooded. There are large beechwoods, pines, and innumerable copses and meadows which offer the bear and the chamois of the Abruzzi excellent shelter and plentiful food. A remarkable fact is that this park still has wolves, carnivorous animals which are practically extinct in most of Europe. In winter they assemble in large bands, howling together and sometimes approaching villages, giving this extraordinary region an intense and wild poetic atmosphere.

Hunting with a camera

A Paillard-Bolex camera.

Hunting with the camera, still and cine, is a new sport which is gaining more and more popularity from year to year. We should be delighted at this fact, as every photograph gives a permanent existence to each instant of life, whereas the rifle can only leave behind it the work of death. In a world where the balance between species, including man, is already gravely threatened, photographing nature and wild animals would seem to provide an answer to an urgent need.

All the photographs in this book have been taken with lenses ranging from the normal-angled lens to the 600 mm telephoto lens. Certain photographs of birds could not have been taken without the possibility of remote control. The 2000th second flash has been invaluable in several instances. The author has also used every type of hide, from the primitive hut made of branches to the ideal tent; he has used every method of approach, every possible trick and every means of camouflage at his disposal. However, all these are useless without a great deal of patience, allied to a profound knowledge of the habits of each species; only such knowledge can be a guarantee of success. The more the photographer knows about the animals which he wishes to photograph, the better will be his chances of success. Here, as elsewhere, personal experience is irreplaceable; each time he sets out, he will learn something new about an animal which he always considered he knew so well. Nothing has been written as yet on the best means of photographing the fauna of mountainous areas and this adds a certain spice to any expedition – in the Alps, the Pyrenees or elsewhere. In the mountains, the feeling of entering a world of unknown possibilities is very much to the forefront and the pleasure of discovery increases that of taking photographs.

Whatever the circumstances may be, eyes and ears must be kept open! Even a sense of smell may help in spotting the recent presence of a fox or a deer in the rutting season. All senses must be constantly alert whenever making an expedition; if the animal being sought does not appear do not be too disappointed. Each photograph taken of a mammal or a bird is, in the words of Alpinus, a 'real conquest'. He was referring of course to hunting! But this is only too true for many reasons: nowhere else in the world is the fauna so wild, nowhere else in the world does it hide in areas which are so difficult of access; the fauna only rarely moves in groups and doubtless owes its survival to its habits of being widely scattered. From this fact stems the special character of hunting with the camera in the mountains, its particular value and excitement which affects even the most indifferent. Another factor which cannot be emphasised too strongly is that this hunt with the camera in even a few hours is so reviving: lungs are freed from pollution and, even more important, all worries can be forgotten. One should be able to profit from this nature cure and lose oneself amongst the rocks, the juniper, edelweiss and the rhododendrons, slowly absorbing the healing perfume of the plants.

One will become ones real self again. Then the problems of the town will appear rather small, disappearing like snow melting in the sun. One will take

197

pleasure in the grasshopper chirruping, in the bumble bee hovering over the flowers, in the ant struggling to drag along its prey which is ten times larger than itself. The photograph which will perhaps be taken will gain its full value. Otherwise what use would this photograph be if, instead of preparing slowly to take it the image was snatched from the mountains? If, instead of planning for the photograph calmly and silently it is taken at any cost, it will be valueless. A profound joy will be lost and the true interest of photography in the mountains will not be found. It is not exaggerating to say that it should be a sort of act of love . . . It cannot be called a simple amusement if photographs are taken successfully after long hours of effort, long days of waiting, long periods of coming to terms with oneself.

Imponderables will always be encountered on even the best prepared mountain expedition. This, however, is no reason for complaint; indeed, the opposite is true. One will always remain at the mercy of a change in wind, or the alarm cry of a startled bird; one will always run the risk of a reflection from the telephoto lens, or worst of all, disturbance by a party of fellow mountaineers. It is important to keep calm

René Pierre Bille watching out for black grouse with a Novo-flex camera.

at such times, recognising that these are an integral part of the risks one must run when hunting with the camera.

The author is convinced, however, that the fauna has habits which are much more regular than may be expected; it keeps to its watering places, its tracks and its favourite resting places . . . one should try all these possible meeting places, and wait there, co-ordinating ones observations, noting the time of day, the wind, the weather and the season. One has to remember, for example, that the rutting season of the deer in the mountains begins at the end of September; that the chamois reaches the height of its mating ardour in November; while the ibex reaches its climax in mid-December. It is as well to take advantage of such occasions, as the amorous animal loses its prudence and becomes mistrustful to a certain extent. It is also possible that the rutting season will take the animal to regions where, for the rest of the year, it would be sought out in vain. Thus, the deer, which remains invisible throughout the summer, suddenly emerges from the forest cover and the male chamois, urged on by passion, sometimes loses its prudence and runs towards an observer who can have little similarity in clothing and appearance with his own species. The telephoto lens, therefore, should be at hand. A second camera with a smaller lens would also be helpful to be used if an animal should suddenly appear. In this way the remorse of having lost an occasion, which will not be easily repeated, can be avoided.

The author considers that the true nature photographer must always work alone whenever possible; the advantages are particularly obvious when approaching an animal or seeking out a hiding place. One is perfectly free to go where one wishes and to stop when one thinks fit, to choose this tree trunk rather than that rock, and remain there for as long as one wishes. Alone one is far better able to concentrate, and ones thoughts and decisions are perfectly independent. Very often one can be guided by intuition to the right spot.

Finally, it is possible to work much more quietly and less trace of human scent is left behind. One can enjoy the wind of liberty, a deep joy which is born of ones surroundings and the wild beauty of the landscape; one listens to the crackle of the lichen beneath ones feet, and the marvellous silence of the true mountain areas. One will, of course, still be aware of the noises of the plains, but they will be very faint and distant. One will not be protected from the harsh rumble of jet aeroplanes, but they will only appear in their true light: useless and luxurious toys born of civilisation and doubtlessly destined to destroy it one day.

There is one last point which the author cannot emphasise too strongly; the mountains should be walked not only when the weather is good, but at all possible times and seasons. To a photographer this may seem a little paradoxical at first. However, ex-

René Pierre Bille in action in the Gran Paradiso park.

perience will show that the majority of alpine animals, with the exception of the marmot and the ibex, avoid strong light. On dull days or when a slight drizzle falls, on snowy days, one will find that animals then emerge from the forests and appear to be less timid, feeding avidly on the damp grass. Even mist can produce some unexpected photographs, full of poetry and fantasy. Owing to the mist one may succeed in approaching certain animals which one never hoped to see. The important point is to be well positioned and to wait for the moment when the mist lifts. Moreover, photography in the mountains would be rather insipid without the mist, without those rapid changes in the wind and temperature which oblige the photographer to remain alert at all times. Everything combines to make hunting with the camera one of the most complete and fascinating of sports, because all factors necessary for successful sport seem to be present; the difficulty of the search, the rugged landscape, the wildness of the majority of the animals, the exceptional beauty of the scenery, and finally that feeling of complete liberty and total satisfaction which cannot be found anywhere else to such a degree.

PHOTOGRAPHIC EQUIPMENT

1
A Noflexar 400 mm lens mounted on a Pigriff grip and Novoflex bellows plus an adaptor ring which allows the Canon body (and most other makes of cameras) to be fitted on. Advantages: it is possible to fit in position the Novoflex 640 mm or 280 mm lenses in place of the Novoflex 400 mm lens. Very rapid focusing by means of the Pigriff grip. Lightness and maximum manoeuvrability. Particularly suitable on photographic excursions when closing in on cautious animals, such as chamois, roe-deer, stags etc.

2
A Noflexar automatic lens 1:4/105, fixed on to Noring extension tubes, which are themselves fixed on to Novoflex bellows. The whole kit is fitted to the Canon body, with a photo-electric cell incorporated, and equipped with a double-release. Particularly suitable for macrophotography. The extension of the bellows can be increased by supplementary tubes which are fitted between the latter and the Noflexar lens.

3
A Curtagon wide-angle lens 1:4/35, equipped with a lens hood and attached to an Alpha Reflex. Particularly suitable for general shots or whenever there is no room to move back. Owing to a special ring near the base, the image can be moved up or down.

4
An adaptor ring enabling the Astro 400 mm telephoto lens (No. 12) to be fitted to the Paillard-Bolex H. 16 Reflex cine-camera (No. 15).

5
A Robot "Royal" fitted with a 135 mm Schneider Xenar telephoto lens. This camera has a powerful spring which allows a dozen shots in succession to be taken within a few seconds. Extremely practical for game surprised at close range (e.g. a hare hurriedly leaving its seat, etc. . .).

6
A nickel-cadmium battery used with the Alpha motor (No. 7b), which is attached to the Alpha Reflex body (No. 7) giving both remote control and transport of the film without the direct intervention of the photographer. It can be recharged on an ordinary electric point. A cable, 160 or 330 ft (50 or even 100 m) long (No. 20).

7
An average telephoto lens, possibly the Kinoptik Apochromat 100 mm fitted on to this Alpha body. Extremely useful in long distance work for the nests of sparrows or other birds, and for particularly wary mammals.

8
A normal Summicron 50 mm lens with a lens cap and hood. This lens is fitted on to the Leicaflex (No. 10).

9
The base plate of the Astro 400 mm telephoto lens (No. 12) for the Paillard-Bolex H. 16 Reflex cine-camera. In the centre of the plate there is an adaptor ring which enables the Leicaflex to be fitted both to the bellows and to the Novoflex Pigriff grip (No. 1).

10
A Leicaflex body fitted to the Astro telephoto lens (No. 12) by means of a special ring. Especially suited for hidden observation work from a cabin or a tent. Moreover, the Leicaflex, which fires at 1/2000th of a second, can be used for taking shots of very swift flights.

11
A Telyt 280 mm telephoto lens f/4.8, fitted by means of Leitz rings to the Leicaflex. A telescopic hood. Excellent clearness of detail can be obtained, even at full aperture.

12
An Astro 400 mm telephoto lens fitted either to the Paillard-Bolex H. 16 Reflex cine-camera with the adaptor ring (No. 4) or to the Leicaflex body with the Leitz rings (No. 10).

13
A long Kilfitt 600 mm telephoto lens f/5.5, fitted for general shots to an Alpha Reflex body. It can be adapted with the appropriate rings to the Paillard-Bolex H. 16 cine-camera, as well as to other different makes of cameras. It can be of real use in hidden observation work on a fixed point, e.g. a nest or a lair. Excellent clearness of detail. On the other hand, the excessive weight of this powerful telephoto lens makes for difficult handling and cumbersome transportation, even though it can be dismantled into two or even three parts. A tripod or solid support is indispensable.

14
A Metz electronic flash, which can be recharged on an electric point, allowing numerous flashes to be taken (up to 300 or 400 without recharging). Secondary flash-heads may be fitted. Essential for macrophotography and for shooting nocturnal species.

15
A Paillard-Bolex H. 16 Reflex cine-camera mounted on its turret and equipped with the Yvar 150 mm telephoto lens and the Switar 50 mm lens. Particularly valuable for mountain work on account of its reduced weight and bulk, its ability to stand up to anything, and the relative simplicity of its handling. Thanks to different rings, it can be adapted to the Novoflex Pigriff grip (No. 1), as well as to the 400 mm Astro (No. 12).

16
A strong mountain case in watertight canvas with zip fasteners. This is a necessity for excursions in the Alps.

17
Sound recordings in nature necessitate the use of tape recorders with sturdy, sensitive microphones and, in most cases, parabolic reflectors. For general shots, the latest innovation in sound recording technique is the high-performance Nagra NS. miniature tape-recorder. It weighs about 300 g.

18
Headphones suitable for the Nagra NS. enabling read-out of the tape after recording.

19
A specially sensitive and sturdy microphone fitting on to the cable attached to the Nagra NS.

20
A 160 ft (50 m) cable attached at one end to the nickel-cadmium battery (No. 6), and at the other to the Alpha motor (No. 7b). This allows 500 shots to be taken by remote control. The recharging time is about 15 hours.

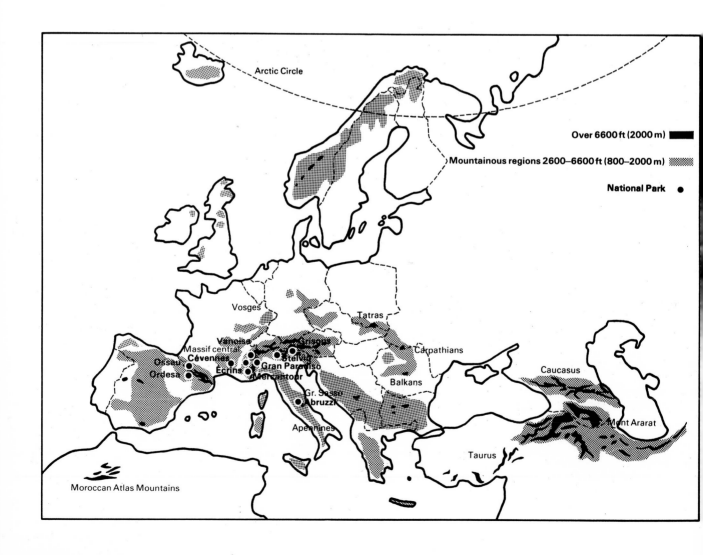

Arctic Circle

Over 6600 ft (2000 m)

Mountainous regions 2600–6600 ft (800–2000 m)

National Park ●

Vosges

Tatras

Carpathians

Caucasus

Vanoise

Massif central

Cévennes

Stelvio

Gran Paradiso

Mercantour

Écrins

Ossau

Ordesa

Gr. Sasso

Abruzzi

Balkans

Mont Ararat

Apennines

Taurus

Moroccan Atlas Mountains

Glossary

A = Arachid
AM = Amphibian
B = Bird
F = Fish
I = Insect
M = Mammal
R = Reptile

Adder (R)
Vipera berus
Food: Small mammals, viviparous lizards, frogs and sometimes birds. Reproduction: Rather similar to that of the asp. The young are born in August or September, in the north or at high altitudes gestation can last as long as two years. There is usually only one litter of approximately twelve young produced; these are from 14–18 cm in length. Sexual maturity is only reached after four or five years, but the asp reaches sexual maturity only after five or six years. Distribution: central and northern Europe, the Apennines, the Balkans, northern Asia up to 3000 m and above. In France the adder is found to the north of the Loire, the Massif Central and the Pyrenees.

Alpine accentor (B)
Prunella collaris
Length: 16.5 cm. Wing span: 30 cm. Average weight: 40 g. Distribution: Alps, Pyrenees, Mont Dore, Corsica, Apennines, Carpathian Mountains, mountain ranges of Asia and the North of Morocco. Four to five turquoise blue eggs hatched by both adults. The young leave the nest after sixteen days without being able to fly well. They hide amongst stones and are often killed by the stoat or the kestrel.

Alpine apollo (I)
Parnassius phoebus
Rather large butterfly of the Papilionidae family, which is related to the Apollo, although it is slightly smaller and characterised by yellowish white wings with black patches and white centred red spots. The fore-wing of the male: 30–33 mm. It is more mountainous in its habitat than the Apollo, and it is also more rare and localised, living near damp areas up to an altitude of 3000 m. The caterpillar feeds on saxifrage and sempervivium. Distribution: Throughout the alpine mountains, both the maritime Alps and the eastern Alps.

Alpine argus (I)
Albulina orbitulus
Small butterfly belonging to the large family of the Lycaenidae. The fore-wing of the male measures from 12–14 mm. The upper part of the wing is a fine light blue with thin borders of black at the edge. The female is brownish. The lower part of the wings of both sexes is light grey, speckled with white patches and dots. These patches lack the black centres normally found in the argus, a fact which allows this mountain species to be identified easily. It is found in high alpine meadows from 1700–2600 m. Distribution: From the Alps to Norway and central Asia.

Alpine bee (I)
Bombus alpinus
One of the insects of the super-family Apoidea, characterised by a furry squat body, a black thorax and a russet abdomen. Length of female: 20–24 mm. The worker is smaller and of varying size, having on an average a length of 15 mm. The species is rather similar to the large red-tailed bumble bee – *Bombus lapidarius* – but is found at much higher altitudes, even in snow regions. Distribution: The entire alpine range but also in northern Europe and in Lapland.

Alpine chough (B)
Pyrrhocorax graculus
Length: 38 cm. Wing span: 75–80 cm. Average weight: 200 g. Distribution: Throughout most of the European mountain ranges (Alps, Pyrenees, Balkans, Apennines), the Caucasus, the Lebanon, the Atlas mountains of Morocco; Himalayan mountains as far as western China, and the Altai. Reproduction: The nest is built inside cracks and inaccessible cavities in rocks and is made from small branches; it is lined with wool and horsehair. Three to five eggs are laid which are whitish and speckled with brown. Hatching is carried out chiefly by the female and lasts for about three weeks. The young birds remain in the nest for about 30 days and follow their parents for a long time after they have learnt to fly. Eggs are laid once annually.

Alpine grayling (I)
Oeneis glacialis
Medium size butterfly of the Satyridae family. The upper surface of the wings are a brownish colour with yellowish stripes towards their extremities; these stripes have several eye markings. The underside of the hind-wings is blackish brown with almost white veins. The fore-wing of the male measures from 25–28 mm. This insect lives in the moraine and rocky areas from 1800–3000 m. The caterpillar lives on various types of grass, amongst others the fescue. It hibernates twice. The species is limited to the Alps and seems particularly common in the Valais.

Alpine grizzled skipper (I)
Pyrgus andromedae
Small butterfly of the Hesperiidae family. The upper part of the wings are brownish, marked at the front with white spots arranged in a definite pattern. Fore-wing of the male: 13–15 mm. This species is typical of the mountains and can be found in the Pyrenees and the Alps from 1500 m up to a very high altitude. It is also present in the mountains of Scandinavia and the North Cape.

Alpine marmot (M)
Marmota marmota
Length of body: 48–56 cm. Tail: 16–20 cm. The weight varies greatly according to the season: In September the average weight is from 4–6 kg, but certain individuals become very fat and can weigh up to 9 kg. Distribution: The marmot inhabits the entire alpine area, from the maritime Alps to Styria. It was introduced into the Carpathian mountains and into the Black Forest. In 1948, at the instigation of Dr Marcel Couturier, from Grenoble, marmots were first released in the Pyrenees, in the valley of Barrada. The colony was subsequently added to and now appears to be flourishing. Other introductions of the marmot have taken place at Troumouse and Pont d'Espagne in the upper Pyrenees. Reproduction: According to recent observation the marmot breeds generally only every second year. Gestation lasts 34 days. Between the middle of May and June, depending on the region, they produce a litter of two to six young. They are born naked and blind, opening their eyes after three weeks and being suckled for six to eight weeks. Longevity: approximately ten years, sometimes as long as twenty years.

Alpine newt (AM)
Triturus alpestris
Length of male: 8 cm. Female: 11–12 cm. Distribution: Europe, as far south as Spain and Tuscany in Italy, and as far north as Denmark. They can be found in the French Alps up to 2600 m.

Alpine salamander (AM)
Salamandra atra
Length: 11–15 cm. Distribution: Alps and Jura, mountainous regions of Wuertemberg and Carinthia; the Balkans, Herzegovina and Albania. Food: Various insects, spiders, worms and small snails.

Alpine shrew (M)
Sorex alpinus
This is very similar in size to the common shrew. It can be identified from the latter by its tail, which is at least a third longer, 6.5–8 cm and its fur which is slate grey and almost uniform. Head and body: 6–8 cm. Average weight: 8.5 g. Distribution: Only in the mountainous regions of central and eastern Europe, in particular the alpine ranges, Jura, Vosges, the Carpathians and the Transylvanian Alps. It can be found in very localised areas in the central Pyrenees and in the high areas of Yugoslavia. It usually favours damper areas than the common shrew, that is the mountain meadows at the upper limit of the conifers but also can be found in much lower, marshy ground, particularly in central Europe where it has been found between 500 and 3000 m. Reproduction: Similar to the common shrew.

Alpine swift (B)
Apus melba
Length: 22 cm. Average wing span: 54 cm. Average weight: 100 g. The alpine swift is the largest of the European swifts. Distribution: northern Morocco, Iberian Peninsula, Italy, Sardinia, Sicily, Southern Balkans, Crimea and Caucasus for the standard type. In France and in Switzerland the alpine swift inhabits the Jura, Alps, Massif Central, Pyrenees and Corsica. The species is migratory and spends the winter in tropical Africa. It returns to Europe sooner than the black swift (house martin) at the end of March or the beginning of April and also leaves later, in September. Reproduction: The nest is small compared to the size of the bird; it is made of various materials which are moulded together and then firmly attached between rocks or against a wall chosen by the mating pair. Only one clutch of three white elongated eggs is laid annually. Incubation is carried out by both sexes for about twenty days. The young leave the nest at the age of 55 days. Food: Only winged insects. The adults feed their young about twenty times a day with small balls of food made from numerous insects stuck together by the birds' saliva (as many as 600 insects can be found in one ball!).

Alpine tit (B)
Parus atricapillus
Length: 13 cm. Wing span: 19–20 cm. Weight: 11 g. Distribution: This alpine tit exists in two forms: one inhabits the plains and is called the alder tit, the other is in the mountain forests, called the alpine tit. In France and Switzerland the alpine form lives in the Alps and the Jura. The alder form is absent from the south-west of Europe and the Mediterranean countries. It lives in England, southern Scotland, the north of Asia as far as Kamchatka, central Europe, northern and central Italy. It usually makes its nest by digging its own hole in rotten wood. One clutch of seven to nine white eggs, speckled with rust. Incubation is similar to the crested tit. The bird is non-migratory but travels over wide areas.

Alpine vole (M)
Microtus nivalis
Length (head and body): 12–14 cm. Tail: 5–7.5 cm. Weight: 38–55 g. Distribution: Alps, Pyrenees, Massif Central, Apennines, Abruzzi mountains and the Balkans. Reproduction: Two to three litters annually, consisting of three to seven young. Each litter is born in an underground nest made of hay and grass stems. The animal has a short, sharp cry which is rarely repeated.

Alpine white (I)
Synchloë callidice
Medium size butterfly of the Pieridae family, characterised by the veins on the lower sides of the hind-wings, which are thickly powdered with greenish grey, thus assuring a better absorption of the sun's rays. The upper part of the wing is white with some black patches. Fore-wing of the male: 22–26 mm. This butterfly flies very rapidly and, of all the Pieridae, is the most at home in the mountains. It is found near glaciers as high as 3000 m and is rarely found below 2000 m. Distribution: Pyrenees, French Alps, the Alps of Valais, of Austria, and Bavaria. In North America another species *Pontia occidentalis* flies over the high western mountains of Alaska, Colorado and California.

Anonconotus alpinus (I)
Bush-cricket of medium size belonging to the family Tettigoniidae. The male measures between 14 and 18 mm and the female 21 mm (without the egg sac). It is greenish brown, with brown lateral lobes with a yellow edge. The wing sheaths of both sexes are very small, leaving almost the entire abdomen exposed. This species is common in the Alps of south and central France where it reaches the remarkable altitude of 3000 m.

Aphodius alpinus (I)

Small chafer beetle of the family Scarabaeidae. It is rarely larger than 8–12 mm in length with black thorax and reddish wing sheaths. It is found everywhere at high altitudes, particularly in the droppings of cattle.

Aphodius fossor (I)

This species is closely related to the preceding beetle and approximately the same size, but with brilliant black wing sheaths. It is frequently found in the high meadows where it seeks out particularly fresh droppings. Very common everywhere throughout the alpine mountain ranges.

Apollo (I)

Parnassius apollo

Rather large butterfly of the family Papilionidae, with whitish and slightly transparent wings marked with red spots and black patches. The fore-wing of the male measures from 35–41 mm. The abdomen of the male is furry while that of the female is smooth. It can be found in all the sub-alpine meadows, sometimes reaching a height of 2600 m in southern Europe. Distribution: Mountainous regions of Continental Europe, from Scandinavia to Spain and Sicily, and from the Balkans to central Asia.

Arctia flavia (I)

Moth of the Arctiidae family. Fore-wing of the male: 25–28 mm. It is similar to the Parasemia plantaginis, but its size is almost double and the marbling of its fore-wings is disposed in a different way. The back wings are ochre yellow speckled with two dark patches. The species is localised in our mountains from the high Alps to the Grisons.

Arctic charr (F)

Salvelinus alpinus

The weight, size and colour of this fish is extremely variable according to the surroundings in which it lives. It has tiny scales, about 200 on the lateral line, which give it a very smooth appearance. The eggs are smaller than those of the trout, and they hatch from the end of November to the end of January, possibly later at high altitudes.

Arcyptera fusca (I)

Grasshopper of the family Acrididae, rather large in size, being from 23–31 mm in length for the male and from 30–40 mm for the female. Generally yellowish brown in colour for both sexes. The rear thighs are bright red on the inside, as is also the case with the tibia, which is also decorated with a yellow ring at the base. The species is localised, but is quite common in the sub-alpine meadows up to an altitude of 2200 m or even higher. Distribution: Alps, Pyrenees and the mountains of south-east France.

Arran brown (I)

Erebia ligea

Butterfly of the Satyridae family which is considerably larger than *Erebia pandrose*. It is of brown appearance with beige stripes on the fore and hind-wings, and with white centred eye-spots. The underneath of the back wing is brown with white stripes and small eye markings. The fore-wing of the male is 24–28 mm. This butterfly prefers the sub-alpine glades and the scattered woods of mountainous regions up to 1800 m. Distribution: Massif Central, Alps, Jura, Vosges, Carpathians and Balkans as far as Macedonia. It is also found in Scandinavia at low altitudes. It is absent in the Pyrenees, Spain, the Mediterranean islands, Greece and part of Germany.

Asp (R)

Vipera aspis

Food: Mostly small rodents, lizards, frogs and some birds. Reproduction: The adults mate in April or May, sometimes as late as June in the mountains. The female is ovo-viviparous and gives birth to the young (sometimes as many as twelve or more) four months later. These are hatched at the moment of birth and measure from 13–18 cm. They are immediately independent, and their poison glands also function as soon as they are born. They may mate again in the autumn, before hibernation. Distribution: From the south of the Pyrenees to Belgium and the south of the Black Forest in Germany. The alpine range, the pre-alps and the Jura, the north and centre of Italy. The whole of France with the exception of the Channel and the Provence areas.

Badger (M)

Meles meles

Length of body: 61–72 cm. Tail: 15–19 cm. Height to the withers: 30 cm. Weight: from 12–20 kg, sometimes more in the case of large males. Boars in Greece. Distribution: Throughout Europe with the exception of the extreme north: also found in the majority of the Mediterranean islands. In the mountains to a height of 2200 m, but on occasion the animal wanders to higher altitudes. In winter it hibernates often beneath the ground for long periods, living on its reserves of fat, but it does not enter into deep sleep like the marmot. The black and white patches on its face allow this animal to be easily recognised. Cry: Several different kind of yelps, snuffling and growling noises, and sometimes it utters terrible cries! Its breathing habits are little known. Period of gestation is long, from seven to eight months. Three to five young are produced annually, usually born at the end of winter. They are suckled for eight weeks and the young become independent when they are six months old. Longevity: Fifteen years approximately. Food: Omnivorous: insects, molluscs, small vertebrate animals, eggs and fledglings, berries, roots, mushrooms and various seeds.

Bank vole (M)

Clethrionomys glareolus

Length: (including head and body) 8–12 cm. Tail: 3.6–7 cm. Weight: 14–36 g. Distribution: The greater part of Europe, although it is absent from Spain, Greece, and Italy apart from the southern part of this country. Reproduction: Three to four litters annually consisting of from four to eight young. Each litter is born in a spherical nest built of grass stems and leaves. This animal has a short and slightly trembling cry.

Bearded vulture (B)

Gypaetus barbatus

Length: 1–1.50 m. Wing span: 2.70–2.80 m. Weight: 5–6 kg. Distribution: The bearded vulture still nests in Spain, Yugoslavia, Sardinia, Greece, Bulgaria, Asia Minor, north Africa and central Asia. In France only a few couples breed in the Pyrenees and Corsica.

Beech marten (M)

Martes foina

Length: including head and body: 41–49 cm. Tail: 23–26 cm. Average weight: 1–2 kg. Distribution: Throughout Europe with the exception of the British Isles, Scandinavia and north-east Europe. It is found throughout Asia as far as the north-west of China. The animal nests in barns and old abandoned dwellings and hollow trees. In the mountains it is very often found in the rocky areas. The beech marten usually produces two to seven young. There is a first, 'false' rutting season between January and February, then a 'true' rutting season from July to August, which is the beginning of a long gestation period of twelve months. The beech marten, which is more slightly built than the pine marten, can be distinguished from the latter by its paler coloured fur through which the greyish under-fur can be seen, and by a large white bib on its throat and neck which extends to the inner sides of the front legs. This is rarely the case in the pine marten, whose bib is more orangey yellow and does not continue down the legs.

Black apollo (I)

Parnassius mnemosyne

Butterfly of the Pieridae family which is smaller than the Apollo and is characterised by the white wings, which are a little transparent on the edges and marked with two or three black spots, although it has no red patches. The fore-wing of the male: 25–30 mm. Distribution: Widespread throughout western Europe, but localised in the sub-alpine meadows of mountainous regions, between 500–2200 m. The Pyrenees, Massif Central, Savoy, Swiss Alps as far as the Carpathians, the Apennines, western Sicily and the Balkans. It is rarely found in Norway and Finland.

Black grouse (B)

Lyrurus tetrix

Length of male (from the end of the beak to the end of the central rectrices): 51–54 cm. Female: 42–46 cm. Wing span of male: 83–92 cm. Female: 66–77 cm. Weight of male: 1.1–1.5 kg. Weight of female: 700–950 g. Exceptionally to 1 kg. Distribution: The black grouse lives both on the plains in the north of Europe and in the mountains of the Alps. At high altitudes it seeks out the sparse woodlands at the upper limit of the tree line and the area of dwarf bushes and rhododendrons intersected with rocky outcrops. It is widespread in the British Isles (with the exception of Ireland), the Alps, up to 2400 m, and occasionally in the Ardennes. It is non-migratory. Reproduction: Clutch of six to ten creamy coloured eggs, marked with russet or sepia; the eggs are laid in a cavity in the ground, covered with feathers, usually in a spot where they are sheltered by the vegetation. The male does not look after the nest. Incubation is carried out by the female for 24–28 days. The chicks are cared for by the mother with great attention. If there is any sign of danger the mother will fly in front of the enemy and distract its attention by pretending to be wounded. One clutch of eggs is laid annually, but there are frequent replacement clutches produced. Food: Shoots and pine needles form the basis of the winter diet; berries of all sorts, buds and young shoots of alder trees, spruce, birch, larch etc.

Black redstart (B)

Phoenicurus ochruros

Length: 15 cm. Wing span: 26 cm. Average weight: 17 g. Distribution: Alps, western, central and southern Europe; the south of England and of Sweden; Asia Minor; north Africa; the Caucasus; the area of the Himalayas up to the west of China. Migratory: The first birds leave in September and they continue to leave until mid-November. Reproduction: The nest is always placed in a cavity or beneath a roof. It is made of dry twigs and lined with horse-hair and feathers. Clutches of four to six white eggs are laid. They are incubated by the female for fourteen days. The young leave the nest when they are two weeks old. There are two clutches laid annually, even in high altitudes if conditions allow it. Food: Various insects and spiders; wild berries in the autumn.

Black-veined white (I)

Aporia crataegi

Butterfly of the Pieridae family which is quite large in size and characterised by a uniform white or cream colour, with black veins intersecting its wings. The fore-wings of the female are partially transparent. The fore-wing of the male measures 28–34 mm. This species is found in all the sub-alpine meadows up to an altitude of 2000 m. Distribution: From western Europe to Korea and Japan. It is absent in England and in the north of Scandinavia. It is also absent in Corsica and Sardinia.

Black vulture (B)

Aegypius monachus

This is the largest vulture in the Old World. It is very similar to the griffon vulture in shape while flying. It differs, however, in that its tail is a little longer and wedge-shaped. Its plumage is entirely dark brown. Average length: 112 cm. Wing span: 2.65 m–2.87 m. Average weight: 8 kg. Distribution: (Extremely rare in Europe): Spain, Portugal, Majorca, Greece, Bulgaria, the Caucasus and Cyprus; it has probably disappeared from Sardinia and Sicily. Reproduction: One clutch is produced annually between the end of February and mid-March; only one egg is laid, with white marks and reddish brown patches. The egg can weigh as much as 245 g. Incubation is carried out by both adults for 52–54 days. The young bird remains in the nest for about four months. As opposed to the griffon vulture and the Egyptian vulture, the black vulture usually builds its nest at the top of a large tree.

204

Black woodpecker (B)

Dryocopus martius
Total length: 47 cm. Wing span: 70–75 cm. Average weight: 300 g. Distribution: Alps, the mountains of central and eastern Europe, Scandinavia, the Pyrenees, Calabria and the mountainous areas of northern Turkey. In Asia it is found as far as the Pacific between the 50th° and 65th° northern Parallels. In general it is non-migratory, but the young sometimes travel very far from their birthplace. One clutch of eggs is laid annually consisting of three to five white, shining eggs. Incubation is carried out by the male, which is the rule with the majority of woodpeckers. The young leave the nest after 27–30 days.

Brephos parthenias (I)

Small moth belonging to the family Geometridae which are active during the day. The fore-wings are brownish grey with two faint white patches. The back wings are orange in colour, with dark brown marks. This moth flies very early in the spring, from the beginning of March. Distribution: Central and northern France, Pyrenees, Belgium, Switzerland. It is found in the mountains up to a height of 2000 m.

Brown bear (M)

Ursus arctos
The Pyrenean brown bear is relatively small. Its total length according to Couturier: 1.70–2 m. Height to the withers: 0.9–1 m. Weight: adult male; 80–230 kg, adult female 65–170 kg. A male killed in the valley of Ossau on the 16th June 1848 weighed 350 kg. This is however an exception. There is a great variation in the colour of the fur which can range from light brown, almost beige, to darkest brown or grey according to the age of the animal and to individual specimens. Distribution: Apart from the regions already mentioned, east and south-east Europe, Scandinavia, south-west Austria. Mating takes place between April and August. Gestation lasts from seven to eight months. The two or three young, which are born in the winter, are very small and are suckled for three to four months. Sexual maturity from three to four years. Longevity: 35 years.

Brown hare (M)

Lepus europaeus
Length of body varies between 50 and 68 cm. Tail: 7–10 cm. Weight varies from 2.5–6 kg. The brown hare of the east is generally heavier. Distribution: The species is found throughout an immense territory including Africa, Asia and the greater part of Europe with the exception of almost the whole of Scandinavia and Iceland. There are numerous local and geographical forms. The brown hare has been introduced into Northern Ireland. Reproduction: There are three to four litters annually consisting of three to four young which are born with open eyes and covered with fur. Gestation lasts from 42–44 days. The young are weaned during the third or fourth week and the young hare is capable of reproduction at the age of one year. Food: The brown hare feeds only on plants: grasses, roots, berries, buds, bark and small twigs. Longevity: About ten years.

Brown trout (F)

Salmo trutta
The weight and length are very variable. In streams at high altitude there exists a dwarf form which is scarcely ever larger than 15–20 cm. In larger rivers, the brown trout can reach 50 cm in length and weigh between 1 and 2 kg; some specimens may weigh even more. Eggs are usually laid on the gravel bed of running, shallow water. The female prepares for laying by moving on to its side and releases the eggs by a violent movement of its body and tail. The number and size of the honey-coloured eggs varies according to the individual; the eggs usually measure about 4.5 mm, and 220 eggs are an average for a weight of 100 g. The length of incubation is normally 105 days in water at a temperature of 4°.

Buff-tailed bumble bee (I)

Bombus terrestris
One of the largest European bees, commonly found everywhere, both on the plains and in the mountains where it can live up to an altitude of 2900 m. Easily recognisable from its thorax and abdomen which are striped in yellow and black and from the white hairs covering the last segments of the abdomen. The large female can reach a length of 28 mm. In the mountains a smaller, lighter coloured variety exists. Distribution: Throughout Europe.

Bullfinch (B)

Pyrrhula pyrrhula
Length: 16–17 cm. Wing span: 28 cm. Average weight: 30 g. Distribution: Western, central and eastern Europe; absent from the extreme north, Greece, and in the greater part of the Iberian peninsula. The species is found in northern Asia as far as Japan, but it is absent from Corsica and on the Mediterranean plains of France. In Switzerland it can be found everywhere in the mountains and occasionally in the coniferous forests on the plains. Reproduction: The nest is always placed close to the ground, at a height of between 1 and 2 m, in a tufted pine or in a thorny bush. The nest has the appearance of a platform of twigs and roots, decorated in the centre with hairs. Eggs are laid once or twice annually, four to six in number and are pale blue in colour with a few black or chestnut coloured spots. Incubation is carried out by the female and lasts from thirteen to fourteen days; the young leave the nest after seventeen days. Food: All sorts of seeds, flower buds (in winter) and certain insects.

Bullhead (F)

Cottus gobio
The size can vary from 10–20 cm and the weight from 30–50 g. Spawning takes place in February or March, but is much later at high altitudes. This is particularly the case in the pools of the Arve and Durance. Here one can find the bullhead at altitudes of more than 2000 m. The female lays about 100 slimy eggs, placing them between the stones in the river bed, where the male defends them fiercely throughout the incubation period. This strange representative of the fauna of the river bed supplies trout fishermen with excellent bait.

Buzzard (B)

Buteo buteo
Length: 52–55 cm. Wing span: 115–135 cm. Weight varies greatly, from 500 gr–1 kg in the case of the male and from 700 gr–1 kg 350 gr in the case of the female. Distribution: Throughout Europe with the exception of Iceland, the Faroes and the north of Scandinavia. Sub-species inhabit the Canary Islands, the Azores and the Cap Verde Islands. There are also sub-species found in Asia. Reproduction: Two or three white eggs with brown speckles are laid once a year. They are hatched by the female in approximately 34 days.

Caddis-fly (I)

Trichoptera
The caddis-fly undergoes a complete metamorphosis; its larva is aquatic (apart from the very rare exception). The larvae are found in very large numbers in mountain streams up to a high altitude. They live in a cocoon whose form allows them to be recognised on occasion. The cocoon is usually made from grains of sand which are stuck together with a secretion produced by the larva. These larvae can be seen crawling across the beds of streams, where they feed on vegetable matter or decomposed animals. The adult caddis-fly does not move far away from the water and seems rather similar to certain butterflies, especially those belonging to the Psychidae family, such as the *Oreopsyche plumifera*.

Camponotus herculaneus (I)

This is a large, blackish ant with a wide head, a reddish thorax belonging to the family of Formicidae. The animal digs tunnels in dead wood or fallen tree trunks. The females are

Black vulture.

Brephos parthenias.

Larvae of the caddis fly (*Trichoptera*).

Caddis fly (*Trichoptera*).

Chough.

Cicindela gallica.

Coenonympha gardetta.

large and winged, reaching a length of 16mm. The workers are smaller and vary in size. This species is particularly common in the mountains throughout the alpine ranges.

Capercaillie (B).
Tetrao urogallus
Length: 85cm for the male; 60cm for the female. Wing spread: 120–150cm for the male; 100cm for the female. Weight of the male: from 4–5kg in the Alps, Jura, Vosges, Pyrenees; from 5–8kg for the males in Scandinavia and eastern Europe. Average weight of the female: 2.50kg. Distribution: Alps, Pyrenees, Scotland, the large forests of central Europe, Scandinavia, eastern Europe, a large part of Asia. It is non-migratory. Reproduction: Sexual maturity is reached at two years. The nest, which is lined with leaves, is made in a cavity beneath a bush or at the foot of a tree. The capercaillie lays 7–9 beige eggs with brown spots. Incubation: 26–28 days. Food: All sorts of wild berries, buds of conifers and beech trees, alders and birches. Shoots and needles of larch trees and white pines. Seeds, beech nuts, and during summer all types of insects.

Carabus auronitens (I)
A splendid beetle of the Carabidae family, which can reach a length of 28mm. The head and body are of a copper red colour. The wing sheaths are brilliant, bright green with black sides. It is found in the mountains up to the tree line and even beyond. There are numerous local variants. Distribution: Alps, Vosges, Jura, Dauphiné, Massif Central.

Carabus hortensis (I)
A beetle of the Carabidae family which varies quite considerably in colour, although it is most often black with violet spots when found at high altitudes; its length is from 13–18mm. The melanistic species is similar to the dark coloured 'Orinocarabus latreillanus csiki', from the Alps of Valais. It is very common and widely found in Europe (France, Switzerland, Poland, Russia). It is also common in certain areas of the Alps, where the author found it up to an altitude of 2400m.

Chaffinch (B)
Fringilla coelebs
Length: 15cm. Wing span: 26cm. Average weight: 24g. Distribution: The whole of Europe apart from the extreme north; Asia Minor, north Africa, western Siberia. They lay a clutch of three to four eggs of varying colour. Often they are greenish or greyish but sometimes pale beige, marked with brownish red patches surrounded by paler brown and by rust coloured spots. The female incubates the eggs from twelve to thirteen days and the young leave the nest after two weeks. Food: Various insects, cereal seeds and conifer seeds, especially in winter.

Chamois (M)
Rupicapra rupicapra
Length: 1.10–1.30m for the alpine chamois; 1–1.01m for the pyrenean chamois. Height to the withers: 80–85cm for the male, 75–80cm for the female. Average height to the withers: for the pyrenean chamois 70cm. In the summer months, the male weighs from 45–50kg. The female weighs from 30–35kg. The pyrenean chamois is much smaller and lighter than the alpine chamois (on average 10kg lighter). The alarm cry is given by a nasal hissing noise which is much longer than the cry made by the ibex. The chamois pays attention to the whistles of the marmot. Distribution: At present the chamois inhabits the greater part of the alpine range and, in its local geographical form, the Pyrenees. Moreover, during the last twenty years it has colonized large areas of the Swiss Jura and can also be found in the French Jura (peaks of the Mont-Dore and Mont Pontarlier). It has recently been introduced into Germany in the Black Forest and from there has extended into the south-west of Schwaben in Germany and the mountainous regions of the Elbe; in 1956 it also inhabited the Vosges. Other regional types inhabit the Apennines, the Balkan mountains, the Carpathians, and the range of the Tatra. Reproduction: The rutting season finishes in November, and mating

only lasts a few seconds, although the female can be mounted several times by different males. Period of gestation: 160–180 days. The young are born with their eyes open, usually from mid-May to mid-June and are suckled sometimes until November. The female first gives birth at the age of two years. Longevity: Twenty years.

Chough (B)
Pyrrhocorax pyrrhocorax
Length: 35–38cm. Wing span: 76–80cm. Weight: 290g for the female and up to 350g for the male. Distribution: In Switzerland only found in Valais and Grisons. In France: the Alps, the Pyrenees, Causse; some small colonies in Finistère and Morbihan. Mountains of southern Europe, Great Britain, north Africa and Asia. The bird always nests in an inaccessible spot, under an outcrop of rock, in a hole or crack. The nest is made of small branches and decorated with wool and hairs. Three to five eggs are laid, which are creamy white or greenish in colour, speckled with brown. Length of incubation: 21 days. The young leave the nest after 36–40 days. At first their beak is either yellow or slightly orange in colour which makes them easily confused with the alpine chough.

Chrysochloa gloriosa (I)
This beetle belongs to the family of Chrysomelidae and is characterised by the oblong shape and its brilliant colours. It is 8–11mm in length. Its colour can vary a great deal, but it is generally metallic green with blue stripes, or golden green with purple stripes. Distribution: Alpine meadows on the large umbelliferous plants up to an altitude of 2000m. Most of the mountain ranges of central Europe.

Chrysochraon brachyptera (I)
This small cricket belongs to the family of Acrididae and is scarcely ever longer than 20–25mm (female). It has very small wings (3–5mm) and is found in the mountain meadows up to an altitude of 2000m. It is common but localised: the Massif Central, the Alps and the Pyrenees.

Cicindela gallica (I).
This tiger beetle is limited to the high alpine areas of France, Switzerland, Italy, up to an altitude of 2600m. The wing sheaths are dark green or bronze, and are marked with several ivory white crescents and a hooked crossband across the centre. Length: 13–17mm.

Citril finch (B)
Carduelis citrinella
Length: 13cm. Wing span: 22cm. Average weight: 12g. Distribution: The mountains of central and western Europe up to 2300m. The Alps, Vosges, Massif Central, Jura, Pyrenees. It spends the winter in large colonies at the bottom of sunny valleys. The birds travel considerable distances towards the southern slopes of the mountains. They lay four to five greenish blue eggs with brown marks. The incubation is carried out by the female for fourteen days. The young leave the nest after seventeen days. There can be either one or two clutches of eggs produced annually, depending on atmospheric conditions. Food: Seeds of wild plants and conifers, caterpillars and small insects.

Coal tit (B)
Parus ater
Length: 11cm. Wing span: 18cm. Average weight: 9–10g. Distribution: Throughout Europe with the exception of the extreme north. It is rarely found in the west of France and it is absent in south-west plains of the southern area of France. Asia Minor, north Africa, a part of Asia, the Ukraine and the Italian peninsula. In general it is non-migratory except in the north and east of Europe. One clutch of eight to ten white eggs, speckled with rust are laid in a hole in trees or walls. The nest is built of moss, hair and wool. Incubation is carried out by the female for twelve to fourteen days. The young leave the nest after about three weeks and subsequently fly through the forest in small groups together with the adults. In general two clutches of eggs are laid annually.

Coenonympha gardetta (I)

Greyish brown, small butterfly of the Saty-ridae family, whose fore-wings are slightly overlaid with beige. The underneath part of the hind wings is greyish or brownish grey with a pale band, containing six to seven black eye markings, with white centred spots. The fore-wing of the male: 16 mm. This species is common in the high alpine meadows between 1500 and 2400 m. Distribution: Massif Central, northern Alps and the Balkans.

Common frog (AM)

Rana temporaria
Length: up to 10 cm. Distribution: Throughout Europe, from the Pyrenees to the North Cape, although the species is absent in the south of France and Italy. Eggs are laid once a year numbering from 1000–4000. Incubation lasts from three to four weeks, possibly longer at high altitudes, depending on the temperature of the water. The life of the tadpole lasts from three to four months.

Common shrew (M)

Sorex araneus
Length: head and • body: 6–8 cm. Tail: 3.2–5.5 cm. Average weight: 9 g. Distribution: Throughout Europe with the exception of Ireland, Iceland, certain Mediterranean islands and the greater part of the Iberian Peninsula. It is widespread in Asia. Gestation from thirteen to twenty days. The young are born naked in a nest of dry grass, and are suckled for three weeks approximately. There are three to four litters born annually, consisting from five to eight young. They have a very short life: six months to one year at the most.

Common vole (M)

Microtus arvalis
Average length: head and body: 10 cm. Tail: 3.7 cm. Weight varies greatly: from 15–51 g. Distribution: Central and eastern Europe. Absent in the greater part of Britanny and in the British Isles, with the exception of the Orkney Islands, where the largest species can be found. It is also absent in Italy and in the entire Mediterranean periphery. Reproduction: Throughout the year. The nest is built of grass in the shape of a ball, with a large inner cavity measuring up to 50 cm in depth. It is sometimes built on the grassy ground beneath the snow or even beneath a large stone. Gestation lasts twelve days approximately. On average there are five litters born annually, consisting of five to ten young, born naked and blind, growing fur from the sixth day and opening their eyes from the ninth day. The coat of the young is at first light grey on the back and white under the stomach, eventually turning to dark grey and finally beige brown.

Crag martin (B)

Ptyonoprogne rupestris
Length: 16–17 cm. Wing span: 34 cm. Average weight: 21 g. Distribution: Rocky crags of southern Europe, the Alps, Jura, the Massif Central, Pyrenees and Corsica. The bird builds its nest up to an altitude of 1800 m in the Alps. One clutch annually is laid, consisting of four to five white eggs, speckled with rust. The young leave the nest after 25 days.

Cranberry blue (I)

Vacciniina optilete
Small butterfly of the Lycaenidae family, characterised by the upper part of its wings, which are dark violet blue without any other pattern apart from the narrow, black edges. The upper surface of the female's wings are dark brown with traces of violet scales at their base. Forewing of the male: 13–15 mm. The underneath of its wings are yellowish grey in both sexes, and have markings which are found on the argus. The species is widespread throughout the mountain slopes and plains up to 2200 m. Distribution: Central Alps and Arctic Europe as far as Japan.

Crested tit (B)

Parus cristatus
Length: 11–12 cm. Wing span: 20 cm. Weight: 11 g. Distribution: Throughout Europe with the exception of southern Italy, the north of Scandinavia, a part of the Ukraine and the greater part of the British Isles. It is

also absent in Corsica. The bird is non-migratory but travels widely in autumn and winter. It lays one clutch of five to eight white eggs with chestnut coloured marks. The nest, which is placed in a hole of a tree trunk, is made of moss and lichens, lined with horse hair and wool. In the mountains, eggs are laid once annually, very rarely twice. Incubation is carried out by the female and lasts for two weeks. The young fly away after three weeks. Food is similar to that of the coal tit: insects and their eggs or larvae and seeds of conifers in the winter.

Crocota lutearia (I)

Small moth of the Geometridae family, with ochre yellow coloured wings. The fore-wing measures from 18–19 mm. The female is noticeably smaller and lighter in colour than the male. The species is common throughout the whole of the sub-alpine and alpine zones up to an altitude of 2300 m. Distribution: Alps and Massif Central.

Crossbill (B)

Loxia curvirostra
Length: 16 cm. Wing span: 27–30 cm. Average weight: 35 g. Distribution (very wide): Alps, Vosges, Jura, Massif Central, Pyrenees and other parts of Europe; north Africa, Asia and North America. Generally found in coniferous mountain forests, and also in the coniferous trees of parks and gardens in the plains. Reproduction: The bird nests throughout the year, but prefers the months between December and May. The nest is built in a conifer and is always well protected, sometimes at a height of 30 m and sometimes only a few metres away from the ground. It is built of dry twigs, grass, moss, lichens and small roots. Three to four eggs are laid, once or twice annually. These are of a greenish white colour, speckled with brown, black or rust. Incubation begins with the first egg and lasts for two weeks. The young leave their nest at the end of two weeks. Their striped plumage is darker than that of the adult female, which is of a greenish appearance. The young male, when moulting, is a fine yellowish orange or pink.

Cuckoo (B)

Cuculus canorus
Length: 32.5 cm. Wing span: 60 cm. Average weight for the male: 118 g, for the female: 100 g. Distribution: Throughout Europe with the exception of the extreme north-east and the islands in the North Atlantic; almost everywhere in Asia, Africa. The bird is migratory and spends the winter in tropical or southern Africa. Food: various insects, but in particular furry caterpillars which, because of their irritating hairs, are disdained by other birds.

Cynthia's fritillary (I)

Euphydryas cynthia
A butterfly belonging to the Nymphalidae family, of medium size and characterised by marked dimorphism between male and female. The colour of the male on the upper parts of the wings: russet brown on a white background, the white background being marked by black patches; the female is orangey brown, rather uniform in appearance, with transverse blackish lines. The fore-wing of the male: 19–21 mm. This is a typical species of the alpine meadows where juniper bushes end and myrtle bushes grow. It is very common but limited to the Alps and the mountains of Bulgaria at a height of between 600 and 2500 m. In the Alps of Valais it is found up to 2800 m and above. The caterpillar lives on the plantains in the Alps.

Daddy-long-legs (A)

Pholcus phalangiodes
The daddy-long-legs is very similar in appearance to the spider, although it differs in certain structural details. Their legs, which are extremely long and thin, support a tiny body which is normally oval in shape and segmented, the cephalthorax and the abdomen being fused. The two eyes are situated in the centre of the cephalthorax. If seized by an attacker the daddy-long-legs immediately abandons one or more of its very fragile legs and escapes. The abandoned leg continues to move spasmodically and attracts the attention of the attacker. The daddy-long-legs feeds on

Common shrew.

Cranberry blue.

Crocota lutearia.

Cuckoo.

207

Dewy ringlet.

A dipper diving (10 to 30 seconds). After seeking its food at the bottom of the stream, it comes out of the water seemingly dry, owing to its watertight plumage.

Dusky grizzled skipper.

Endrosa aurita.

Erebia

various types of decaying matter which is plentiful in the mountain woods and sub-alpine meadows; certain species are found as high as the snow areas. Distribution: Very wide.

Dark green fritillary (I)
Mesoacidalia charlotta
Large butterfly belonging to the Nymphalidae family. It is characterised by silvery patches on the underside of its back wings; the wings are generally greenish in colour with a more yellowish appearance for the male. The fore-wing of the male measures from 25–29 mm. The upper part of the wing is beige with the black designs which are common to Argynnis. The caterpillar is spiny and feeds on violets. The species is widely spread throughout the woodland meadows and flowery fields, from sea level up to more than 2500 m. Distribution: Throughout Europe up to the North Cape, including England, although it is absent in Crete and the Mediterranean islands with the exception of Sicily.

Dewy ringlet (I)
Erebia pandrose
Medium size butterfly belonging to the enormous family of Satyridae, characterised by the general brownish colour of the upper part of the wings with a large beige patch on the fore-wings, surrounding 4 black spots and a dark coloured transverse line. The underpart of the rear wings is silvery grey in colour crossed by two irregular dark lines. Measurement of the fore-wing of the male: 21–25 mm. The caterpillar feeds on grass. This species is widespread in stony meadows from 1800 m to 2500 m. More frequently found in the alpine ranges and the Pyrenees. It is also found in the arctic regions where it can be seen from the sea level up. It is absent in the Jura and the Vosges.

Dipper (B)
Cinclus cinclus
Length: 18 cm. Wing span: 30 cm. Weight: 50–70 g. The dipper is a typical inhabitant of streams and rivers in the mountains and occasionally near the plains. It builds its nests up to an altitude of 2200 m and can be found even higher. Distribution: Most of Europe and Asia, and also north Africa. Average number of smooth, white eggs laid is five. Length of incubation: about two weeks. The young leave the nest after 20–25 days in May or in June, depending on the altitude. It appears normal for eggs to be laid a second time during the summer.

Dotterel (B)
Charadrius morinellus
Length: 21 cm. Wing span: 45–47 cm. Weight: 120 g. The mating plumage is very different and much more colourful than the autumn plumage. The wide eyebrow and throat appear much whiter and the sides of the neck and the front of the chest, which are greyish brown, are separated from the bright red of the breast and sides by a black and white arc. The base of the stomach is black and the area under the caudal feathers is white; the legs are brownish yellow in the adult and olive yellow in the young. The nest is a simple hollow between stones or in low vegetation. The dotterel lays three olive coloured eggs spotted with black. Once the eggs have been laid it is the male who takes on incubation as well as raising the young! The European dotterel is a descendant of the ice age and lives on the summits of the mountains of Styria, Carinthia and Transylvania. But the species is now becoming rare. The fact that it builds its nests in the Alps, especially in Grisons, Switzerland, was proved for the first time in 1965, by Dr J. Burnier of Geneva.

Dragonfly (I)
Aeschna juncea
This insect usually appears in the second half of July. Eggs are laid a few days after it completes its metamorphosis, and the laying season can continue from July to mid-October, according to altitude. In sub-alpine areas the dragonfly can appear at the beginning of July. Usually the larvae go through seven to eight moults and spend the first winter in the water, leaving it at the beginning

of July to complete the chrysalis stage. At this time great numbers of dragonflies appear on the borders of numerous alpine lakes. The eggs are laid from July to September, but chiefly in August, and these do not hatch until the following year. The complete cycle therefore lasts two years. Distribution: Throughout northern Europe and Asia as far as Kamchatka, in the central European mountains, from 800 to 2400 m.

Dunnock (B)
Prunella modularis
Length: 15 cm. Wing span: 21 cm. Average weight: 20 g. Distribution: Europe, apart from the extreme north and south, and Asia Minor. Found in the Alps up to an altitude of 2200 m. An interesting fact is that this bird, although exclusively restricted to the mountains in Switzerland, is often found in France in the plains near the Atlantic coast, where it is non-migratory. Those birds inhabiting the mountains migrate partly to the south, although many of them descend to the plains for the winter if the climate is suitable. Incubation period: Thirteen to fourteen days. The young leave the nest after about twelve days. Eggs are sometimes laid twice a year, even in the mountains. Food: Small insects and larvae, spiders, molluscs, and the seeds of wild plants.

Dusky grizzled skipper (I)
Pyrgus cacaliae
This species is only found in the high mountains from 1990 to 3000 m. It has one generation which lives in July and August. The fore-wing of the male: 13–15 mm. Distribution: Maritime Alps, High Alps, Alps of Valais etc. It has been found in the Bucegi mountains in the Carpathians and the Pyrenees. The caterpillar feeds on coltsfoot.

Eagle owl (B)
Bubo bubo
Length: 52–72 cm. Wing span: 1.60–1.80 cm. Weight of male: 2–2.5 kg. Weight of female: 2.5–3.20 kg. Distribution: Alps, the southern Massif Central, the Pyrenees, Provence. The bird appears to be extinct in the Jura, Burgundy and the Vosges. It is absent also from the British Isles, Holland, Denmark and most of the Mediterranean islands. The species still nests in Austria, the Harz mountains, Saxony and the Balkans, but it is becoming rare everywhere, in particular in Scandinavia and Finland. It is also present in Asia and north Africa. It is very sedentary and remains faithful to its breeding site. In the Alps, the eyrie is generally built on a rocky crag, protected by a sheer rock, facing the south. Two or three greyish white eggs are laid in a cavity in the ground, scratched out by the female. Length of incubation: 34–36 days. The young leave the nest after ten weeks approximately.

Egyptian vulture (B)
Neophron percnopterus
Length: 60–68 cm. Average wing span: 1.50 m. Average weight: 2 kg. Distribution: Southern Europe, Africa, Asia Minor, India. In France the Egyptian vulture is migratory and spends winter in the south of the Sahara. Reproduction: The nest is placed in a hole of a rock face in fairly high mountains. One clutch is produced annually and there are one or two whitish eggs, speckled with brown; these are laid on a pile of small branches, lined with rubbish and wool. Incubation is carried out by both adults for 42 days. The young, when completely covered with a dark brown plumage, leave the nest after two months and a half and gradually become lighter in colour after each moult, although they do not assume the adult plumage until they are five years old.

Endrosa aurita (I)
Small tiger moth belonging to the Arctiidae. It is russet yellow with black spots on the fore-wing, which, in the male, measures from 13–14 mm. The female is smaller and the black spots are less pronounced. At high altitudes these moths have thick stripes along the veins instead of the black spots, and they are smaller in size, with paler coloured wings. The species is found in the rocky areas of the Alps and the Jura from 800–2600 m.

Erebia cassioides (I)

Butterfly of the Satyridae family, brownish in colour with short beige stripes on the upper part of the wings and with very visible eye markings with black eye spots on the fore-wings. Length: 17–19 mm for the fore-wing. Common on the grassy slopes of the sub-alpine meadows up to 1900 m. Distribution: The species is limited to Europe from the Cantabrian mountains to the Balkans.

Erebia euryale (I)

This species is related to the preceding one, but is larger. Length: 21–23 mm for the fore-wing of the male. There are blank eye spots in the beige stripes, which are much clearer on the upper side of the wings, the latter being bordered with a fringe. There are eye markings with white spots on the underside of the wings. The insect lives in glades and sparse woods from 1000–2000 m. Distribution: Pyrenees, Massif Central, Carpathian mountains, Alps and Balkans.

Erebia euryale adyte (I)

Very similar to the preceding species. It differs through the eye markings on the upper part of the wings which are generally provided with white spots. The same habitat. Distribution: (See text on the Insects of the sub-alpine meadows).

Erebia gorge (I)

Smaller than the preceding species. The fore-wing of the male measures from 17–20 mm. It has a satin-like appearance and is brightly coloured. Light grey alternates with dark grey on the under-part of the hind-wings. It is found at higher altitudes than *Erebia euryale*; it inhabits the moraine and rocky slopes up to 3000 m. Distribution: It is limited to the rocky mountain areas of Europe.

Erebia nivalis (I)

This species is closely related to *Erebia gorge*. The size is slightly smaller. The fore-wing of the male is 15–17 mm. The eye markings of the fore-wings are very small and have white centres. The underneath of the hind-wings is marbled in grey with characteristic bluish reflections. It lives chiefly in the upper edges of the alpine forests between 2000 and 2200 m. It is limited to the Alps.

Eresus niger (A)

Very handsome spider measuring, in the case of the male, from 8–9 mm and in the case of the female, which is much larger, from 19–28 mm. The male is black, with a bright red or orange abdomen marked with four black patches. The female is completely black. This remarkable and rather rare species belongs to the group of primitive spiders. It appears to prefer dry ground, rocky areas or the slopes of valleys which are well-exposed to the sun, and it is found in the Alps up to an altitude of 2200 m. It can also be found on the plains, especially in Provence. Its exact distribution is still unknown.

Ergates faber (I)

One of the largest European beetles, belonging to the family of Cerambycidae. It has long wing sheaths and very developed antennae, especially in the male, which measures from 30–45 mm, whereas the female is sometimes larger than 50 mm. The wing sheaths of the male is reddish brown, usually dark, with the thorax showing laterally two shining patches. The female is blackish brown with a much rougher thorax. It is found chiefly in pine forests, in the mountains up to an altitude of 2000 m. The larva digs tunnels in the wood and takes several years to reach its full size. Distribution: Western Pyrenees, maritime Alps, Alsace, and the southern slopes of the alpine ranges.

Eudia pavonia (I)

Rather large butterfly with a strong hairy body, belonging to the family Attacidae, although its activity is diurnal. The female is noticeably larger than the male and is brownish in colour without any trace of yellow or orange on its lower wings. The antennae of the male are short but forked, which allows it to seek out newly born females in full sunlight. This fine species is found up to 2200 m and above in the mountains, seeking out the slopes exposed to the sun, and throughout almost the entire alpine ranges.

European lynx (M)

Lynx lynx

Total length: 1–1.30 m. Height to the withers: 60–70 cm. Weight: 20–30 kg. The northern lynx is larger and the male can exceed 35 kg in weight. Distribution: North and north-west of Europe, Tatras Mountains, Carpathians. It was reintroduced into the Swiss Alps in 1970. Reproduction: Rutting season in February–March. Length of gestation: 70 days. 2–4 young are produced, which open their eyes after two weeks. They are suckled for approximately 2 months. One litter is produced annually. Longevity: 16–18 years. Food: Chiefly mammals up to the size of the deer, various birds, in particular the grouse. Its large prey is killed by a bite through the back of the neck. The lynx does not generally attack man except when wounded or in defence of its young when they are threatened.

Field vole (M)

Microtus agrestis

Average length (head and body): 11 cm. Tail: 3.7 cm. Weight varies greatly between 16 and 62 g. Distribution: Throughout Europe with the exception of the greater part of the mediterranean basin and the south east. It is also absent in the greater part of Spain and is not found at all in either Ireland or Iceland. Reproduction: Similar to the common vole.

Fox (M)

Vulpes vulpes

Length of body: 60–70 cm. Tail: 32–43 cm. Average height to the withers: 37 cm. Weight varies between 6 and 10 kg. Cry: Apart from the hoarse bark, the fox yelps and, during the rutting season, utters plaintive cries which are penetrating and grunting in character. Distribution: Throughout Europe with the exception of Iceland and Crete. Reproduction: The rutting season takes place from January to March and lasts until April in the mountains. Gestation is 50–52 days. The female gives birth in her lair, having built a nest of grass and hair; three to eight young are produced, and they are born blind, opening their eyes after two weeks. They are suckled for one month, sometimes longer, and are then fed chiefly by the female, and occasionally by the male. One litter is produced annually. The fox can live up to about ten years. Food: The fox is more or less omnivorous. It feeds chiefly, however, on small rodents, worms, insects and, in particular, the grasshopper in the mountains, young chicks of gallinaceous birds and young birds, squirrels, fawns, and even adult deer in winter, which the fox attacks while they are alive, but enfeebled by the snow. In autumn it feeds on fruit and wild berries and during the winter months dead carcases and refuse. In the mountains the author has often found broken shells of pine seeds in the winter droppings of the fox. The rôle of the fox as a predatory animal is important and necessary, as it eliminates automatically sick animals and prevents the dangers of epidemics. Nevertheless, its numbers must be limited and kept under control.

Garden dormouse (M)

Eliomys quercinus

Length of body: 14 cm. Tail: 12 cm. Weight varies according to season: from 50–120 g. There is a large amount of fat acquired in the autumn before hibernation and the animal is much thinner when it reawakens in the spring. Distribution: North Africa, throughout Europe, with the exception of the British Isles, Scandinavia (where it only exists in the south of Finland), the north of Germany and the coast line areas of the North Sea and the Baltic. It has a loud plaintive cry which is uttered frequently, especially during the rutting season. Length of gestation: 23 days. Three to seven young are produced and these are naked and blind, only opening their eyes eighteen days after birth; the female suckles them for ten months.

Geotrupes vernalis alpinus (I)

Beetle of the Scarabaeidae family, very similar to the common Geotrupes of the plains, although the former is smaller with more convex, smoother wing sheaths which are greenish black in colour and more shiny. Length: 12–20 mm. Distribution: The entire alpine ranges where it can be found up to an altitude of 2500 m.

Giant wood wasp (I)

Urocerus gigas

A large member of the Uroceridae family which has an orange yellow abdomen marked with black in the case of the female. The female is always much larger than the male and can reach a length of 40 mm, not including the terebra, while the length of the male varies between 10 and 25 mm. This wasp-like creature introduces its eggs into the wood of the coniferous trees by means of its powerful terebra. The larvae develop slowly and dig long tunnels in the wood tissue. They are, however, often attacked by the *Ichneumon rhyssa persuasoria*. The giant wood wasp is common in the mountains throughout the alpine ranges.

Glandon blue (I)

Agriades glandon

Small butterfly with greyish blue upper surfaces or brown in the female. Fore-wing of male measuring from 13–15 mm. The species belongs to the vast family of Lycaenidae, commonly known as Argus. It prefers the mountains, inhabiting alpine meadows between 1800 and 2500 m. Distribution: Alps, Pyrenees, Balkans, Sierra Nevada.

Goldcrest (B)

Regulus regulus

Length: 8–10 cm. Weight: 4–5 g. Distribution: The Azores, the greater part of Europe, Asia as far as China (it is absent in the north of Scandinavia, the north and south of Russia and the greater part of Spain). It is found more frequently in the mountains than on the plains and the goldcrest is a typical inhabitant of the coniferous forests, in particular of the spruce forests. It is generally non-migratory in the Alps. Reproduction: seven to ten whitish eggs, spotted with brown. The female incubates them for sixteen days and the young leave the nest after fifteen to eighteen days according to the atmospheric conditions. There are usually two clutches produced annually. Food: Small insects and larvae or cocoons, spiders, greenfly etc.

Golden eagle (B)

Aquila chrysaëtus

Length of male: 80–87 cm. Wing span: 188–212 cm. Weight: 3550–4400 g. Length of female: 90–95 cm. Wing span: 215–230 cm. Weight: 4050–5720 g. The young, two to three year old eagle is much darker than the adult. It is almost black, with broad white patches on its wings and at the base of its tail. The adult rarely utters its cry, although in the spring whistling, mewing cries, rather like those of a buzzard, can sometimes be heard. When it is alarmed, near its eyrie, it utters a sort of muffled bark. The eyrie is generally built on an inaccessible ledge beneath a vertical rock face, between 1500 and 2400 m. In the Alps it consists of dry branches and fresh twigs. It lays one or two whitish eggs speckled with brown, particularly at one end. Incubation is carried out by the female and lasts about 40 days. The young eagle leaves the eyrie only after 75 days. It reaches sexual maturity after four to five years. Distribution: Very wide geographical distribution: Scotland, Ireland, Alps, Pyrenees, Massif Central, Apennines, Iberian peninsula, Scandinavia, eastern Europe, a large part of Asia and North America, north Africa. It is very rare in western Europe.

Goshawk (B)

Accipiter gentilis

Length of male: 55 cm. Female: 70 cm. Average weight of the male: 700 g. Average weight of the female: 1100 g. Wing span: 100–120 cm. Distribution: All of Europe apart from Iceland and the extreme north-east. In Great Britain only found in the south.

Asia, North America. The goshawk has become rare in France. Reproduction: The bird lays eggs once annually, producing two to four white or greenish eggs. Incubated by the female from 35–40 days. The young leave the nest after five or six weeks. Non-migratory, at least in central Europe.

Grayling (I)
Hipparchia semele
Butterfly belonging to the very large family of Satyridae found, in particular, in the temperate zones of the Old World. The fore-wing of the male measures between 27 and 30 mm. The female is larger, with beige patterns on the upper part of the wings. The species prefers dry ground and rocky woods well exposed to the sun, between 1000 and 2000 m, and above, from May throughout the summer. Distribution: Balkans, Alps, Pyrenees, central and southern Europe. Numerous local variants.

Great spotted woodpecker (B)
Dendrocopus major
Length: 22 cm. Wing span: 42 cm. Average weight: 80 g. Distribution: Throughout Europe with the exception of northern Scandinavia and Ireland. North Africa, Asia Minor and the greater part of Asia. It is non-migratory in the Alps up to the tree line. Reproduction: The hole which leads to its cavity measures from 4–5 cm in diameter and 22–30 cm in depth. Four to six shining, white eggs are laid and these are occasionally placed on a few twigs. Incubation: Eleven to twelve days. The young leave the nest after 22 days on an average.

Greater horseshoe bat (M)
Rhinolophus ferrumequinum
Average length of the body: 6.5 cm. Length of the front leg: 5.6 cm. Average weight: 22–25 g. The female, in general, is a little heavier than the male. The fur is a reddish brown on the back and pinkish grey on the ventral surface. The species is rather large, with well-developed ears, but it is most remarkable for the extraordinary nasal appendage which is in the form of the upper part of a violin. This nasal characteristic serves as a sound board which channels ultrasonic sounds, emitted through the nostrils. Muscular contractions allow its shape to be changed, so that the animal can utter either intense or diffused sounds. The ears are constantly moving and act as receivers. The greater horseshoe bat can detect isolated obstacles by noting the differences in the intensity of echoes. Therefore it utters regular prolonged sounds directed towards the objects which surround it. In order that the echo may be well-received, its ears must be constantly moving. Distribution: Throughout Europe, with the exception of the north and the north-east. The animal is present in southern England and Wales. It is particularly common in the mediterranean basin, in north Africa and in Egypt. It is also found in Asia as far as China and Japan, and in the Alps up to an altitude of 2000 m, where, at this height, it hibernates in deep caves. Reproduction: The rutting season takes place in autumn, but true fertilization takes place when the animal emerges from hibernation, through the sperm which is stored in a special pouch and which is used when the ovary is released. Gestation is about 75 days. Usually only one young bat is born, and immediately after birth it seizes the maternal fur and attaches itself firmly to the false pubic nipples, only leaving them in order to suckle. Its suckling teeth are perfectly formed at birth and are soon lost. The female greater horseshoe bat takes her offspring with her during her nocturnal flights, at least for the first few days. The author has seen a mother, who had been disturbed in a cavern, carrying a young bat which was almost as large as herself, and was attached to the false pubic nipples of the adult in an upside down position. The young bat is naked at birth and opens its eyes after a week. It is able to fly only after four weeks, but can reproduce at the end of the first year. Longevity: About twenty years. Food: Various insects which are usually caught while the bat is in flight, although they are sometimes taken from the branches or leaves of trees. The greater horseshoe bat

takes water from the surface of calm pools and rivers.

Green tiger beetle (I)
Cicindela campestris
Beetle belonging to the family of the Cicindelinae. Of average size with large head armed with powerful drawers, protruding eyes, long, thin legs; it is very agile and carnivorous, taking flight at the least sight of danger. Length: 12–15 mm. The wing sheaths are greenish with yellowish white patches, varying in size. It is found in the mountains up to the tree line and beyond. There are numerous local variations. Distribution: Alps, Pyrenees, relatively common throughout France and in a large part of Switzerland.

Green woodpecker (B)
Picus viridis
Total length: 31 cm. Length of beak: 4–5 cm. Wing span: 50 cm. Weight: up to 200 g. Habitat: Small woods in the plains, but also mountain forests up to 2000 m (especially in the Alps of Valais). This species is closely related to the black woodpecker, being distinguished from the latter by its smaller size and its more greyish plumage. The male has a small red patch on the front of its head. The female's black 'moustaches' are narrower. This woodpecker is never found as high as the green woodpecker in the Alps. Distribution: As the green woodpecker, in the Alps and generally throughout Europe up to Lat. 60° N. Asia Minor, West Iran. It is non-migratory. One clutch annually of five to eight pure white eggs is laid. The young leave the nest after three weeks.

Grey wagtail (B)
Motacilla cinerea
Length: 21 cm. Wing span: 29 cm. Average weight: 18–19 g. Distribution: All of Europe apart from the east and the larger part of Scandinavia. North Africa, Asia Minor and Asia as far as Japan. Reproduction: Eggs are laid twice annually (once only at high altitude). There are between four and six whitish eggs, speckled with russet brown, and they are incubated by both adults for two weeks.

Griffon vulture (B)
Gyps fulvus
Average length: 1 m. Wing span: 2.57 m. Average weight: 7 kg. Distribution: In France it is found only in the Pyrenees, where it is becoming rare. It is also found in Spain, Sardinia, Sicily, north Africa, Asia Minor and central Asia, South Africa, Egypt. Reproduction: The nest is usually built on an inaccessible cliff and is made up of branches, hair and dry grass. The griffon vulture nests and lives in colonies. One clutch of eggs annually. The single egg produced is whitish in colour, with brownish red marks. It is incubated by the female for 52 days. The young leave the eyrie after two months, generally in July. The laying season begins either at the end of January or in February.

Hazel hen (B)
Tetrastes bonasia
Length: 35–36 cm. Wing span: 54–65 cm. Weight: 329–440 g. Distribution: Alps, Central Europe, Scandinavia, Russia and a large part of Asia. It is non-migratory and remains very attached to its local territory. Eight to ten shining, russet coloured eggs with a number of brown patches. Length of incubation: 21 days. Food: All types of wild berries, insects, molluscs, worms in winter, young shoots, buds and pine needles.

Honey buzzard (B)
Pernis apivorus
Average length: 55 cm. Wing span: 117–125 cm. Weight: 600–950 g. Distribution: Throughout almost all of Europe apart from the north-east and the north of Scandinavia. The species does not exist in Iceland. In France it is less common than the buzzard, but is still found throughout the country apart from Corsica and the extreme south. It is also found in Switzerland, in the higher areas of Belgium and Holland, but is very rare in Great Britain. Two eggs of a dark, russet brown colour, are laid annually. The young

leave their nest after six weeks.

Ibex or wild goat (M)
Capra ibex
Length of body: 1.30–1.50 m for the male and 1.05–1.25 m for the female. Tail: 12–14 cm. Height to the withers: 70–90 cm. Average weight of the male: 90–105 kg, but certain specimens, becoming particularly fat in the autumn, can reach a weight of 130 kg. The female is much lighter; her average weight varies between 45 and 50 kg. Length of horns: 85 cm to 1 m. Average weight of the male adult horn, according to Couturier: 3256 kg. Distribution: The ibex is only found in the French, Swiss and Austrian Alps, in Germany, Italy, Yugoslavia, the mountain areas of the Tatras. Recently, it has, however, been introduced into numerous regions. Summer coat: fine grey. Female: yellowish beige. Winter coat: chestnut brown or chocolate. There is one moult in the spring. Rutting season is from November to January. Gestation lasts from 21–23 weeks. The female gives birth to one or two kids, but not necessarily every year. The young are given milk for approximately six months. Sexual maturity is reached in both sexes at the age of eighteen months. Most active reproduction, according to Couturier, takes place from the age of $2\frac{1}{2}$ or $3\frac{1}{2}$ years. Longevity: up to twenty years, sometimes even longer. Food: Chiefly fescue, various alpine plants, lichens, twigs of small bushes and young shoots of conifers. The ibex sometimes descends to the forests in winter, but generally lives above the tree line for the greater part of the year, climbing to the areas of snow in the summer. Highest altitude at which the ibex has been found is 4061 m, at the summit of the Gran Paradiso.

Ichneumon (I)
General name given to insects of the family Ichneumonidae, which are extremely widespread throughout the whole world. In France alone there are more than 5000 species. Their size is variable, but rarely smaller than 5 mm, and they often exceed 20 mm. Many are dark in colour, but several of them have yellow and black striped abdomens, recalling to a certain extent the appearance of a wasp. They all lay eggs which develop as parasites on the bodies of larvae of other insects, usually inside the latter, although they are occasionally to be found on the outside. The ichneumon plays a very important rôle in nature, by controlling the number of many harmful insects such as butterflies, beetles, spiders.

Idas blue (I)
Lycaeides idas
Small butterfly of the Lycaenidae family, characterised by the upper part of the wings, which are a brilliant blue colour in the case of the male and brown for the female. The underpart of the wings have points normally associated with the argus and black spots along their edges with greenish blue centres. The fore-wing of the male is 15–16 mm. The caterpillar lives in symbiosis with different species of ants. The idas blue is widely distributed over the mountain slopes up to an altitude of 2200 m. Distribution: Throughout western and central Europe, including Scandinavia.

Jay (B)
Garrulus glandarius
Length: 33 cm. Wing span: 52–54 cm. Average weight: 170 g. Distribution: Throughout Europe with the exception of the extreme north; Asia Minor, west of Iran, Asia as far as Japan and north Africa. Reproduction: The bird builds its nest of small branches and roots, generally at a height of between two and five metres in large bushes or small trees, occasionally against the trunk of a tree. Four to seven eggs are laid once a year; they are greenish grey in colour, finely speckled with brown. They are laid in May, but sometimes later in the mountains. Incubation is carried out by both members of the pair and lasts seventeen days. The young leave the nest after twenty days approximately.

Kestrel (B)
Falco tinnunculus
Average length: 35 cm. Wing span:

70–80 cm. Average weight: 200 g. The female is slightly heavier than the male. Distribution: Very wide, throughout Europe with the exception of the extreme north-east and Iceland; almost throughout Asia, Africa and Arabia. Reproduction: Eggs are laid once a year, numbering four to six, which are russet coloured. The female incubates them for about 30 days.

Large skipper (I)
Ochlodes venata
This is a small butterfly of the Hesperidae family characterised by its head, which is as wide as the thorax, its triangular fore-wings and its general beige colour, with russet yellow or greenish undersides of its hind-wings. This species inhabits the grassy slopes and alpine meadows up to 2500 m. Distribution: Very widespread throughout Europe up to 60° N. It is also found in Sicily, but is absent in the Mediterranean islands.

Leptura dubia (I)
Medium sized beetle, belonging to the Cerambycidae family, which is very common in the mountains and is found on the flowers of the sub-alpine meadows. Length: 12–18 mm. This longhorned beetle is related to the *Leptura rubra* and is an inhabitant of the coniferous forests, as its larvae develop in the stumps or trunks of the white pine, the larch and sometimes the spruce. It is widespread, but is localised in the Alps and the Pyrenees up to the tree line.

Leptura melanura (I)
Small beetle of the Cerambycidae family, which is recognised by its elongated wing sheaths, narrowing towards the end of the abdomen. The male which measures 7 mm in length, has reddish brown wing sheaths; the russet, orangy brown female is larger, measuring 9 mm in length. The wing sheaths and joints of both male and female are blackish, while the head and body are also of the same colour. This longhorned beetle is widespread and frequently found on umbelliferous plants as well as on scabious flowers and on the centaury plant; they are found in the mountain meadows throughout the alpine range.

Leptura sexmaculata (I)
Medium sized beetle of the Cerambycidae family, 12–18 mm long and characterised by sheer yellow wing sheaths decorated with six black patches. This insect is rarer than the ordinary *Leptura maculata*, which is frequently found in the alpine glades. The species is found in the eastern Alps and in a section of the southern Alps as well as in the Alps of Valais. The insect is always rather localised and found in small numbers.

Little blue (I)
Cupido minimus
Very small butterfly of the family Lycaenidae. The upper part of the wings are brown, and the male has silvery blue scales at the base of both fore and hind wings. The fore-wing of the male measures 10–12 mm. Very common and widely distributed, from sea level to more than 2000 m. Vast distribution: from the centre of Spain and France to Asia. Not found in a section of the interior of Scandinavia.

Lygris populata (I)
Small moth of the Geometridae family, which is commonly found throughout the alpine plains at the end of summer. It is similar in appearance to the *Camptogramma bilineata*, but is larger and paler in colour with a longer abdomen. It is sulphur yellow with brownish stripes and patterns on both wings. The caterpillar feeds on the dwarf alder and various types of bilberries. Distribution: In the Alps of Valais up to a height of 2400 m.

Malacosoma alpicola (I)
Small lackey moth belonging to the family of Lasiocampidae, which has a strong body, covered with thick hairs and greyish wings. The caterpillar is striped lengthwise and often lives in large colonies on dwarf alders. The female is always larger than the male. This species is sometimes found in large numbers on the alpine meadows of the mountainous areas of central Europe.

Malacosoma castrensis (I)
This species is very similar to the one above, but is a little larger. The fore-wing of the male: 11–13 mm. The fore-wing of the female: 20–22 mm. It is reddish brown, beige or greyish brown, according to sex, habitat and altitude. The female is always much larger than the male, but its size decreases on the higher meadows. The eggs are very resistant, and are laid in rings around the stems of low plants. The caterpillar turns into a chrysalis inside a yellow cocoon, but it is often attacked by a small parasitic Ichneumon. Distribution: Throughout the alpine mountain ranges up to an altitude of 2700 m; elsewhere it is also found on the plains.

Marbled white (I)
Melanargia galathea
A butterfly of the Satyridae family, characterised by the black and white designs similar to a chess board, covering the upper side of the wings. The species is common on the meadows and in the woods, from sea level up to more than 2000 m. The female is larger than the male and its fore-wing can reach a length of 28 mm. Distribution: From western Europe through southern Russia to the Caucasus and the north of Iran. It is absent in Scandinavia, Finland and Lithuania.

Mellicta varia (I)
This butterfly is slightly smaller than the spotted fritillary and is less reddish in colour. The upper part of the male's wings are brighter beige than that of the female's, which is usually dark brown. The fore-wing of the male: 15–17 mm. This is a typical inhabitant of the alpine meadows, usually living between 1800 and 2700 m. The caterpillar feeds on gentian. Distribution: The species is limited to the Alps and the Apennines.

Metrioptera roeseli (I)
Medium sized grasshopper of the family Tettigoniidae, characterised by a general brownish or greenish colour. The head is decorated with brown and black stripes, and the lateral lobes of the pronotum are bordered with yellow and green. Length of male: 14 mm. Length of female without the egg tube: 19 mm. Egg tube: 7–8 mm. The wing sheaths of the female half cover the abdomen, while those of the male cover it almost entirely. The species is very common throughout the woodland meadows and the alpine plains of mountainous areas up to 2200 m and above.

Minnow (F)
Phoxinus phoxinus
Length: 9–12 cm. The female is larger than the male. This fish has very tiny scales. Eggs, numbering from 200–1000 are laid in clear water on a gravel or pebble bed, and the fry are active as soon as they are born. This fish is the only cyprine which exists in alpine lakes, together with the trout. Very wide distribution, but in Europe it is absent in the south of Spain and Italy.

Mistle thrush (B)

Turdus viscivorus
Length: 26 cm. Wing span: 45–46 cm. Weight: 113 g. Distribution: Throughout Europe with the exception of the extreme north. Asia Minor; western Asia, north Africa. The bird is partially migratory. Reproduction: Three to five eggs, which are generally greenish blue speckled with brown, rust or violet grey spots. Incubation is carried out by the female and lasts for fifteen days. The young leave their nest after twelve to fifteen days, unable to fly well. One or two clutches of eggs are laid annually. In the mountains eggs are frequently laid to replace those destroyed.

Moorland clouded yellow (I)
Colias palaeno
Medium size butterfly of the Pieridae family, characterised by the sulphur yellow coloured upper part of the wings (the European form is found at high altitudes). The fore-wing of the male: 23–25 mm. The underside of the hind wing is often covered with dark coloured scales. This butterfly is found on slopes where myrtle and rhododendron bushes grow, from 1600–2500 m and above. The sub-species

Greater horseshoe bat.

Ichneumon.

Large skipper.

Leptura melanura.

211

Musk beetle (*Callidium violaceum*).

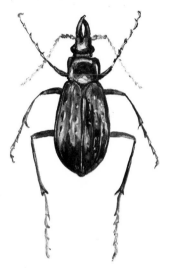

Orinocarabus latreillanus
(magnification 2×).

Painted lady.

Parasemia plantaginis.

Colias p. palaeno flies at low altitudes in Scandinavia and Finland. The upper part of its wings is much paler, and that of the female has the typical greenish white background.

Mouflon (M)
Ovis musimon
Length of body: 1.10–1.30 m. Height to the withers: 65–75 cm. The weight of the wild sheep living in Corsica varies between 25 and 35 kg, and the weight of those which have been introduced into France, Germany and Czechoslovakia, is between 30 and 50 kg. Distribution: This animal was originally from Corsica and Sardinia. It has at present been introduced into many regions of France where it numbers approximately 4000. There are 10 000 wild sheep in Germany, and approximately 6000 in Czechoslovakia. Reproduction: Gestation lasts approximately five months. There is usually only one young born, which is suckled for six months. Longevity: fifteen to twenty years.

Mountain clouded yellow (I)
Colias phicomone
Butterfly belonging to the family of Pieridae, and very common throughout the alpine and sub-alpine meadows up to an altitude of 2600 m. The upper part of its wings is yellowish or greenish white, sparsely speckled with dark grey spots, especially the male's, whose front wing measures 20–25 mm. Distribution: From the Alps to the Carpathian mountains, the Pyrenees, the Cantabrian mountains. It is absent in the Jura, the Apennines and the south of the Balkans.

Mountain hare (M)
Lepus timidus
Length including head and body: 50–65 cm. Average weight of animals found in the Alps: 2 kg. Individuals weighing more than 3 kg are exceptional. Distribution: Alps, northern and north-eastern Europe, Iceland, Ireland, Scotland. Northern part of Asia as far as Japan. It is widespread in North America. It is interesting to note that the mountain hare of Scotland and of the Scandinavian forests only turns partially white in winter, whereas in Ireland and on the Faroe Islands it remains more or less brown. Moreover, the summer fur is more reddish in colour in Ireland than in Scotland. The mountain hare of Scandinavia is larger. Reproduction: From April to August. Young can be found as late as September. Gestation lasts for about 50 days. The female gives birth in the shelter of a rock or any other cover and produces two to five young, which are born with their eyes open and covered with fur. The young are extremely precautious and start eating their first shoots of grass when they are only ten days old; they are independent after three or four weeks. Two litters are usually born annually and a third is not excluded.

Musk beetle (I)
Callidium violaceum
A longhorn beetle of the family Cerambycidae, which has a magnificent dark blue or violet colour. This insect is a typical inhabitant of the coniferous woods. Its length is 12–15 mm. The species is easily recognised from its brilliant colour and its enlarged thighs. The antennae and legs are blackish. The larvae are found in the dry trunks of the white pine and the larch. Distribution: Alps, Massif Central, Vosges, Jura.

Nutcracker (B)
Nucifraga caryocatactes
Length: 32–35 cm. Wing span: 55 cm. Average weight: 175 g. Distribution: Alps, Vosges, Jura; mountains of central and eastern Europe, the south of Scandinavia, the Baltic countries, northern Russia, Siberia, as far as Japan between the 40th and 70th parallels. Three to four pale green eggs are laid, which are speckled with small brown spots. Incubation is carried out largely by the female, who is regularly fed by the male. Length of incubation is on an average eighteen days, and the young leave the nest after 24 days.

Nuthatch (B)
Sitta europaea
Total length: 14 cm. Wing span: 26–27 cm. Weight: 20–25 g. The nuthatch is found more or less throughout the plains and is therefore not a typical mountain bird, although it can be seen in the Alps up to the tree line, preferring the larch and pine tree to the spruce or white pine. Distribution: Throughout Europe with the exception of Scotland, Ireland and the greater part of Scandinavia. The bird is also absent in Corsica, where a smaller species, known as the Corsican nuthatch, takes its place.

Oeropsyche plumifera (I)
Small moth of Psychidae family. The male is characterised by a furry blackish appearance, its antennae being widely forked. The female is wingless and never leaves its larva cocoon. The caterpillar of the Psychidae spends its entire life in a silk cocoon covered with bristles. The males are generally active in the day. The insect is born early, even at high altitudes, which can be as high as 2300 m in the Alps of Valais. Distribution: Vosges, Jura, Alps, Massif Central and Pyrenees.

Orinocarabus latreillanus (I)
Beetle of the Carabidae family, which is very dark in colour and localised in Valais. Length: 12–18 mm. This insect can be found as high as 2700 m in the meadows of the Alps of Valais and seems rather localised. Its distribution is unknown.

Otter (M)
Lutra lutra
Length of body: 65–80 cm. Tail: 40–50 cm. Height to the withers: Approximately 30 cm. Weight varies between 6 and 16 kg. Distribution: Throughout Europe with the exception of Iceland and the majority of the Mediterranean islands. It is almost extinct in several regions. Reproduction: The female gives birth to two to five young in a burrow. The young open their eyes after one month and are suckled for seven to eight weeks. They remain with their mother for a long time. One litter is produced annually, but young otters can be found throughout the year. The biology of the species is still little known. Food: Apart from fish the otter also eats frogs, crayfish, water birds and other mammals. Longevity: 15–20 years.

Painted Lady (I)
Vanessa cardui
Rather large butterfly of the family Nymphalidae. The colour of its wings is a characteristic beige pink. There are small white patches on the black sections of the fore-wings. Forewing of male: 27–29 mm. This fine butterfly is capable of long migratory flights and is found everywhere, from sea level to more than 2500 m. The species is found throughout the world, apart from South America.

Pale clouded yellow (I)
Colias hyale
Closely related to the moorland clouded yellow and can be distinguished by the silvery white spot, often doubled, on the underneath of the hind-wing. This spot is always surrounded by brownish red, whereas the disc on the *Colias palaeno* is smaller and seems somehow lost in the sulphur yellow or ochre yellow colour of the rest of the wing, which is also speckled with grey. The fore-wing of the male: 21–25 mm. Very common throughout the flowery meadows from sea level up to more than 2400 m in the Alps of Valais. Distribution: Throughout Europe as far as 62° N. Partly absent from Spain and Italy.

Parasemia plantaginis (I)
Moth of the Arctiidae family, whose forewings are black, marbled with white. The male's hind-wings are yellow marked in black and the female's are marked in orange. The caterpillar feeds on plantains. The species is common from the plains right up to the highest alpine meadows. Size of the fore-wing of the male: 17–19 mm.

Peregrine (B)
Falco peregrinus
Varying length: 38–48 cm according to sex and age; the same is true for the wing span which varies between 80 and 115 cm. Average weight of the male: 608 g. Average

weight of the female: 962 g. Distribution: Very wide; the peregrine is found on every continent. There are numerous sub-species. The peregrine inhabits the whole of Europe, its islands, (with the exception of Iceland) and western Siberia. In France the bird is becoming more common in the Mediterranean area. In Switzerland certain cliffs in the Jura seem to have a larger population, and the species appears to resist the effect of pesticides better in the Alps, where it builds its nest on the rocky cliff faces of the sub-alpine region. Reproduction: The two or three reddish or russet coloured eggs (occasionally four) are laid on the ground on an outcrop of rock or in the abandoned nest of a bird of prey in the forests. Incubation lasts about 30 days and is carried out largely by the female, the male taking over from time to time. The young leave the nest after five weeks. Food: Almost exclusively birds seized in flight (pigeons, jays, crows, thrushes, etc.).

Pied wagtail (B)
Motacilla alba
Length: 19 cm. Wing span: 30 cm. Average weight: 23 g. Distribution: Found throughout almost the whole of Eurasia, north Africa. It is common in France, but rare in Corsica. Reproduction: Eggs are laid twice annually, numbering between five and six which are whitish, speckled with grey and brown; they are incubated by both adults for between twelve and fourteen days. The young leave the nest after two weeks.

Pine marten (M)
Martes martes
Average length: 80 cm of which the tail takes up 25 cm. Weight varies between 1 and 2.50 kg. Distribution: Throughout Europe with the exception of Iceland, the extreme north, the south-east and the greater part of the Iberian Peninsula. In the Alps, as far as the tree line. The young, numbering two to five are born in April or in May in the mountains. They are born naked and blind, opening their eyes after 35 days, and being suckled for seven to eight weeks; they are independent at three months.

Podisma alpina (I)
Medium size grasshopper of the Acrididae family, characterised by a slightly furry body of a fine green colour decorated with rust and black markings. The wing sheaths are atrophied in both sexes and only traces of them exist. The male is always smaller than the female and rarely grows longer than 18–20 mm. The female, however, can reach a length of 30 mm. This alpine grasshopper is widespread throughout the alpine ranges, from 1000 m up to the tree line, particularly in areas where wheat and myrtle grow.

Podisma pedestris (I)
Grasshopper of medium size belonging to the Acrididae family and very closely related to the previous species, although it is of a Boreo-alpine origin. Its colour varies, but in general it is rust brown or yellowish brown with a black stripe along the sides of the pronotum and on the abdomen. The hind tibias and tarsus are bright dark blue. The wing sheaths are scarcely ever longer than 3–4 mm. This species is widespread towards the end of summer, throughout the dry Alps of the south, in Valais and in the Pyrenees from 1000–3000 m. It is, however, always more or less localised.

Procris statices (I)
Small butterfly of the Zygaenidae family, without any design on its wings and coloured in fine shades of metallic green or blue, which can change under the influence of atmospheric humidity. They can often be found mating on thistle or scabious flowers. Common everywhere from the plains to 2300 m and above in the Alps.

Psodos alpinata (I)
Charming small moth of the Geometridae family which is easily recognised from its black wings, each bearing a large orange patch. Fore-wing of the male: 11–13 mm. This mountain moth is particularly common in the zones of bilberries up to 2400 m. Distribution: Alps, Vosges, Jura, Massif Central and Pyrenees.

Psophus stridulus (I)
Grasshopper of the family Acrididae. Males can measure up to 25 mm and females up to 30–40 mm. Their abdomen, when swollen with eggs, extends well beyond the wing sheaths. It has a strong general appearance, and is brown or blackish in colour. The lower wings are brick red with a large black patch. The male chirrups loudly when taking flight. Widely found throughout all the mountainous regions of central Europe up to an altitude of 2400 m.

Ptarmigan (B)
Lagopus mutus
Length: 35 cm. Average weight: 400–430 g. Wing span: 55–62 cm. The female is roughly the same size as the male or slightly smaller. The ptarmigan of the Pyrenees is heavier than the alpine ptarmigan. Distribution: Alps and Pyrenees from 2000 to 3500 m. It also inhabits the north of Scotland, Scandinavia, Spitzberg, Greenland, northern Siberia. Subspecies inhabit Japan and the arctic regions of North America. Reproduction: The alpine ptarmigan has only one mate. One clutch of eggs annually consisting of 4–9, which are yellowish white in colour and heavily speckled with darker spots shaped like russet brown splash marks; these are sometimes blackish in colour. The eggs are incubated by the females for three weeks and are laid in a cavity in the earth. If the eggs are destroyed, a second clutch, smaller in number, is laid to replace them.

Pygmy owl (B)
Glaucidium passerinum
Length: 16 cm. Wing span: 35 cm. Average weight: 60–65 g. This bird is occasionally active during the day. Distribution: Alps, foothills of the Alps, Jura, Vosges, the mountains of central and eastern Europe. Scandinavia, Asia and North America. Reproduction: Nests are built in the old holes of woodpeckers. Four to eight eggs are laid once annually; they are white and are incubated by the female for 28 days. The male takes care of feeding; the young leave the hole after about one month. It is difficult to find this bird, because of its small size and rarity. Food: Mostly rodents like the vole and common shrew; also small sparrows of the coniferous forests including the willow tit, the goldcrest, the tree creeper; sometimes insects.

Pygmy shrew (M)
Sorex minutus
This insect-eating relation of the common shrew can be distinguished from the latter by its smaller size, its lighter coloured fur, which is almost grey and usually uniform in appearance. Head and body measures 4–6.4 cm. Tail: 3–4.5 cm. Its cry is sharper than that of the common shrew. It is also much rarer than the latter, but is found throughout almost all of Europe, apart from Spain, Corsica, Sardinia and Sicily. The alpine shrew is larger, being the size of the common shrew with a slate grey fur and much longer tail.

Pyrenean desman (M)
Galemys pyrenaica
Length of head and body: 11–14 cm. Tail: 12–15 cm. Feet are broad and webbed. This is a small insect-eating mammal, which is exclusive to the pyrenean mountains and is the size of a mole. It is almost blind and has a very mobile nose. The desman leads a nocturnal and aquatic life and feeds mainly on larvae of the Trichoptera (caddis flies).

Rainbow trout (F)
Salmo gairdneri
This fish is raised artificially. After two years the rainbow trout can weigh up to 700 g. Introduced from America in 1882 and widely found in Europe and north Africa.

Raven (B)
Corvus corax
Length: 64 cm. Wing span: 125–130 cm. Average weight: 1.15 kg. Distribution: The raven is found throughout Europe with the exception of certain central and western areas, where it has been exterminated. It is also found in the greater part of Asia, north Africa, Asia Minor, North America and on the coast line of Greenland. Since the development of tourism it has been increasing in number in the Alps, the Pyrenees and the Massif Central. From time to time it can be found in the Jura. Usually its nest is placed on a rock face, but if there are no cliffs, the nest is also built on pine trees. It is made of small branches, decorated with wool, dry grass and moss. From mid-March onwards three to six blue green eggs with brown and black marks are laid, once a year, at high altitudes, incubated for three weeks by the female who is fed by the male from regurgitated food. The young leave the nest after a fortnight. Sexual maturity is reached at two years.

Red ant (I)
Formica rufa
Member of the Formicidae family, which is extremely widespread throughout all the coniferous forests. The size of the worker varies from 4–6 mm. The female is larger, with a thicker thorax – 9 mm. The species is also called the red ant, because its thorax and base of its abdomen are reddish in colour. The males are entirely brown. The nest is built below the ground and is surmounted by a large dome of twigs, which can reach a height of 1.25 m. The interior of the nest is a very complex collection of tunnels and living areas, which are intercommunicating and are built on different levels, being occupied by tens of thousands of ants amongst which there is a reasonably large number of queens. Distribution: Extremely wide. The wood ant is found in almost every coniferous forest of Europe. It destroys large numbers of other insects and therefore plays a very important rôle in maintaining the balance of nature.

Red deer (M)
Cervus elaphus
Length of body: 1.70–2.50 m. Tail: 12–15 cm. Height to the withers: 1.20–1.50 m. Weight varies between 100 and 220 kg. The red deer of eastern Europe is heavier and larger. The female, in general, is a third smaller than the male. Distribution: Common in certain areas of the Alps, especially in Switzerland, Grisons and in a more general way throughout central Europe. Elsewhere the animal is found sporadically. Its habitat extends to the west of Norway and to the British Isles. In western Europe, especially in the mountain forests up to an altitude of 2000 m or higher. It is also found in the northern half of Asia and in north Africa. Elsewhere the species prefers the forests and is most active during the night or at dusk, resting for the greater part of the day, apart from the rutting season when certain individuals are very active throughout the day. The red deer of both sexes like to wallow regularly in mud baths. The place where they do this is called a 'wallow.' The male loses its horns every year in March; however, they grow again rapidly, protected by a skin which is very rich in blood vessels and is called the 'velvet.' Generally speaking the new horns are more beautiful, stronger and with more branches than their predecessors. The growth of the horns depend on the influence of hormones. With the arrival of old age the horns become smaller. Once the horns have completed their growth, the animal is obliged to get rid of the velvet which covers the horns and rubs them against bushes in the forest. In the rutting season a gland situated in front of the eye secretes a strong smelling viscous liquid, which flows like sticky tears. The deer smears its coat with this substance produced by its 'tear duct', and then rubs itself at length against young tree trunks and branches in order to mark out its territory. The adult male surrounds itself with several hinds and defends them vigorously against any other claimants. On occasion fierce struggles take place for possession of the females. Gestation: 230–238 days. The fawns are born in May or June and have a coat which is patched with white. They are suckled for three or four months. The coat of the adult is a reddish brown colour in summer and brownish grey in winter. When disturbed, the female utters a loud raucous bark. Life span: more than twenty years.

Redpoll (B)

Carduelis flammea

Length: 13 cm. Wing span: 21 cm. Average weight: 15 g. Distribution: Alps, British Isles (for the smaller sub-species), the north of Scandinavia and Russia, Siberia, North America, Greenland, (wood redpoll and the white redpoll). The bird is partially migratory. In the winter months, flocks of wood redpolls descend from the north into central Europe, while the smaller redpolls come down from the mountains into the plains and attack the birch and alder trees. Reproduction: One or two clutches annually consisting of three to six eggs, which are a very fine pale blue colour, sometimes being slightly greenish and speckled with russet brown. The incubation is carried out by the female who is fed by the male; the incubation lasts from eleven days to a fortnight. The young leave the nest after twelve days to a fortnight. Food: Mostly the seeds of conifers, in particular those of the larch, seeds of alpine plants and in the winter the seeds of the birch and alder trees. In spring and summer the redpoll also eats small insects.

Red squirrel (M)

Sciurus vulgaris

Length of body: 22–26 cm. Tail: 15–22 cm. Average weight: approximately 300 g. Distribution: Throughout the Alps up to the tree line. The black or dark brown variety seems to be dominant. The red variety lives chiefly on the plains. It inhabits the whole of Europe with the exception of the extreme northern islands and those of the Mediterranean. In England the American grey squirrel has replaced the red squirrel in large areas. The winter coat is thicker and darker than the summer coat. Reproduction: After a gestation period of 38–40 days the female produces three to seven young in a spherical nest, which is heavily lined with lichens and wool. The young are naked and blind. They open their eyes after one month and are suckled for six weeks. They are able to reproduce after one year. If disturbed by man, the female carries her young to another nest.

Rhagium inquisitor (I)

Medium sized beetle, belonging to the Cerambycidae family, which can reach a length of 15–16 mm. It is brownish in colour with grey hairs and wing sheaths with two black transverse stripes. The species is mostly seen in coniferous forests up to the mountain tree line. It is quite common throughout the entire alpine range.

Rhyssa persuasoria (I)

This fine member of the Ichneumonidae family can measure up to 30 mm (not including the terebra). The female lays eggs inside the larvae of the giant wood wasp – *Uroceridae*. With its very long egg tube it can penetrate wood fibres measuring several centimetres. The larva of the *Rhyssa persuasoria* remains outside its host's body, only attacking the vital organs when it is fully developed. This superb ichneumon is relatively common in all the coniferous forests of the Alps.

Ring ouzel (B)

Turdus torquatus

Length: 27 cm. Wing span: 42 cm. Average weight: 110 g. Distribution: Alps, Jura, Pyrenees, Massif Central, Mountains of the British Isles and Scandinavia, Carpathians, Balkans, Caucasus and the north of Iran. The nest is quite large and built of dry grass, moss and earth, often being placed against the trunk of a coniferous tree at a low height (2–5 m). One clutch of three to six eggs, which are pale blue or greenish in colour, speckled with chestnut. Incubation is carried out by the female, and lasts thirteen days to a fortnight. The young leave the nest after two weeks, before being able to fly well. In general only one clutch is laid annually at high altitudes. Food: Insects, earthworms and wild berries in autumn. The bird is migratory.

Robin (B)

Erithacus rubecula

Length: 13.5 cm. Wing span: 22 cm. Average weight: 16 g. Distribution: Throughout Europe with the exception of the north of Scandinavia and Russia and the south-east of the Ukraine. Sub-species also inhabit Asia Minor, eastern Siberia and north Africa. Reproduction: They normally lay two clutches annually, consisting of four to eight eggs. These are incubated by the female for thirteen days to a fortnight. The young leave the nest after two weeks. Food: The robin feeds mainly while on the ground: it eats various insects, earthworms, small molluscs; wild berries in autumn, small seeds, crumbs and fat placed on bird tables in winter.

Rock bunting (B)

Emberiza cia

Length: 15–16 cm. Wing span: 23 cm. Average weight: 20 g. Distribution: Alps, Vosges, Jura, Massif Central, Pyrenees. Asia Minor, north Africa, central Asia. Food: Insects and seeds. Usually four eggs are laid twice a year; they are pale violet grey with brownish thread-like markings. The young leave the nest after ten or twelve days, without being able to fly.

Rock partridge (B)

Alectoris graeca

Length: 35 cm. Wing span: 55 cm. Average weight: 500–600 g. Distribution: Alps, Apennines, Sicily, south-east Europe and Asia. A clutch of ten to fifteen eggs is laid, which are shining yellowish white in colour, very finely marked with pale brown. The nest is built in a cavity, dug by the female beneath a rock, at the base of a tree trunk, or underneath a juniper bush. Length of incubation: Approximately 25 days.

Rock pipit (B)

Anthus spinoletta

Length: 16 cm. Wing span: 28 cm. Weight: 22 g. Distribution: Alps, Vosges, Pyrenees, Massif Central, Cévennes; the mountains of: Spain, Italy, Corsica, Sardinia, Germany, Czechoslovakia, Poland and of the Balkans. Sub-species exist in Asia, eastern Siberia, and North America (there is also a maritime pipit which is closely related to the rock pipit, but is different from it both geographically and ecologically. Generally its appearance is darker than the alpine species and it inhabits the coast line and rocky islands of northern and western Europe, from the White Sea to France). Reproduction: The nest is very similar to that of the tree pipit and is usually built in the cavity of a small tree trunk or beneath a rock. It is always well protected from possible snow falls. This bird is sometimes found up to 2700 m, but also much lower, especially in the Jura. One clutch is laid annually at high altitudes, and two clutches in more favourable regions. There are four to five greyish or greenish eggs, which are heavily marked with black or brown. The incubation is carried out by the female for two weeks; the young leave the nest after two weeks.

Rock thrush (B)

Monticola saxitilis

Length: 18–19 cm. Wing span: 35 cm. Average weight: 65 g. Distribution: Southern Europe, Alps, Massif Central, Corsica, Sardinia, the Mediterranean area and the Pyrenees; Asia Minor, north Africa, Caucasus, Iran, the Altai Mountains, extending to China. Winter is spent in tropical Africa. The rock thrush leaves Europe in September and returns in mid-May to the mountains. Reproduction: The nest is built largely of dried, finely interwoven grass. One clutch of eggs laid annually, numbering four to six, which are pale blue, sometimes slightly greenish in colour, marked with a few russet coloured spots. Incubation is carried out by the female alone and lasts for two weeks. The young leave the nest after fourteen to sixteen days. Food: Various insects, caterpillars, earthworms and small molluscs.

Roe deer (M)

Capreolus capreolus

Head and body: 91–135 cm. Tail: 2–3 cm. Height to withers: 60–80 cm. Weight from 15–30 kg. The female is usually much lighter than the male. Bright reddish brown colour in summer; greyish brown in winter. The animal is very inquisitive, but timid and has a well-developed sense of hearing. Distribution: The whole of Europe, from the Mediterranean coast to central Sweden, Asia Minor, Siberia, Manchuria, Chinese Turkestan. It is found in the mountains and in the Alps up to the tree line. Reproduction: The roe deer appears polygamous, but generally lives in pairs. In April–May (June at high altitudes) the female gives birth to one or two fawns and on rare occasions to three. The rutting season of the roe deer lasts from the end of July and throughout August, occasionally extending even into September. The horns of the male grow on a sort of axis and fall off every autumn between October and December. In January there appears a swelling on the axis, covered with a tissue containing many blood vessels. From this swelling grow two branches, which consist at first of cartilage and finally become bone. The process of becoming bone lasts from January to the end of April. When it is complete the velvety skin which covers the horns, and which is called 'velvet', dries up and gradually strips off. The true horns appear and then last until the autumn.

Rove-beetle (I)

Staphylinus caesarus

Beetle of the Staphylinidae family, characterised by its black head and abdomen, its rust coloured wing sheaths, which cover one third to one half of the stomach. Length: 18–25 mm. The rear side of the body and the segments of the upper side of the abdomen are decorated with tufts of golden hairs. It is very common and widespread, both on the plains and in the mountains up to a high altitude.

Savi's pygmy shrew (M)

Suncus etruscus

This shrew is the smallest known mammal. It weighs only 1 or 2 g and measures, including the head and the body, between 3 and 5 cm. It is therefore smaller than the pygmy shrew. We should hasten to add that the species is never found in the mountains but only in the Mediterranean basin, the Mediterranean islands and the Iberian peninsula.

Shepherd's fritillary (I)

Boloria pales

Rather small butterfly of the Nymphalidae family, characterised by reddish brown patches, which can also be dark red on the underpart of the back wings; the upper side is a bright beige colour with black designs. The fore-wing of the male: 17–19 mm. This is a typical species of the Alps, inhabiting the plains and meadows covered with myrtle and bilberries – from 1800–2300 m. The caterpillar feeds on the spurred violet and the polygonum. Distribution: The alpine level of the Pyrenees, the Cantabrian mountains, the Alps, the Carpathians and the Caucasus as far as central Asia.

Siberian cricket (I)

Aeropus sibiricus

Medium sized insect of the family Acrididae, from 19–25 mm. The colour varies between green and brown. This is a typical siberian-alpine species and is particularly common in the high mountains on alpine meadows between 2000 and 3000 m. An interesting feature is the swelling of the front tibia in the male, which forms a small ball. Distribution: Alps, Vosges, Pyrenees.

Silver-spotted skipper (I)

Hesperia comma

Small butterfly of the Hesperidae family, characterised by its head which is almost as large as the thorax, and by almost triangular wings, beige in colour with wide dark brown borders on the upper sides. The underneath of the hind-wings are olive green with yellowish spots and patches. The fore-wing of the male: 14–15 mm. Distribution: Grassy slopes and meadows from sea level up to 2500 m. Distribution: Northern Spain, central and northern Europe as far as Asia in the temperate zones and in north-west America. Absent from southern Italy, Corsica and Sardinia.

Siskin (B)

Carduelis spinus

Length: 11 cm. Wing span: 21 cm. Average weight: 13 g. Distribution: Central and eastern

Europe, part of Scandinavia, the north of the British Isles, western Siberia. It appears occasionally in the Alps, the Vosges, Jura, Massif Central and Pyrenees, and builds nests infrequently and in a sporadic fashion. Reproduction: The nest, which is very small, is built very high, towards the end of a lateral branch of a conifer and is very well concealed in the tufts of needles. The four or five pale blue eggs, speckled with reddish spots, are very similar to the eggs of the goldfinch. The female carries out incubation for eleven days, while the male feeds her. The young leave the nest after twelve days. There are often two clutches of eggs laid annually.

Six-spot burnet (I)
Zygaena filipendulae
Medium sized moth belonging to the Zygaenidae family. It is characterised by a very large body, a heavy and rectilinear flight, and by its front wings which are either black or greenish blue, heavily decorated with red spots on the fore and hind wings. All types of Zygaena compensate for the slowness of their movements by the presence of caustic juices, which are produced by their bodies as soon as they are seized by an enemy, a faculty which assures them real protection against attackers. The species is extremely common and widespread, from the plains to the mountains up to 2300 m. They are very frequently found on scabious and centaury flowers, where occasionally, as many as five or six individual moths can be seen at the same time. The forewing: 15–17 mm. Distribution: Alps, Jura, Vosges etc.

Small tortoiseshell (I)
Aglais urticae
Rather large butterfly of the Nymphalidae family, which is extremely widespread everywhere, from sea level up to more than 3000 m. The upper part of the wings is beige or reddish in colour, marked with small black patches or blue crescents. Distribution: Throughout western Europe up to the North Cape. It is absent in north Africa. The fore-wing of the male: 22–25 mm. The small tortoiseshell is certainly one of the first butterflies to be seen flying through the mountains in spring. The caterpillar is black and spiny with yellow lateral bands. The chrysalis is suspended and is brownish in colour with silver spots. This species has been known to migrate over large distances across certain ridges of the Alps.

Small wood nymph (I)
Hipparchia alcyone
Large butterfly of the Satyridae family, which is of a generally brownish appearance, with the upper and lower sides of its wings decorated with yellowish or whitish stripes, more pronounced in the female than in the male. Fore-wing: 27–35 mm. The small wood nymph inhabits rocks and ravines exposed to the sun up to a height of 2000 m. Distribution: North Africa, central and southern Europe, Asia Minor from the Lebanon to the Caucasus and to Kurdistan. A closely related species, the *Hipparchia fagi* is larger, but seems less fond of the mountains than the *Hipparchia alcyone*, as it is hardly ever found above 1400 m.

Smooth snake (R)
Coronella austriaca
Reproduction: Oviparous; the young are born in August or September. This takes place once a year and there are five to six young measuring up to 15 cm. Distribution: Europe from the north of the Iberian peninsula to Scandinavia and Lat. 64° N. In the south-east as far as the Caucasus.

Snow finch (B)
Montifringilla nivalis
Length: 16 cm. Wing span: 33 cm. Average weight: 37 g. Distribution: Alps and Pyrenees; the high mountains of southern Europe; the Caucus; central Asia. Nests have been found on the Jungfrau (Switzerland) as high as 3470 m. It is non-migratory, but in winter the snow finch moves from one mountain side to another or descends to the foothills and high villages. Reproduction: Its nest is made of dry

twigs and roots with feathers lining the interior. Four to five white eggs are incubated by the female for two weeks. The young leave the nest after three weeks. One clutch laid annually. Food: Various insects and seeds.

Song thrush (B)
Turdus philomelos
Length: 23 cm. Wing span: 35 cm. Weight: 75 g. Distribution: Throughout Europe except for the extreme north, the greater part of the Iberian peninsula, the south of Italy and the Balkans. Asia Minor and western Asia. Winters are spent in places similar to those chosen by the mistle thrush, including north Africa and the Mediterranean islands. The bird is partially migratory. Two clutches of eggs are laid annually (only one at high altitudes); the clutch consists of three to five greenish blue eggs; incubation takes twelve days to a fortnight. The young leave the nest after two weeks.

Sooty ringlet (I)
Erebia pluto
Larger than the *Erebia nivalis*. The fore-wing of the male measures from 23–25 mm. The upper part of the wing is covered with a velvety black, sometimes with white centred eye markings. (*E. pluto alecto*.) The female is paler than the male, and sometimes has beige patches on both wings. Habitat: Rocky outcrops and moraine, from 2000–2800 m. Distribution: Limited to the Alps.

Sparrow hawk (B)
Accipiter nisus
Length of the male: 28 cm. Length of the female: 38 cm. Weight of the male: 130–140 g. Weight of the female: 240 g approximately. Wing span: 60–80 cm. Distribution: Throughout Europe with the exception of Iceland, the Faroes, the extreme north and north-east; north Africa, Asia. The bird is generally non-migratory in the Alps. In winter it is more common on the plains, to which it migrates from the north. Reproduction: The male, while performing its nuptial flights, glides at very high altitudes. The nest is built by both adults. Eggs are laid once a year, numbering four to six; they are dirty white in colour, speckled with rust. Incubation period lasts about 41 days and is carried out by the female who is fed by the male near the nest. The young leave the nest after four weeks.

Spotted fritillary (I)
Melitaea didyma
Small butterfly of the Nymphalidae family. The male is characterised by the upper part of its wings, which are reddish beige all over with black patterns. The female is larger and the edges of the fore-wings paler in colour, often being speckled with grey. The fore-wing of the male: 17–21 mm. This species is extremely widespread throughout all the woodland meadows and the alpine meadows up to 2600 m. Very wide distribution covering the north of Africa and western and central Europe up to Lat. 55° N. It is absent in England, Holland, in Denmark, in the Scandinavian countries and the greater part of Germany.

Spurge hawk (I)
Celerio euphorbiae
Moth of the Sphingidae family, characterised by its thick furry body, its large size, its triangular, elongated fore-wings, its much shorter hind-wings and its bright pink colouring, with a transversal, black line. If this moth is disturbed, it suddenly opens its wings and shows the reddish or pink colours of the hindwings which obviously act as a deterrent to its enemies. The fore-wing of the male measures about 35 mm. The caterpillar is one of the finest in existence; it is velvety black in colour, speckled with small, yellow dots and decorated along the sides with two lines of gold coloured eye markings, a magnificent short red stripe also runs along its back and ends with a small horn of the same colour on the last abdominal segment. This remarkable moth is relatively common on the slopes of all the valleys of the southern Alps, where it can be seen as high as 2000 m. A related species, but much rarer, is the *Celerio vestpertilio*; this

Musk beetle (*Rhagium inquisitor*).

Siberian cricket (*Aeropus sibiricus*).

Silver-spotted skipper.

Smooth snake.

Stenobothrus.

Tawny owl.

Three-toed
woodpecker.

Titania schrankiana.

has grey fore-wings, and is found in the mountains more often than the *Celerio euphorbiae* – sometimes at very high altitudes.

Stauroderus scalaris (I)
Grasshopper of medium size, belonging to the Acrididae family which is easily recognised due to the characteristic chirruping which the male produces during flight. This chirruping, however, is not so loud as that produced by the male of the *Psophus stridulus*, which is much larger in size and darker in colour, with brick red backwings. The *Stauroderus scalaris* is dark olive brown, with blackish wing sheaths of which the front parts are enlarged in the male. The wings themselves are smoky coloured. The male measures 18–22 mm and the female 23–30 mm. In certain summers it becomes so widespread that it causes real damage to the mountain vegetation. Not long ago religious processions were organised in the high alpine villages of Valais, and prayers were said in order to overcome this pest.

Stenobothrus (I)
A type of small grasshopper, of which there are numerous species and which are difficult to identify. This insect is characterised by the size of its wing sheaths, which are straight and do not form a lobe towards the base. It is also distinguished by the valves of the egg tube which are scalloped on the outside edges.

Stoat (M)
Mustela erminea
Length of head and body (dwarf form): 200 mm approximately. Tail: 105 mm. Weight: 125–200 g. The female is smaller than the male. The stoat of the plains is larger and its weight can reach 300 g. Distribution: Throughout Europe with the exception of Iceland, the islands of the Arctic and the greater part of southern Europe. The stoat is not found to be on the Pyrenees, the north west mountains of Spain, and east of the Dalmatian mountains. It is also found in Asia, Algeria, and North America. Reproduction: The young are produced once annually and consist of four to eight (sometimes more). The young open their eyes after 40–45 days and are suckled for seven weeks. They are independent after three or four months and are able to reproduce at two years of age.

Swallowtail (I)
Papilio machaon
Butterfly of large size belonging to the Papilionidae family. This is one of the most beautiful butterflies of Europe. The fore-wing of the male: 32–39 mm. The background colour of the wings is yellowish gold, and there are different designs and blackish patches on them partly covered with yellow scales. There are blue and black patches and a single orangy patch on the hind-wings, which end in points. The caterpillar is greenish in colour with transverse black stripes and orange spots. The caterpillar feeds on various umbelliferous plants. The species is widespread throughout all the sunny meadows. In the mountains it can be found well above the tree line, (as high as 2300 m in the Alps of Valais). Distribution: Very wide; throughout Europe and in the temperate areas of Asia. It is also found in north Africa. There are very closely related sub-species in North America.

Tawny owl (B)
Strix aluco
Length: 37–45 cm. Wing span: 91–100 cm. Weight: 500 g. Distribution: Throughout Europe with the exception of the north-east, the north of Scandinavia, Ireland, Iceland and Corsica. North Africa, Asia. Common in France, Switzerland, Belgium, Germany, etc. It is more rare in the mountains. Reproduction: Inhabits all types of cavities, sometimes the old nests of crows or diurnal birds of prey. It is also found in ruins or abandoned buildings. Eggs are laid once annually numbering two to six; they are white and rounded and are incubated for 28 days by the female while the male feeds her. Rather slow development of the young: they leave the nest after four or five weeks, sometimes even later, without being able to fly well. Food: Extremely

varied, depending on the area inhabited. In the mountains food consists of small rodents, shrews, squirrels, weasels and mountain hares; various types of sparrow are also eaten and brown frogs, insects, etc.

Tengmalm's owl (B)
Aegolius funereus
Length: 26 cm. Average wing span: 58 cm. Average weight: of the female: 168 g and of the male: 120 g. Distribution: Alps, Jura, Vosges, mountains of central and eastern Europe, Scandinavia, Caucasus, Siberia, North America. The bird is non-migratory. Reproduction: This owl uses the old holes of the black woodpecker and the green woodpecker. Three to seven white eggs are laid once annually, which are hatched by the female for 28 days. The young leave the nest after 50–55 days. Their plumage is then quite different from that of the adult as it is much darker and chocolate brown in colour. Food: Mostly rodents and small sparrows, including insects from time to time.

Testediolum glacialis (I)
Small beetle of the Carabidae family, often measuring less than 5 mm in length. The species lives at high altitudes, beneath the stones of the glacial moraine. It is extremely widespread at this altitude throughout the alpine range.

Three-toed woodpecker (B)
Picoides tridactylus
Length: 21 cm. Wing span: 37–40 cm. Average weight: 65 g. This bird is approximately the same size as the great spotted woodpecker. It differs, however, from all other types of woodpecker in Europe because of the complete absence of red patches, by almost entirely black wings, by the wide whitish band along the back and by the black cheeks which are striped with white. The top of the male's head is yellow. The front of the female's head is whitish with a black patch on the top of the head. The bird utters its cries more frequently and in a softer manner than the great spotted woodpecker. Reproduction: Similar to the great spotted woodpecker. Distribution: The three-toed woodpecker is a descendant of the ice age and inhabits the Alps, the Carpathians, Scandinavia and Russia. Scattered and sporadic presence in the Swiss Alps and Savoy.

Titania phrygialis (I)
Small butterfly whose fore-wing measures not more than 10 mm. It is micaceous in appearance. This insect is often seen in large numbers near pools or the sandy banks of streams in the mountains up to 2600 m and above. It is very common throughout the alpine ranges.

Titania schrankiana (I)
This species is closely related to the preceding one, but has brownish designs on its front wings which are much more clearly marked, and does not have the micaceous reflections which characterise the *Titania phrygialis*. This tiny butterfly seems also more localised, although it is found in large numbers in certain areas of the Alps, in particular the area of the climbing juniper bushes in Valais.

Tree-creeper (B)
Certhia familiaris
Total length of bird: 11–13 cm. Wing span: 19–20 cm. Weight: 7–10 g. The tree-creeper is found over an extremely wide geographical area which includes Eurasia and North America; in the Alps it can be found to the tree line, (2200 m), approximately. However, its true home is the coniferous forest: the woods of larch trees, pine trees, spruce and mountain firs. Only its song, which is sweeter and less rhythmical than that of the short-toed tree-creeper, allows it to be identified with certainty. Its nest is usually built in the space beneath a loose piece of bark or a narrow crack at a fork of two branches. It is made of pieces of bark, twigs, moss, and dry grass with a lining of feathers and horsehair. Five or six eggs are laid, which are white and finely speckled with dark brown spots. At high alti-

tudes there is probably only one clutch of eggs laid. The young leave the nest after sixteen or seventeen days. The tree-creeper feeds almost exclusively on insects hidden beneath the bark, on their eggs and their larvae. They do, however, also eat spiders, beetles, centipedes and small molluscs and occasionally consume seeds. They are fairly tame and rather inquisitive by nature. The tree-creeper is not afraid of approaching a person to examine it closely, while still being able to conceal itself at the first sign of danger. In winter it can often be seen in the company of tits and goldcrests, which live near fallen trees in the mountains, in search of the tiny insects.

Tree pipit (B)
Anthus trivialis
Length: 15 cm. Wing span: 26–27 cm. Average weight: 22 g. Distribution: Throughout Europe, Asia from the Urals and Asia Minor as far as the Lena. It does not nest on the Mediterranean plains nor south of the Spanish Pyrenees. In the mountains the tree pipit seeks out sub-alpine meadows and the borders of woods up to 2000 m and above. It is migratory and spends the winter on the plains of tropical Africa, returning to Europe in April and leaving again at the end of August. Normally one clutch of eggs is laid annually in the mountains. The young leave the nest before being able to fly, about twelve days after their birth. Food: Small insects and larvae, caterpillars, spiders, molluscs and the seeds of wild plants.

Trichius fasciatus (I)
This is a medium sized beetle of the Scarabaeidae family, and is easily recognised by the three black stripes which decorate its fine golden yellow wing sheaths. The *Trichius fasciatus* has yellow or russet hairs on its head and body. Length: 10–13 mm. This beetle usually prefers to live on the centaury plant or the thistle, which are found in the sub-alpine glades up to 2000 m. It is common throughout the alpine ranges, although it is sometimes localised.

Viviparous lizard (R)
Lacerta vivipara
Length: 15–18 cm. Distribution: Central and northern Europe up to Lat. 70° N. Asia as far as the island of Sakhalin.

Wall creeper (B)
Tichodroma muraria
Length (excluding the beak): 13–14 cm. Wing span: 26–27 cm. Average weight: 19–20 g. Distribution: Throughout the mountains of Europe; the high mountains of Asia Minor and Iran and from the Himalayas to western China. Reproduction: a large nest is built in a rocky fissure; it is made of moss, stems of grass and lichen, sometimes lined with feathers. One clutch of four to five white eggs with rust coloured marks annually. The young grow rather slowly and do not leave the nest until they are about 26 days old.

Wart-biter (I)
Decticus verrucivorus
A large insect of the Tettigoniidae family. Length of male: 24–38 mm. Female from 28–45 mm. The egg-laying tube of the female is shaped like a curved sabre and its length is 18–25 mm. This large grasshopper, which is mainly carnivorous in diet and very variable in colour, is common in the sub-alpine zone up to the tree line, sometimes even higher.

Wasp beetle (I)
Clytus ariatis
Small longhorn beetle of the family Cerambycidae, which can be found very often on the flowers of umbelliferous plants. Length: 10–16 mm. This insect explores trunks of fallen trees before laying its eggs. Its jerky movements and the yellow stripes which decorate its wing sheaths make it similar to a wasp when seen from some distance, and the insect in fact imitates the wasp's behaviour. Quite common in the sub-alpine meadows and the clearings of coniferous forests.

Weasel (M)
Mustela nivalis
Total length: Male 22–27 cm. Female 20–24 cm. Average weight: Male 90–120 g. Female 45–70 g. There is a large variation in the sizes found in this species. In the north and centre of Europe it is a pygmy race. It is more nocturnal than the stoat. The weasel builds an underground nest beneath stones, in a hollow trunk or inside a wall. It has a sharp and piercing alarm cry. The animal produces between five and six young on average. Distribution: All of Europe. It is not found in Ireland, Iceland and in certain other islands.

Wheatear (B)
Oenanthe oenanthe
Length: 14 cm. Wing span: 24 cm. Weight: 26–30 g. Distribution: Throughout Europe, the Alps, Iceland, Asia to the 35th parallel south, the coastline of Greenland and a section of North America. It is migratory; from August to September the wheatear moves down to the African plains to spend the winter. It returns to Europe at the end of March, and to the Alps in April or May. Reproduction: One clutch of four to five eggs laid annually, which are of a magnificent pale blue, sometimes with small brown spots. Incubation is carried out by the female for two weeks, and the young leave the nest after fourteen to sixteen days.

Wild cat (M)
Felis silvestris
Length of body: 47–70 cm. Tail: 26–37 cm. Height to the withers: 35–40 cm. The animal is much larger than the domestic cat. Distribution: Scotland, localised in western and central Europe, in Spain and in the south-east of Europe. The species appears to have spread into certain areas of Germany (Harz, the Taunus mountains etc.). Reproduction: Mating takes place in February. Gestation lasts from 63–65 days; there is one litter annually which consists of three to five young, who open their eyes after ten to twelve days and are suckled for at least four weeks. Sexual maturity is reached at the age of one year. Longevity: twelve to fifteen years. The wild cat purrs, meeows and squeals like a domestic cat but its cry is more powerful and deeper.

Winchat (B)
Saxicola rubetra
Length: 12–13 cm. Wing span: 24 cm. Average weight: 18 g. Distribution: Europe with the exception of the southern peninsulas, the north of Scandinavia and Russia; Caucasus; western Siberia. The bird is migratory; it arrives in Europe at the end of April and leaves in August or September for tropical Africa. It is a typical inhabitant of the sub-alpine meadows in the mountains, where pairs can be found nesting up to the tree line. In general one clutch of five to six eggs is laid annually. They are turquoise blue and are amongst the most beautiful to be found. Incubation is carried out by the female and lasts for two weeks. The young leave the nest after a fortnight. The song of the winchat is not loud, but is very pleasant and it imitates the cries of other birds.

Wolf (M)
Canis lupus
The size of the wolf is similar to that of a large alsatian dog, which it resembles. It has a tufted tail and is probably the ancestor of the domestic dog. Length of body: 1.10–1.30 m. Tail: 30–40 cm. Height to the withers: 70–80 cm. Weight: 25–50 kg. The female is slightly smaller. It utters long howls, especially during winter nights, and these cries are known as the choir of wolves. Distribution: It is practically extinct in the greater part of Europe. It still exists in Scandinavia, in eastern Europe, the Balkans, Italy, in the Apennines, and the Abruzzi. It is found in greater numbers in Asia and North America. Reproduction: The rutting season takes place in winter. Gestation lasts for 63 days. In the spring the female gives birth to three or six young in a 'bed' concealed beneath a rock or under brushwood. The young are blind at first and open their eyes after ten to twelve days: they are suckled for two months. There is one litter annually. Longevity: fourteen to sixteen years.

Woodcock (B)
Scolopax rusticola
Length: 35 cm. Wing span: 60–65 cm. Weight: 300–340 g. Distribution: All of Europe, with the exception of the Iberian peninsula; northern Scandinavia; Russia; Asia. The species likes deciduous and coniferous woods with damp soil, both on the plains and in the mountains up to an altitude of 2000 m. It nests in a depression in the ground which is lined with leaves. Eggs are laid twice annually. Food: Especially earthworms, insects and their larvae and small molluscs.

Wren (B)
Troglodytes troglodytes
Length: 9–10 cm. Wing span: 14.5 cm. Average weight: 9 g. Distribution: Western, central and southern Europe; it is absent in the north of Scandinavia and the east of Russia; North Africa; Asia Minor; Central Asia; from Alaska to Labrador in North America. It is generally sedentary, but the species living in the north and even in central areas do migrate when autumn arrives. The wrens living in the mountains can also be found in the plains. Food: Small insects, larvae and spiders. Two clutches of five to eight eggs laid annually, which are white, speckled with rust. The incubation is carried out by the female alone and lasts from fourteen to fifteen days. The young leave the nest after sixteen to eighteen days. The young are then looked after by the male who guards them and in the evening leads them to one of the numerous sleeping and nesting areas.

Yellow-necked mouse (M)
Apodemus flavicollis
Length of body: 9–13 cm. Tail: 9–13.5 cm. Weight: 22–40 g. Distribution: Northern and eastern France, Pyrenees, the low and high Alps; central and eastern Europe as far as Greece, northern Italy and also Asia Minor. Gestation: 23 days. The young open their eyes after a fortnight and can reproduce after eight weeks.

Zygaena exulans (I)
Related to *Zygaena filipendulae*, but the upper parts of the fore-wings have more red marks, and the background is lighter and more greenish in colour. The abdomen is shorter and much more furry. The species is extremely widespread in the meadows of the Alps and the Pyrenees up to 3200 m and above. The caterpillar is blackish in colour with yellow rings on the suture lines. It lives on different short plants on the higher parts of the mountains. It hibernates twice in succession. The chrysalis is enclosed in a bulbous shiny white cocoon, and is attached to a stone; it is sometimes found pressed close to dozens of other cocoons of the same type.

Zygaena purpuralis (I)
This species is related to the *Zygaena exulans*, but is characterised by wider, red patches on its upper wings. Moreover, it does not fly as high as the preceding moth and is rarely found at greater altitudes than 1800 m in the Alps; in this area it is found less frequently than the *Zygaena filipendulae*. The male caterpillar is bluish in colour and the female is pale yellow with two lines of black spots. It hibernates two years in succession. The chrysalis is found in a yellowish cocoon hidden beneath mosses. It lives in the sub-alpine meadows and glades where wild thyme grows.

A capercaillie during its mating period.

Bibliography

Auber L.: *Coléoptères de France* (tomes I, II, III), N. Boubée, (Paris, 1958)

Bourlière F.: *Natural History of Mammals* (3rd edition), (London, 1964)

Brink van den F. H.: *A Field Guide to the Mammals of Britain and Europe* (London, 1967)

Brown L., Amadon D.: *Eagles, Hawks and Falcons of the World* (2 vols.) (London, 1968)

Burton M.: *Systematic Dictionary of Mammals of the World*, (London, 1962)

Chapman R. F.: *The Insects — Structure and Function*, (London, 1969)

Couturier M.: *Le Gibier des montagnes françaises*, Arthaud (1964). *Le Bouquetin des Alpes*, Imp Allier (1962)

Didier R., Rode P.: *Les mammifères de France*, (Paris, 1935)

Dorst J.: *The Migration of Birds*, (London, 1962)

Dottrens E.: *Batraciens et reptiles d'Europe*, Delachaux & Niestlé (1963)

Ford E. B.: *The World of Butterflies and Moths*, (London, 1945)

Geroudet P.: *Les Rapaces d'Europe*, Delachaux & Niestlé (1965). *Les Passereaux* (tomes I, II, III), Delachaux & Niestlé (1951–1957)

Graf J.: *Animal Life of Europe*, (London, 1968)

Guggisberg C. A. W.: *Les Alpes*, Petit Atlas Payot, (Lausanne, 1945)

Hanzak J. et al, *Encyclopaedia of Animals*, (London, 1968)

Harper F.: *Extinct and vanishing Mammals of the Old World*, (New York, 1945)

Higgins L. G., Riley N. D.: *Guide des papillons d'Europe*, Delachaux et Niestlé (1971)

Klots A. B.: *The World of Butterflies and Moths*, (London, 1963)

Konig C.: *Mammifères d'Europe*, Hatier (1970), *Oiseaux d'Europe* (tomes I, II, III), Hatier (1968–1971)

Larousse: *Encyclopaedia of Animal Life*, (London, 1967)

Pesson P.: *The World of Insects*, (London, 1959)

Peterson R. T.: *A Field Guide to the Birds of Britain and Europe*, (London, 1954)

Rougeot P. C.: *Guide du naturaliste dans les Alpes*, Delachaux & Niestlé (1972)

Stanek V. J.: *The Pictorial Encyclopaedia of Insects*, (London, 1969)

Vanden Eeckhoudt J. P.: *Fleurs et petite faune de l'Alpe*, l'École des Loisirs (Paris, 1968)

Walker E.: *Mammals of the World* (2 vols.), (Baltimore, 1964)

Wigglesworth V. B.: *The Life of Insects*, (London, 1964)

Photos by René-Pierre Bille, except those on p. 167,
189 and 199, which are by A. Marconato,
B. Richard and A. Guilhery.

Drawings and diagrams by Thérèse Bille.